HEALTH AND DISEASE
IN CHAD

THE JOHNS HOPKINS MONOGRAPHS IN INTERNATIONAL HEALTH

HEALTH MANPOWER IN A DEVELOPING ECONOMY
Taiwan, A Case Study in Planning. 1967.
    by Timothy D. Baker and Mark Perlman

THE HEALTH CENTER DOCTOR IN INDIA. 1967.
    by Harbans S. Takulia, Carl E. Taylor, S. Prakash Sangal,
    and Joseph D. Alter

HEALTH MANPOWER PLANNING IN TURKEY
An International Research Case Study. 1968.
    by Carl E. Taylor, Rahmi Dirican, and Kurt W. Deuschle

HEALTH AND DISEASE IN FOUR PERUVIAN VILLAGES
Contrasts in Epidemiology. 1968.
    by Alfred A. Buck, Tom T. Sasaki, and Robert I. Anderson

HEALTH MANPOWER IN PERU
A Case Study in Planning. 1969.
    by Thomas L. Hall

HEALTH AND DISEASE IN CHAD

*Epidemiology, Culture, and
Environment in Five Villages*

Alfred A. Buck, Robert I. Anderson,
Tom T. Sasaki, and Kazuyoshi Kawata

The Johns Hopkins Press, Baltimore and London

Copyright © 1970 by The Johns Hopkins Press
All rights reserved
Manufactured in the United States of America

The Johns Hopkins Press, Baltimore, Maryland 21218
The Johns Hopkins Press Ltd., London

Library of Congress Catalog Card Number 73-116348

ISBN-0-8018-1172-4

To Dr. Philip E. Sartwell,
teacher of epidemiology,
for his advice and encouragement

FOREWORD

Modern tools in public health assessment always require extensive testing in field operations in order to demonstrate both validity and usefulness. As sophisticated planning comes increasingly into play, it becomes more and more important to distinguish between historical assumptions as to the epidemiology of diseases and the realities of their occurrence and their transmission. Similarly, long accepted notions as to the impact of geography, culture, and general ways of life on disease incidence necessarily waited for verification upon the development of easily applied immunologic tests and the field scrutiny of situations by multidiscipline teams.

Dr. Buck and his associates made an excellent exploratory start, using the total forces already noted, in their studies of Health and Disease in Four Peruvian Villages. They have now extended their inquiries to a series of settlements in Chad.

The present volume discloses once more the fascinating conclusion that a priori predictions as to the spectrum of disease in a given population frequently may be in error. This is strikingly illustrated in the case of the absence of ascariasis where insanitary conditions of the environment might have indicated their prevalence. It still remains to be explained why this is so, although climatic circumstances, such as sunlight and relatively high temperatures, may have successfully inhibited the growth of ova.

In any event, the findings, extensive and rich in content, suggest almost as many epidemiological questions as they resolve. As these studies are pursued further in other geographic areas, the tools will become more refined, and in fact more applicable to the rapid diagnosis of population disease incidence and dynamics. It is essential that such studies as these produce maximum simplification of field methodologies, since the cost of present multidiscipline teams and their auxiliaries is still relatively high.

It is anticipated that, after several more field expeditions, the authors will produce a reasonably complete interpretive volume in which the salient conclusions as to epidemiological method and immunologic applications are spelled out. The public health planner would welcome such a crystallization.

The specialist in the fields covered by both the Peruvian and the Chad studies need not await such a summary. Both volumes provide a mass of exciting findings. They present a mine of data challenging the testing and interpretation of the experienced worker.

As was the case in Peru, all of the work in Chad was carried out in complete cooperation with the health authorities and associated agencies in the Chad region. Not the least significance of such operations lies in the cooperative successes which they generate with central and local public bodies and with the people themselves. Patience, imagination, and sympathetic understanding are ingredients which do not lend themselves to statistical tables or text. Without them, however, these efforts would fail.

Abel Wolman
Emeritus Professor
The Johns Hopkins University

PREFACE

The Republic of Chad was the second of five countries selected for comprehensive epidemiological studies by a team of the Geographic Epidemiology Unit of The Johns Hopkins School of Hygiene and Public Health. Following the pattern of the first study, in Peru, preparations for the Chad survey included introductory visits to government officials of the Republic of Chad, an extensive pilot study, and logistic preparations by an advance team. The protocols and methods employed in the study were essentially the same as those used previously. This will permit international comparisons of selected indices determined by the same standardized techniques.

Nevertheless, some modifications facilitating adaptation to the special situation of Chad were necessary. These included additional tests for the diagnosis of some of the regionally important endemic diseases and infections; changes in the composition of the field team to broaden the diagnostic and therapeutic capabilities of the research group while working in areas without medical facilities; and improvements of the general camping and research equipment which would permit the team to operate independently under the extremely rugged conditions encountered in some of the areas selected for study.

The field team of the Geographic Epidemiology Unit was composed of a physician-epidemiologist, an ophthalmologist, a laboratory scientist, a senior laboratory technician, a social anthropologist, a sanitary engineer, an entomologist, and two nurses. The Ministry of Public Health and Social Affairs of the Republic of Chad assigned two male nurses who were fluent in French, Sara (an African native dialect), Arabic, and in some of the other local languages spoken by residents of the five villages selected to represent major subareas of the Republic. The two nurses were trained in the conduct of interviews that are part of the standard international-study protocol. Non-professional members of the field team included a cook and his assistant and from three to five camp aides hired locally in each of the five communities.

Major improvements in scientific field equipment included new liquid nitrogen freezers, with a holding time of approximately thirty-five days and a storage capacity for 450 six-milliliter serum specimens, as well as transportation containers for the liquid nitrogen, which was supplied from Paris. Another significant improvement was the availability of a portable field bio-microscope for eye examinations in a country where trachoma and ocular lesions of onchocerciasis abound.

Of the many diseases and infections observed in Chad, some were particularly interesting because of their unusual clinical manifestations (onchocerciasis), occurrence (infestation with *Capillaria hepatica*), distribution (African tick-borne typhus), or their interaction with basic host responses (suppression of delayed-type skin reactions in onchocerciasis).

The success of the study would not have been possible without the continued assistance, advice, and cooperation of many individuals in the United States and in Chad. We are deeply indebted to Maj. Gen. J. Blumberg (Retired), commanding officer of the Medical Research and Development Command, U.S. Army, under whose sponsorship the studies were carried out. We wish to thank His Excellency, M. Maurice Adoum, minister of public health and social affairs, and Dr. Guy Diebolt, senior public health adviser to the minister, for their directions and advice. Our special thanks are due to Dr. Pierre Ziegler and his associates of the Service des Grandes Endémies in Chad for their continued professional assistance, logistic support, and expert advice. We would like to express our thanks to the officers of the U.S. Embassy in Fort Lamy for their cooperation and assistance, which was always generously given when needed. We would also like to express our gratitude to the freight agents of Air Afrique and Pan American Airways, without whose ingenuity the fast and regular shipments of sensitive specimens from the field to Baltimore would not have been possible.

Special thanks are due to the commanding officer of the French armed forces stationed in Fort Lamy, who furnished free air transportation for the team and equipment from Fort Lamy to Faya-Largeau, and to Dr. Denis Marchioni, medical officer in Faya-Largeau, who extended many courtesies to the team. Finally, great appreciation is expressed for the help of the many government officials who volunteered to assist the team in various phases of its work, and especially to the hundreds of persons who by patiently participating in the studies provided most of the data on which this work is based.

Of the many individuals in the United States whose assistance and cooperation were essential for conducting the study, only a few can be mentioned. The authors wish to thank Dr. Martin Donner, Dr. Gunter von Noorden, and Dr. Samuel Boyer of The Johns Hopkins School of Medicine; Dr. James Hitchcock, Dr. Winston Price, Dr. Philip Sartwell, and Dr. Lloyd Rozeboom of The Johns Hopkins School of Hygiene and Public Health; Dr. Lydia Edwards, Dr. Irving Kagan, and Dr. Libcro Ajello of the U.S. Public Health Service; Lt. Col. Robert T. Cutting and the staff of the Medical Research and Development Command, U.S. Army; Lt. Col. Budd Appleton of the Walter Reed General Hospital; Mr. Earl Fife and Dr. Elvio Sadun of the Walter Reed Army Institute of Research; and Dr. Leo Jachowski of the University of Maryland. Special thanks are due Dr. Curtis W. Sabrosky of the Systematic Entomology Laboratory, U.S. Department of Agriculture, for reviewing Chapter 3, "Arthropods of Medical Importance," and to Dr. Harry Hoogstraal of the Naval Medical Research Unit No. 2 for identifying the ticks collected in Chad.

Last but not least, we wish to express our deep gratitude to our silent co-authors, the members of the field team. Despite heat, dust, and lack of basic comforts, they worked from dawn until deep in the night, without a single free weekend in four long months. Very special thanks are due to our two nurses Kay Buck and Jean Hewitt, to Priscilla Washington, our laboratory technician, and to Emile N'Garmirtri and Adoum Kardja, our two Chadian nurses and friends.

CONTENTS

MAPS

ILLUSTRATIONS

HEALTH AND DISEASE
IN CHAD

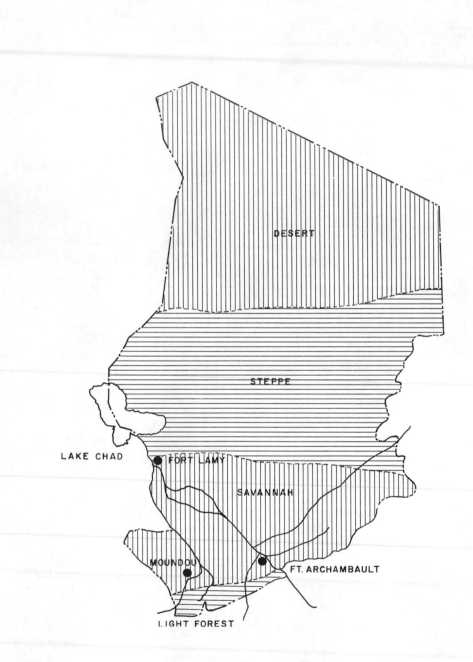

DESERT

STEPPE

LAKE CHAD

FORT LAMY

SAVANNAH

MOUNDOU

FT. ARCHAMBAULT

LIGHT FOREST

Natural Regions of Chad

1

THE COMMUNITIES

The Republic of Chad covers 495,000 square miles of former French Equatorial Africa between 23°27′ and 7°30′ north latitudes, and 13° and 24° east longitudes. The country is bounded by Libya on the north; the Central African Republic on the south; and Niger, Nigeria, and Cameroon on the west and southwest; in the east it shares 650 miles of border with Sudan.

There are three major natural regions. The northern territory, representing almost half the country, is part of the Sahara Desert (*Zone désertique*) and is characterized by extreme dryness, with little or no rainfall even during the rainy season, and scattered oases. The steppe (*Zone sahélienne*) in the middle part of the country is characterized by spiny scrub vegetation, interspersed with green islands and borders around Lake Chad, along the three main rivers, and in the vicinity of the many small streams and creeks. Farther to the south, the savannah (*Zone soudanienne*) begins gradually, and the vegetation grows progressively more lush as one approaches the border of the Central African Republic. The climate in the southern half of the country is dominated by two major seasons that are dependent upon the monsoon winds. The wet season lasts from June until October, when the wind comes from the southwest bringing tornadoes and heavy rains. Between November and January, and again between March and June, two additional seasonally shifting pressure systems give rise to the harmattan, a strong, desiccating

1

easterly wind which blows on and off through the dry season. The alize, a cool north wind, blows in January and February.

The total population of the Republic in 1965 was 2,936,219, a figure based on an official census (Ministry of Public Health, 1966). The population can be divided roughly into two groups—that is, mixed-blood Negroes of the Sahara, or Black Arabs (Thompson and Adloff, 1960, pp. 426–27), who speak Arabic and the languages of the Kanuric stock (Murdock, 1959, p. 129), and tribes south of the Sahara whose physical characteristics are fully Negroid and who speak the languages of the central subfamily of the Sudanic stock (Murdock, 1959, p. 225–26). Each consists of numerous tribes and subtribes, thus adding to the division of the country caused by geographic contrast, and the residences of the two groups are concentrated in different areas.

The official language is French. Arabic is spoken widely in the north, while Sara prevails in the south. In addition, there are numerous languages and dialects spoken by smaller tribal groups. These have caused great difficulty in communication. Approximately 75 percent of the population are Muslim; the remainder are Christians and animists from the southern part of Chad.

The Republic has only a few natural resources. Ninety-five percent of the population are either farmers or seminomadic herdsmen. Staple crops include cotton, millet, peanuts, ground peas, manioc, and gum arabic. Corn, wheat, and rice are being successfully introduced into irrigated or seasonally inundated areas. Principal livestock includes zebu cattle, sheep, goats, and camels. Around Lake Chad and along the main rivers fish are abundant. They are smoked, dried, and marketed in the vicinity of the areas where they are caught.

Chad has approximately 18,600 miles of roads connecting principal towns. Most are unpaved, with the exception of a few miles in and around the major cities. One thousand miles are considered "all-weather" roads. During the rainy season many roads collapse or are washed out, leaving the country a raft of isolated islands surrounded by mud and water or desert. Free travel through all parts of the Republic is possible only during the major part of the dry season, and even then it is often difficult. The landlocked country depends on trucks and airplanes—and during parts of the rainy season on river boats—for heavy transport. There are no railroads.

During the pilot study numerous communities in all the major zones of Chad were visited by the epidemiologist, laboratory direc-

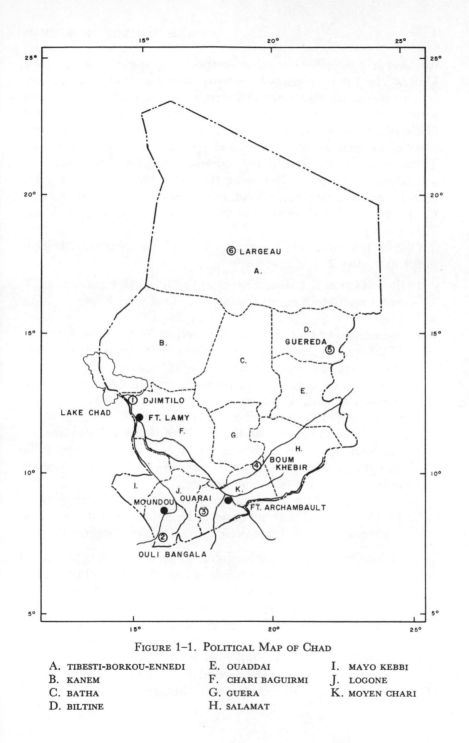

FIGURE 1–1. POLITICAL MAP OF CHAD

A. TIBESTI-BORKOU-ENNEDI   E. OUADDAI   I. MAYO KEBBI
B. KANEM   F. CHARI BAGUIRMI   J. LOGONE
C. BATHA   G. GUERA   K. MOYEN CHARI
D. BILTINE   H. SALAMAT

tor, and a public health nurse of the Geographic Epidemiology Unit of The Johns Hopkins University. Based on their preliminary investigations, six distinctly different areas were identified which were considered representative of contrasts in the environment and in the ethnic, religious, and occupational characteristics of the population, as well as of the regional spectra of endemic diseases. These six areas represented the Sahara, the Lake Chad area, the southernmost tip of the Republic, the fertile south-central region, the remote and almost inaccessible shores of Lake Iro in eastern Chad, and the arid mountainous territory of the Ouaddai (see Figure 1–1).

One study community was finally selected for each area, as indicated in Figure 1–1. These were:

1. the village of Djimtilo, located at 12°50′ north latitude, 14°39′ east longitude, near the mouth of the Chari River at Lake Chad;
2. the village of Ouli Bangala, located at 7°50′ north latitude, 15°52′ east longitude, in the southernmost part of the country;
3. the village of Ouarai, located at 8°48′ north latitude, 17°45′ east longitude, in the south-central area of Chad just southeast of the town of Koumra;
4. the village of Boum Khebir, located at 10°10′ north latitude, 19°25′ east longitude; on the northern shore of Lake Iro;
5. the town of Guéréda, located at 14°30′ north latitude, 21°5′ east longitude, in the prefecture of Biltine, twenty-seven miles west of the Sudanese border;
6. the town of Faya-Largeau, located at 17°55′ north latitude, 19°10′ east longitude, an oasis in the Sahara and the administrative seat for the huge prefecture of Tibesti-Borkou-Ennedi.

A combination of unfavorable circumstances, including increased guerrilla activities in the area north of Lake Iro, the refusal of our drivers to pass through this territory, and the early beginning of the rainy season, which made the poor roads impassable, did not permit a study of the population of Guéréda. Because of weight limitations in transporting the team and equipment from Fort Lamy to Largeau by aircraft, the epidemiological investigations in that Saharan community had to be carried out by a smaller team, which did not include the entomologist and sanitary engineer.

Djimtilo

Djimtilo, with a population of approximately four hundred, is located about 134 kilometers north of Fort Lamy, in the canton of Mani, subprefecture of Fort Lamy, prefecture of Chari Baguirmi. To the west of the village flows the Chari River, and due north, 8 kilometers away, is Lake Chad. As can be seen from Figure 1–2, one edge of the village is bordered by the marshland that becomes part of the river during the rainy season. Otherwise the marsh can be seen as a stretch of stagnant water covered with tule and other vegetation. The closest fishing village is on an island at the mouth of the Chari River and is the working base for about twenty persons from Djimtilo.

The village of Djimtilo is compact. There is a large cleared plaza around which are built the houses and compounds, many of them enclosed by tall woven reed fences. This plaza serves as a gathering place for meetings and for the weekly market, which is held in Djimtilo on Thursdays. The compound belonging to the chief is centrally located and faces the market place.

The terrain is flat, the soil is sandy loam, and, with scattered thorny trees and squat palm trees, the vegetation is typical of the savannah region.

Djimtilo is about three hundred meters above sea level and has two distinct seasons, the dry and the rainy. The thirty-year average annual rainfall for this region is 500 millimeters (Direction de la Météorologie Nationale, 1955). Located near the edge of the Sahara, Djimtilo is subject to hot winds from the desert, often accompanied by blowing sandstorms in November and December and from March until June. In February the temperature at the medical campsite ranged between 54°F and 101° F.

Wildlife consists of a wide variety of animals since Djimtilo is situated only thirty kilometers from the Réserve de Faune du Bas Chari. Only antelope, wart hogs (*phacochére*), and hippopotami, however, are in evidence. There are a great many species of fish in the Chari River, including the *capitaine* (*Lates microlepis*) and the fish known locally as the *tetradont*, which are smoked and dried for the local as well as the national and international markets. Reptiles, scorpions, and insects are numerous.

The inhabitants of Djimtilo identify themselves as belonging to the Arab Salamat tribe and claim that the village is about 150

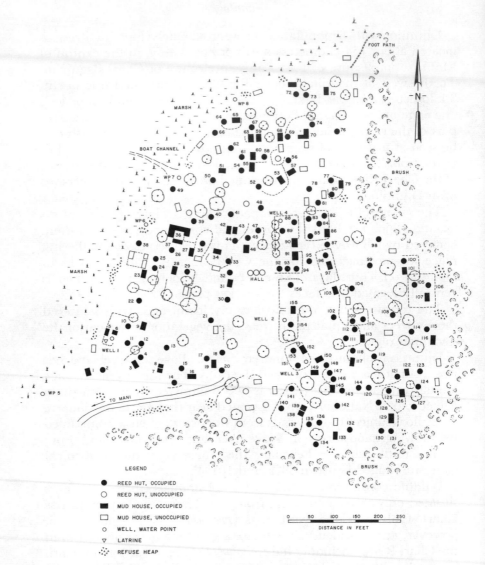

LEGEND

● REED HUT, OCCUPIED
○ REED HUT, UNOCCUPIED
■ MUD HOUSE, OCCUPIED
□ MUD HOUSE, UNOCCUPIED
○ WELL, WATER POINT
▽ LATRINE
⁖ REFUSE HEAP

FIGURE 1-2. MAP OF DJIMTILO

years old. The language spoken is Arabic, and all but two of the household heads interviewed claimed to belong to the Muslim faith. Although the village is located at the end of an unimproved road and appears to be isolated, the people's lives are intimately linked with those who live in neighboring villages, across the Chari River in the Cameroons, and in Fort Lamy. Because markets are held in different villages successively every day of the week, there is much visiting back and forth among the people of these communities. A Fort Lamy bus operator makes two trips a week from that town to Djimtilo and Mani, bringing news and trade goods to the villages. Although there have been extensive contacts with the external world, Djimtilo residents adhere to traditional Arabic customs. The village chieftainship is hereditary, with the chief's allegiance being divided between his obligation to the sultan, who is located in Mani, and his loyalty to the national government. Religious leaders are consulted frequently by the chief and village council, and they influence every aspect of the villagers' social life.

Ouli Bangala

Ouli Bangala is a community of about eight hundred people located in the southernmost part of western Chad in the canton of Bessao, subprefecture of Baibokoum. The village can be reached from Moundou, provincial capital of the prefecture of East Logone, by traveling 116 kilometers southward over graded road. The Lim River, which splits the village, serves as a natural boundary between the rocky hills and mountains to the south and the rolling sandy grassland to the north (Figure 1–3).

The center of the village is at the junction of the main Moundou-Baibokoum road and one that leads to Pandzangue. The houses, totaling about two hundred, lie on either side of the roads. About one hundred meters northeast of the crossroads are the school and its athletic field, and directly south of the school on the opposite side of the road is a United Evangelical church. That part of the village known as Ouli Bangala I, with a population of 401, was selected for research purposes. In recent years there has been a small but steady influx of families from the bush into the village. These families established their homes on the northern periphery of Ouli Bangala, an unoccupied section of land east of the Lim River (see Figure 1–3).

The household heads interviewed were from Ouli Bangala I and were principally Laka tribesmen (88.3 percent); the remaining nine of the seventy-seven respondents indicated that they belonged to the M'Boum, Sara Kaba, N'Gama, M'Gamba, and Moundang tribes. Partly because the village is located on the main roads to the

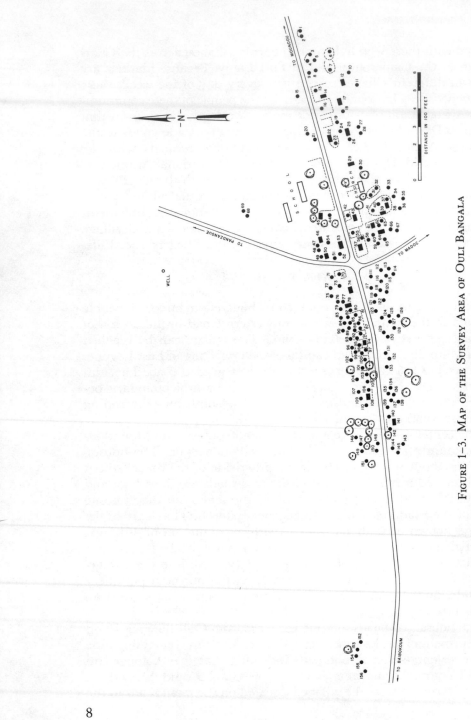

FIGURE 1–3. MAP OF THE SURVEY AREA OF OULI BANGALA

subprefecture office of Baibokoum and the thriving town of Pand-zangue, and partly because of the intensive activities sponsored by both the Catholic and Protestant missionaries, many indigenous customs have been either lost or modified: all male given names have their origins in the Bible; the native rites of passage for pubescent boys have been abandoned; and most young children can understand and speak simple basic French. The subsistence base is agriculture, but here, as elsewhere, there is a wide range of incomes and expenditures among the residents (the more affluent being the teachers and a retired veteran of the French army). Long contact with non-native elements in Ouli Bangala has had its effect on the political structure. Today the community relies more heavily on the officials who represent the national government, and on those persons with foreign training or experience, than on the wis-dom and power of the hereditary chief.

Here, as elsewhere in the southern half of Chad, there are dis-tinct rainy and dry seasons. The thirty-year average annual rainfall in this region is 1,250 millimeters, with most of it coming between April and October (Direction de la Météorologie Nationale, 1955). During the period of the team's residence in late February and early March, the minimum temperature was 50° F, the maximum 105° F.

Ouarai

The village of Ouarai, not indicated on the official map of Chad, is situated about one hundred kilometers southwest of Fort Arch-ambault, the second largest city in the country (Figure 1–4). The village is located in the subprefecture of Koumra, prefecture of Middle Chari, twenty-six kilometers south of the town of Koumra, and can be reached by a road which is open only during the dry months, from January through June.

Ouarai is divided into two political units, Ouarai I and Ouarai II, because of a recent split which will be described in the section on political structure. No discernible geographic feature separates the two units, but the villagers themselves know where the bound-ary is. There is some overlap in the residence patterns of the approximately six hundred inhabitants, with a few Ouarai II families living among those affiliated with Ouarai I.

Ouarai is a compact village (Ouarai I measures 1,200,000 square feet) and is surrounded by fields. Most houses, as shown in

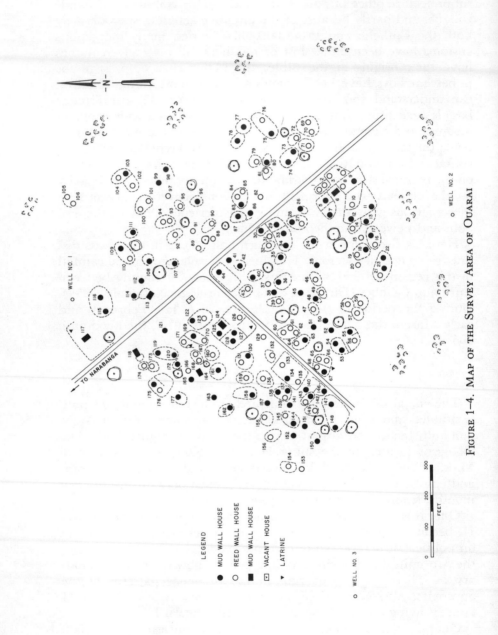

FIGURE 1–4. MAP OF THE SURVEY AREA OF OUARAI

Figure 1–4, are either enclosed by high reed fences or encircled by branches. The latter houses belong to widows whose husbands did not weave the fences and who thus have been left with the task.

The region in which Ouarai is located is representative of the southwestern half of the prefecture of Middle Chari. The savannah is covered with grass and small trees, with occasional tall kapok trees and Y-shaped palms. In some villages there are mango trees. The tributaries of the Lower Chari and Ouham rivers inundate most of the region during the rainy season and leave it moist, swampy, and insect-ridden even during the dry season.

According to readings taken in the medical camp in March, the maximum temperature was 106° F and the minimum 63° F. The thirty-year average annual rainfall in this region was 1,200 millimeters (Direction de la Météorologie Nationale, 1955).

Long contact with European and American missionaries and the foreign travel experiences of veterans of the French army had not had the disorganizing effect on the social system in Ouarai that they had had in Ouli Bangala. Except for two household heads of the eighty-four studied, all belonged to the Sara Vare tribe. The most influential community leaders—namely, the retired veterans and several individuals who had received training in the mission schools—were also the most westernized; at the time of the present study, the mission trainees were government-sanctioned officials. These leaders were the more affluent and were influential in introducing mango trees, thus enabling most people to have fruit, and in promoting labor-saving methods through the purchase of bullocks and carts. Since the village is located near the marsh, its inhabitants have easy access to land capable of producing garden vegetables and to the river, which supplies fish.

As in Ouli Bangala there had been growth in the size of the village. In Ouarai, however, as a result of power struggles between the two chieftains, there had been an exodus of one chief and his followers, who later returned to establish that portion of the village known as Ouarai II.

The spread in wealth among the Ouarai villagers was as great as that found in Djimtilo and Ouli Bangala, but the basis for it was different. Unlike Djimtilo, where wealth was gained solely through the efforts of individuals such as the religious and political leaders, and Ouli Bangala, where the wealthier individuals were civil servants and therefore received their incomes from the central government, the affluent segment in Ouarai received its income primarily from pensions paid to veterans who had served in the French army. That there were perhaps more persons of affluence living in Ouarai than the other villages was evidenced by the larger number of animals, both large and small, galvanized iron roofs for houses, and bullock carts.

Boum Khebir

Boum Khebir, with approximately nine hundred inhabitants, is located 260 kilometers northeast of Fort Archambault in the sub-prefecture of Kyabe, prefecture of Middle Chari (Figure 1–5). The road leading to the village from Kyabe passes through rolling brush-covered plains and through marshland with soil of a deep, spongy consistency.

Prior to 1961, houses in the village were constructed with no apparent order in small clusters enclosed by high reed fences. As the families grew in size, and particularly as the sons married, new homes and compounds were established adjacent to the fathers' compound. In 1964 the village was surveyed and streets were laid in a block pattern (Figure 1–5). Houses that interfered with the street plans were relocated on the south side of the main road.

The main road leading out of Boum Khebir toward Singako and Kyabe separates the old section of the village from the new. At the eastern terminus of the road is a plaza where the canton head-quarters and buildings for guests are located. This area also serves as a town meeting place, the location for the market, and as the place where cotton is brought for sale to the Cotonfran (Compagnie Cotonnière Equatoriale Francaise), a European-owned company which has a monopoly to collect, process, transport, and export cotton harvested in Chad, in return for a percentage of the profits set each year by the government (Thompson and Adloff, 1960, p. 176).

The road between Singako and the shore of Lake Iro is closed during the rainy season, from about the first of May through January. The total annual rainfall reported for 1959 was 768.5 milli-meters. The maximum temperature in Boum Khebir during the period of residence of the medical team was 111° F, and minimum 68° F.

The region is a zone of transition between the savannah and steppeland. Boum Khebir is one of twelve villages located in the canton of Iro at 387 meters above sea level and is approximately

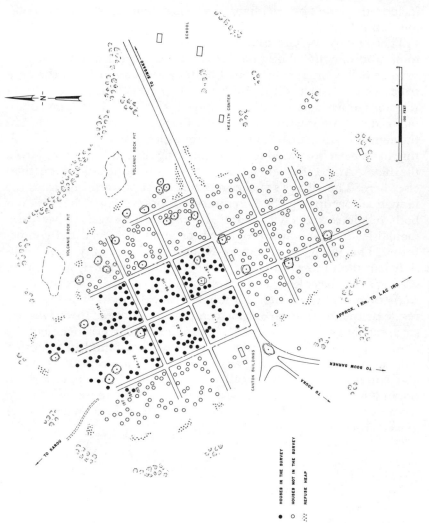

TO GARON

VOLCANIC ROCK PIT

VOLCANIC ROCK PIT

SCHOOL

HEALTH CENTER

TO GONDEY

107-116

117-154

73-97

55-72

1-18

19-43

44-72

CANTON BUILDINGS

TO BOUNA

TO BOUM BARHER

APPROX. I Km. TO LAC IRO

HOUSES IN THE SURVEY

HOUSES NOT IN THE SURVEY

REFUSE HEAP

100 FEET

FIGURE 1–5. MAP OF BOUM KHEBIR

13

one kilometer north of Lake Iro. The lake is the main water source for the villagers and for the numerous animals in the area, which include the antelope, elephant, wart hog, lion, giraffe, hippopotamus, and gazelle.

The most physically isolated village, Boum Khebir is also the most traditionally aboriginal in its social organization and subsistence behavior. It is inhabited by the Goula subtribe of the Sara tribe, whose dialect is little understood by outsiders; few Goulas in the community speak Arabic, despite the existence of long-standing trade relations with the nomadic Black Arab groups which pass through the village. Although certain aspects of the villagers' culture have been borrowed from neighboring Sara subtribes and from the Black Arabs, foreign influences are less noticeable here than elsewhere. The village's spokesman and most powerful figure is the individual occupying the hereditary position of chief; he serves as both religious and civil leader. There are, however, other ceremonial leaders who are recognized for areas of specialized competence. The villagers of Boum Khebir are generally more self-sufficient than those living in the other villages studied, with barter serving as the basis for exchange of various types of artifacts for foodstuffs or other necessities. Although a weekly market is held, the residents spend little except for condiments; indeed, there was less cash exchange here than elsewhere. The living arrangements of family members do not conform to the pattern found in the other villages, where there are separate structures for sleeping, cooking, and entertaining guests. Small children and older single girls in Boum Khebir live with their parents in one-room houses which also serve as kitchens. Older unattached boys sleep in quarters far removed from their parents.

Faya-Largeau

Administrative seat of the prefecture of Tibesti-Borkou-Ennedi, Faya-Largeau is about 1,085 kilometers northeast of Fort Lamy and is located in the largest oasis of the Chadian Sahara. The city is situated centrally on a narrow strip of cultivated land about thirty kilometers long and from two to five kilometers wide and is surrounded by numerous small villages.

Faya-Largeau is 233 meters above sea level. On the basis of a twenty-one-year record, the average maximum temperature (108° F) occurs in June, the average minimum (56° F) in January. The

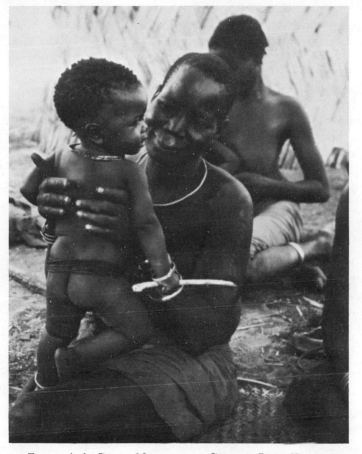

FIGURE 1–6. GOULA MOTHER AND CHILD IN BOUM KHEBIR

rainfall recorded over twenty-two years indicates that June, July, and August are the rainy months, although the amount of rain is negligible (Ministry of Public Health, 1966). The spring-fed oasis produces the finest dates in the region and also enables the inhabitants to grow cereals, truck vegetables, and fruits.

The two communities selected for study are located at the southern edge of the city. Komoro-e is a new village of settlers from the eastern part of the city. They were forced to move to the new location because shifting dunes had begun to cover their houses and because the area had become uninhabitable as a result of the rapid increase in the numbers of scorpions and vipers. The inhabitants of Komoro-e are largely members of a semiservile caste known as the Kamadja (Chapelle, 1957, p. 7). In times past they were slaves to the nomadic tribes and served as cultivators of the soil. More recently they have gained their freedom and have formed a canton headed by their own chief.

The second village, Garba, located several kilometers east of Komoro-e, is the permanent settlement of the nomadic Anakaza tribesmen. The Anakazas have only recently begun to build mud brick houses, and each compound still retains some elliptical-shaped tents.

Although each village is populated predominantly by the tribal groups mentioned above, other tribes are represented: Bornou, Arab-Marige, Arab-Ouled-Rachid, and Guida.

HOUSEHOLD AND FAMILY

The population pyramids for the five villages are asymmetrical, and pronounced differences are found in specific age-sex categories. There were markedly more females than males in all the villages except Ouarai, where the sex ratio (male to female) was 97.2 (see Table 1–1).

TABLE 1–1. SEX RATIO IN THE FIVE CHADIAN VILLAGES

	Djimtilo		Ouli Bangala		Ouarai		Boum Khebir		Faya-Largeau	
Males	162	74.7	184	84.8	180	97.2	172	83.1	97	80.8
Females	217		217		185		207		120	
Total	379		401		365		379		217	

The enumerated sample in Djimtilo was 379 persons, of whom 162 were males and 217 females (a sex ratio of 74.7). As shown in Figure 1–7, there were more females than males in all age categories except that of over fifty.

The proportion of males above the age of forty was much greater than that of the females; conversely, it was lower in the ten-to-forty-years categories. Informants revealed that many males in the latter age groups had migrated permanently either to Fort Lamy or across the Chari River to the Cameroons to avoid paying the head tax.

Explanations for the excess of ten-to-thirty-year-old females in Djimtilo included the males' desire to earn money in urban areas

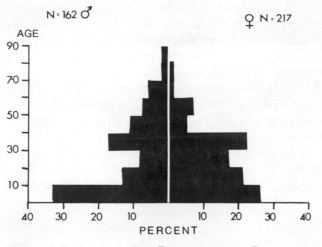

FIGURE 1–7. AGE AND SEX DISTRIBUTION OF POPULATION
SAMPLE, DJIMTILO

so that the bride price could be met. For the five villages, irregularities in the age distribution of females might also be attributed to factors such as polygyny and sex differences in mortality.

The sample in Ouli Bangala included 184 males and 217 females, the total population of the section known as Ouli I. The sex ratio was 84.8 (Figure 1–8). Only in the twenty-and-below and sixty-and-above age categories were there more males than females.

The health survey sample selected in Ouarai for study included 365 individuals, of whom 180 were males and 185 females, a sex

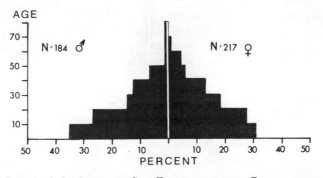

FIGURE 1–8. AGE AND SEX DISTRIBUTION OF POPULATION
SAMPLE, OULI BANGALA

ratio of 97.2 (see Figure 1–9). Males predominated in the twenty-and-younger, females in the fifty-and-older, age categories.

The population of Boum Khebir in 1960 was 859 (Pairault, 1966). The study sample included 379 persons belonging to ninety-two nuclear families living in the north-central part of the village (see Figure 1–10). In the sample 172 were males and 207 females, which gives a male-to-female ratio of 83.1.   As can be seen in Figure 1–10, there were proportionately more females in each age group except the birth-to-twenty-years category.

The sample for the study in Faya-Largeau included 217 persons, 98 from the Kamadja village of Komoro-e and 115 from the Anakaza village of Garba. There were 97 males and 120 females,

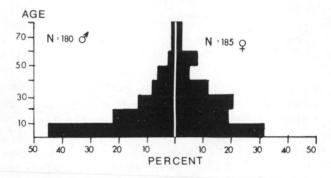

FIGURE 1–9. AGE AND SEX DISTRIBUTION OF POPULATION
SAMPLE, OUARAI

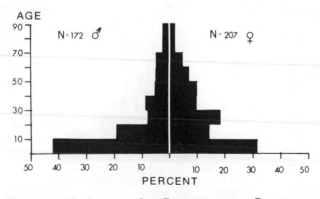

FIGURE 1–10. AGE AND SEX DISTRIBUTION OF POPULATION
SAMPLE, BOUM KHEBIR

resulting in a sex ratio of 80.8. Women predominated in all age groups except the birth-to-ten-years category (see Figure 1–11).

The residents in the communities studied, except those in Faya-Largeau, had lived most of their lives in the vicinity of their villages (Table 1–2). The inhabitants of Djimtilo had dwelled the highest proportion (96.4 percent) of time in that village, followed by those of Ouarai (91.9 percent), Boum Khebir (91.5 percent), Ouli Bangala (74.9 percent), and Faya-Largeau (17.4 percent). According to a respondent in Ouli Bangala, many villagers throughout Chad had fled from their homes in order to escape work as cargo carriers and plantation laborers during the French occupation. The evidence, however, indicates that this was perhaps true only in Ouli Bangala, where those in the thirty-years-and-older category had spent less than 55.6 percent of their lifetimes in the village, whereas in the remaining three communities, aside from Faya-Largeau, the percentages are significantly higher. As will be revealed, the Faya-Largeau Arabs are migratory, a fact which accounts for the fewest number of years spent in the village.

Not only had the villagers lived most of their lives in the vicinity of their respective villages, but few had made trips during the year preceding the study. The wet season is considered to be the period for planting and cultivating crops, while during the dry season the men busy themselves with harvesting crops and with repairing and/or rebuilding houses and fences. Household members are thus kept busy throughout the year. It is not surprising, then, that only a small percentage of the household heads had spent time away from their villages (Table 1–3). Of the southern villages, only in Ouli

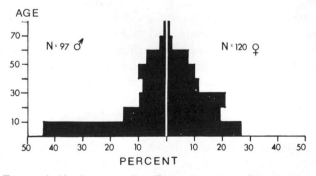

FIGURE 1–11. AGE AND SEX DISTRIBUTION OF POPULATION
SAMPLE, FAYA-LARGEAU

TABLE 1–2. RESIDENCE HISTORY BY AGE GROUPS: AVERAGE
PROPORTION OF LIFETIME SPENT IN VILLAGES

Age Groups	Djimtilo	Ouli Bangala	Ouarai	Boum Khebir	Faya-Largeau
Birth–9	97.6	93.0	95.7	100.0	12.5
10–19	98.6	73.5	93.6	90.7	29.5
20–29	95.9	64.8	87.2	82.8	12.9
30–39	94.2	52.2	90.1	80.4	23.3
40–49	95.6	50.1	90.9	84.8	9.6
50–59	99.6	41.3	78.1	90.4	24.0
60–69	84.7	55.6	89.0	100.0	30.7
70–79	100.0	—	100.0	100.0	10.2
All Age Groups	96.4[a]	74.9[a]	91.9[a]	91.5[a]	17.4[a]

[a] Age-weighted proportion of total lifetimes spent in the villages.

TABLE 1–3. PERCENTAGE OF MALE HOUSEHOLD HEADS WHO HAD SPENT TIME
AWAY FROM THE VILLAGE DURING THE YEAR PRECEDING THE INTERVIEW

	Djimtilo	Ouli Bangala	Ouarai	Boum Khebir	Faya-Largeau
Dry season	4.3	6.6	3.8	4.8	78.3
Wet season	2.9	27.9	1.9	12.9	

Bangala did a sizable proportion (34.5 percent) leave the village, with most of these making their trips during the wet season (27.9 percent) and for a period of a week or less (21.7 percent).

The residents of the villages in Faya-Largeau are highly mobile, particularly during the caravan season. After the date harvest in early winter, the caravans leave for other parts of Chad with dates which are exchanged for grain and other goods. When this trading is completed the caravans return to their villages in Faya-Largeau (Chapelle, 1957, pp. 123–25). Of the forty-six household heads who responded to the question regarding their absence from the village during the previous year, 65.2 percent indicated that they had been away for between two and four months. Ten, or 21.7 percent, revealed that they had not left the village. When the Kamadjas were compared with the Anakazas, it was found that nine (64.3 percent) of the former and twenty-three (92.0 percent) of the latter had been away for one month or longer, with the majority having spent from two to four months in caravan travel.

Marital Status

Early marriage is expected, and, if possible, males prefer to have more than one wife. They tend to remarry when relationships are broken by divorce or death. As will be discussed later, men remarry more often than women, particularly when widowing occurs.

In Djimtilo, in the sample of eighty-five household heads, sixty-five of the seventy males, or 92.9 percent, and three of the fifteen females, or 20 percent, were married (see Table 1–4). The percentage of male family heads in the remaining three southern villages was close to that for Djimtilo. Of the forty-two household heads in Faya-Largeau on whom data are available, twenty-six males and sixteen females, 96.2 percent of the former and 81.3 percent of the latter, were married. Among the female household heads from whom interviews were obtained, the proportion of unattached women varied, with the number being highest in Ouli Bangala (93.8 percent) and lowest in Faya-Largeau (18.7 percent).

The reasons for the absence of spouses of female household heads during the study period are numerous. Djimtilo absentees were in Bol to collect debts or were at the fishing village. The ten husbands in Ouarai were in either Fort Lamy, Koumra, or Baibokoum, and no specific reasons were given for their absence. Boum Khebir male household heads were at fishing streams some distance away from the village. The reasons for absence from the Faya-Largeau villages were not obtained.

TABLE 1–4. COMPARISON OF MARITAL STATUS OF HOUSEHOLD HEADS

Marital Status	Djimtilo		Ouli Bangala		Ouarai		Boum Khebir		Faya-Largeau	
	No.	%	No.	%	No.	%	No.	%	No.	%
Unattached M	5	7.1	8	13.3	5	11.5	2	3.3	1	3.8
Married M	65	92.9	52	86.7	46	88.5	59	96.7	25	96.2
Unattached F	12	80.0	15	93.8	18	64.3	9	29.0	3	18.7
Married F	3	20.0	1	6.2	10	35.7	22	71.0	13	81.3

In each of the villages polygyny is the preferred marital arrangement, although it is too expensive for all but a limited number of males. Custom varies with respect to the selection of the first wife, except that the initial marriage occurs as soon as possible after the onset of puberty, with the bride price and dowry being made available by the parents. In practice, however, postponement of the marriage until the late teens is more usual since neither the families nor intended bridegrooms ordinarily have the bride price in hand.

The financial responsibility for securing the second or third wife is that of the male desirous of acquiring additional wives. Succeeding wives are generally younger than the first, and virgins who have just reached menarche are preferred. Polygyny is considered advantageous for both men and women. Men do not engage in many of the chores necessary for the daily maintenance of the household, such as pounding millet, hauling water, keeping the compound clean, and cooking. For the women, the more wives there are, the more hands there are to share in this work. A second or third wife enables the husband to have more children and also permits him to have sexual outlets with those wives who are not pregnant, since taboos forbid sexual intercourse with pregnant and lactating women. Another benefit to the husband is extra help in tilling the fields.

The polygynous arrangement, although desirable, can be undertaken only by those wealthy enough to pay the additional bride price. When the marital status of males in the five communities was compared, Boum Khebir had the highest percentage—32.8— of males having more than one wife, followed by Ouli Bangala, 25 percent, Ouarai, 19.2 percent, Faya-Largeau, 18.2 percent, and Djimtilo, 8.1 percent (Table 1–5).

TABLE 1–5. NUMBER OF WIVES OF HOUSEHOLD HEADS

No. of Wives	Djimtilo %	Ouli Bangala %	Ouarai %	Boum Khebir %	Faya-Largeau %
One	91.9	75.0	80.8	67.2	81.8
Two	8.1	19.2 } 25.0	9.6 } 19.2	27.9 } 32.8	13.6 } 18.2
Three	—	5.8	9.6	4.9	4.6
	100.0	100.0	100.0	100.0	100.0

The extent of dissolution of marriage by divorce varied among the villages. Djimtilo had the lowest percentage of divorced males, but the evidence indicates that during their lifetimes they had more wives serially. Of the household heads, 65.7 percent of the males and 80.0 percent of the females had been divorced at least once (Table 1–6). The lowest percentage of divorces—11.1 percent of the males and 15.6 percent of the females—was reported in Boum Khebir. Divorce rates of the male household heads of Ouli Bangala (37.7 percent) and Ouarai (34.6 percent) took an intermediate position, while the rate in Faya-Largeau (59.3 percent of the males and 26.3 percent of the females) was close to the rate in Djimtilo. The similarity of the figures for Djimtilo and Faya-Largeau could reflect the common cultural heritage of these Muslim villages.

TABLE 1-6. PERCENTAGE OF DIVORCES AMONG HOUSEHOLD HEADS

	Djimtilo %	Ouli Bangala %	Ouarai %	Boum Khebir %	Faya-Largeau %
Males	65.7	37.7	34.6	11.1	59.3
Females	80.0	56.3	27.6	15.6	26.3

The percentage of male and female household heads in the five villages who had experienced widowhood was lowest in Djimtilo (10.6 percent) and highest in Ouarai (35.8 percent). In Boum Khebir and Faya-Largeau a little more than one-fourth of the household heads (27.4 percent and 26.1 percent respectively), and in Ouli Bangala 18.2 percent, had lost their spouses. When male and female household heads were compared, the proportion of losses was almost the same in Faya-Largeau. The percentage of females who had lost their spouses was higher in Ouli Bangala, Ouarai, and Boum Khebir, and lower in Djimtilo (see Table 1-7).

TABLE 1-7. PERCENTAGE OF HOUSEHOLD HEADS WIDOWED

	Djimtilo %	Ouli Bangala %	Ouarai %	Boum Khebir %	Faya-Largeau %
Males	11.4	14.8	26.9	17.5	25.9
Females	6.7	31.3	51.7	46.9	26.3

Family Life

The basic social unit in each of the five villages is the nuclear family, which consists of the male head of household, his wife or wives, children, and, occasionally, unattached adults. As indicated in the previous section, marriages in the five communities are not stable, and remarriages are frequent, except in the case of widows in Ouarai. Still, the percentage of families with single parents, some temporarily separated, was high—44 percent in Ouarai, 33.3 percent in Ouli Bangala, 32.9 percent in Boum Khebir, 24.2 percent in Djimtilo, and 9.7 percent in Faya Largeau.

The size of the household, which includes the male head and members of his family, varies with the number of wives, as shown in Table 1–8. The average number for the five villages during this study was 4.0 persons.

Living arrangements in each of the villages are dictated by custom. In Djimtilo it is customary for the man to have his own adobe house as well as a separate one for each wife and her children. In addition, there is a hut set aside for the kitchen and an open shelter used to entertain male visitors. Unattached adult single persons have their own houses but generally eat their meals with relatives; still, they claim to have only one house. Owners of single houses thus accounted for 36.7 percent of the households surveyed, while another 26.5 percent of the household heads claimed two houses, and the remainder (36.8 percent) owned three or more (Table 1–9).

In Ouli Bangala and Ouarai similar living arrangements are found, with married adult members of the extended family having their own houses but sharing a common kitchen. Thus almost half (48.3 percent) of the household heads in Ouarai and approximately 41 percent in Ouli Bangala owned only one house, with the remainder (51.7 percent in Ouarai, 59.1 percent in Ouli Bangala) owning two or more.

In Boum Khebir it is more usual for the household head to have only one house. It serves as a living, dining, and sleeping room, and, unless the male head has more than one wife, no other quarters are established. However, since members of the extended family live within the same compound, one other shelter may be found; it is used as the kitchen. When boys reach puberty, and following their initiation rites, they live in separate houses built some distance away from those belonging to their parents. Slightly less than 75 percent of the household heads interviewed owned only one house.

The division of labor between the sexes was found to be the same in the five villages. Male household heads are expected to provide most of their families' subsistence needs, build houses and keep them in livable condition, and are responsible for securing the funds necessary for initiation rites and the bride price for their sons. Women work with their menfolk in the fields. In addition, they

TABLE 1–8. AVERAGE SIZE OF FAMILIES IN THE FIVE VILLAGES

	Djimtilo			Ouli Bangala			Ouarai			Boum Khebir			Faya-Largeau		
	No.	Av. Size	%	No.	Av. Size	%	No.	Av. Size	%	No.	Av. Size	%	No.	Av. Size	%
Single parent	20	2.1	24.2	26	2.9	33.3	37	2.1	44.0	30	2.8	32.9	4	4.0	9.7
One wife	58	3.6	69.8	38	3.9	48.8	38	4.2	45.2	41	3.9	45.1	30	4.4	73.2
Two wives	5	6.0	6.0	10	6.4	12.8	7	7.7	8.3	17	6.4	18.7	3	8.0	7.3
Three wives				4	8.8	5.1	1	8.0	1.2	3	4.7	3.3	4	6.0	9.7
Four wives							1	14.0	1.2						
	83	3.4	100.0	78	4.2	100.0	84	3.8	99.9	91	4.0	100.0	41	4.8	99.9

TABLE 1–9. HOUSE OWNERSHIP IN FOUR[a] VILLAGES

No. of Houses	Djimtilo %	Ouli Bangala %	Ouarai %	Boum Khebir %
1	36.7	40.8	48.3	74.3
2	26.5	44.5	29.2	17.8
3	19.1	7.4	12.4	4.9
4	11.8	5.4	6.7	2.0
5	5.9	1.8	3.4	1.0
	100.0	99.9	100.0	100.0

[a]No data available for Faya-Largeau.

process foodstuffs and prepare meals for the family, and are expected to haul water for domestic use. From the standpoint of time spent in the fields and in household maintenance, women are much more occupied than men.

There is little crossover in sex roles among the villagers, a fact which exerts pressure on the males to obtain wives, although the reverse does not necessarily hold. Men will neither prepare their own food nor haul water, and therefore they either seek a mate to do these chores or rely on their female relatives. On the other hand, while building houses and building or mending fences is considered men's work, widows and other unattached women do engage in these activities, often, however, with the help of male relatives.

While there are general similarities in the household and family life of the villagers, the differences in some respects are quite marked. A more detailed comparison of the process of family formation and of the attitudes and values related to the status and roles of individuals in the family unit reveals two distinct cultural patterns for the villages under study—the Muslim pattern, which exists in Djimtilo and Faya-Largeau, and the southern tribal pattern, which shapes life in Ouli Bangala, Ouarai, and Boum Khebir. The following sections describe family life in Djimtilo and Ouli Bangala.

Djimtilo

Conjugal life in Djimtilo begins at an early age for both boys and girls, and it is the culmination of a series of childhood rites that are conducted prior to marriage.

The results of scarifying the face twenty-six days after birth are observable among older teen-age girls. This practice was taken over by the Arabs from the Kotoko fishermen who live in the region. In more recent years scarification as a mark of beauty has become less popular. This, however, is not true of the practice of the excision of the clitoris, which occurs between the ages of six and twenty, more often between the ages of eleven and fourteen. The operation is considered proper, and those who have not submitted to this rite are kept separate during meals and are subject to ridicule by other girls and women.

Boys are circumcised after the age of three, most commonly when they reach the age of seven. When a father has enough money to pay the fee, about $30.00, he announces his readiness to have his son circumcised. The funds are used to pay the surgeon and to defray the cost of the festivities, which last for four days. Other fathers who have sons may join as co-sponsors, thus reducing the cost of the ceremony. Boys who have lost their fathers, or whose parents have been too poor to have the rite performed, must wait to be circumcised until they have earned enough money to pay the fee themselves. An uncircumcised male may not pray with others.

A boy's father will select a wife for his son when he has reached his fourteenth year. The father pays the bride price of $40.00 or more, depending upon the beauty, personality, and hard-working qualities of the future daughter-in-law. The girl's parents also have obligations, as they must furnish her with a bed and food to last for three months. If the boy's father does not have the bride price ready, or if the bride's parents do not have the dowry, the wedding may still be held, but the date for the consummation of the marriage may be postponed for months. However, regardless of the parents' financial capabilities, there is a minimum waiting time of seven days between the marriage ceremony and the consummation date. During this period the bride is kept in the seclusion of her father's house to insure her delivery as a virgin.

When both parties are ready for the marriage ceremony, a dance is held in the courtyard of the girl's home with most of the village present. Flutists and drummers accompany young dancing girls selected from members of the girl's dance group. These dances are formal and stylistic, but in the evening informal dances are held. Placed within the enclosure are items which the girl will carry with her to her new home. Multicolored pans, loaned for this purpose by either the imam or other wealthy persons, are filled with millet, rice, ground nuts, and condiments. Bags of corn, numerous bottles of oil, and the bed and bedding all are on display.

FIGURE 1–12. WEDDING FESTIVITY IN DJIMTILO

After the waiting period, the bridegroom arrives to claim his bride, and a procession of the bride's female relatives transport her dowry to the bridegroom's home. Once there, more ceremonies are held, and the bride's relatives wait outside the nuptial hut for the announcement that the bride is a virgin. If she is a virgin, family life begins. If she is found not to be a virgin, the groom may either send her home or accept her at a lower bride price. In the event the groom sends her home, the father will seek to discover the person who deflowered his daughter. The accused, if discovered to be guilty, will then pay a fine to the father.

The husband is obligated to provide the necessities for the livelihood of the family. Likewise, the wife has obligations, not only to her husband, but to her husband's parents. Daily she must take a portion of the meal she prepares to her mother-in-law. She further assists in the hauling of water, in keeping the compound clean, in doing the washing, and in working in the fields with her husband. Orders are not passed directly to the daughter-in-law from either of her parents-in-law but are channeled through her husband; this practice tends to reduce friction which might otherwise develop. If the daughter-in-law finds herself exploited, or if the husband's subsistence is found wanting, the wife will refuse to take food to her mother-in-law and, under extreme circumstances, will return to her father's house.

When the wife of the head of the household dies, the daughter-in-law is obligated to prepare food for her husband's father and she becomes the matriarch. When the head of the household dies, the widow is given only her house, and the remainder of the property is divided among the sons. If there are many grown married sons, each will become the head of his own household and may elect to build his own compound elsewhere.

Marriage is brittle in Djimtilo, and few couples live a lifetime together. Rather than enter into a polygynous relationship, an accepted practice in this village, men tend to have their wives serially. Of twenty household heads who were asked how many times they had been divorced, nine were noted to have been divorced at least once, and one replied that he had been divorced eleven times.

When a woman is divorced, she spends 100 days in the seclusion of her father's house. The waiting period permits the man to claim his child should his divorced wife prove to be pregnant. After the waiting period, a woman may either remain in her father's household, declaring that she is available for marriage, or she may become "a woman for everyone."

Since girls are considered an economic burden to the head of the household, early marriages are encouraged so that the bride price may be forthcoming. A girl who has no prospects is given to the imam, who performs the defloration ceremony. Thereafter she is considered available to other men as a prostitute and is thus able to support herself.

Most family activities are sex linked, although some may be engaged in by both sexes. Males are required to build houses, weave fences, fish, farm, and engage in other income-producing activities. Boys from the age of eight to ten begin to learn these skills. During the dry season the workday begins at dawn and ends at 10 A.M., although the men may return to the fields in the late afternoon. Because of the limited number of work activities engaged in by the males, they spend much of their time in the shade of trees, drinking tea and generally at leisure. Women, on the other hand, besides working with the men in the fields, are required to perform the maintenance chores for the household. Thus, when they are not in the fields, from early morning, throughout the day, and on into the early evenings they pound corn or millet, carry water, wash clothes, and sweep the compound. On market days the women display their wares for sale and spend their time gossiping and visiting.

As indicated earlier, a family or several nuclear families that live within a single compound comprise the household. Individual members of this unit are the head of the household, his sons and their spouses, unmarried children, and other relatives. New households are created when the head dies and older sons and their families move to other locations within the village.

The household works its fields cooperatively, and members participate in mutual-aid activities such as helping to raise the bride price or the dowry.

Ouli Bangala

The Ouli Bangala household is composed of those nuclear families who live together in a single compound and are related through blood lines, marriage, or friendship. Households are important in that their members, together with other household units, engage in many types of cooperative ventures—they hunt, fish, and work in the fields as a unit. Financial support is given for ceremonial and social functions, and more intensive social interactions occur within the group(s) than with outsiders.

FIGURE 1–13. MARKET DAY IN DJIMTILO

The nuclear family is established at an early age in Ouli Bangala. Boys at fifteen and girls at menarche are considered ready for marriage. Youths are capable of performing all of the duties required for the maintenance of the family. A boy of fifteen already has built himself a house, worked in the fields, and learned how to hunt and fish. He, like his friends, has had some experience with girls, and he seeks as a prospective mate a girl who has proved her capacity for work, who does not have a sharp tongue, and who is considered beautiful.

The courtship begins when the suitor sends his sister or, in her absence, a brother to determine whether the girl will accept him as a potential husband. If she agrees, the boy, accompanied by a younger brother or friend, visits the girl and stays at her parents' house for from three to five days. If the girl has more than one suitor, each of them will remain with her parents and work for them in the fields, in the house, or at fence building. Eventually the competitors are told which of them has been selected, and the others are dismissed.

At this point the couple's parents or, in their absence, the bride's paternal uncle will negotiate the bride price. The bride price is about $100.00, and the boy's father and relatives are obligated to help him obtain his first wife. Should there not be sufficient funds available, the boy will continue to work for his father, and at the same time he will work two or three days each week with the girl's father. It may be two or three years before the amount agreed upon is accumulated. The bride price is dependent upon the affluence of the prospective husband and/or his family, and it functions as a control over the spouse. A husband who pays little for his bride cannot make the same demands of her as one who spends a large sum.

When the bride price is in hand, the boy's cousin takes a goat and two chickens to the girl's residence. The goat is given to the girl's paternal uncle, who kills it and prepares it for the members of the extended family. If any member is absent, one calabash filled with millet and meat will be saved. The chickens are prepared and served to the members of the immediate family and to the cousins of the girl.

The day following the wedding ceremony, a village-wide dance is held. The girl's parents, accompanied by her sisters and cousins, take two goats and millet to the boy's house. The village chief is invited, and the festivities, which consist largely of drinking millet beer and dancing, will continue for three or four days. The young bride then settles in to live in her father-in-law's compound.

Controls are exerted by both the girl and her father. The father's choice may not be that of his daughter. While the bride price may be fully paid by the selected suitor, the girl may insist that the first child be that of the suitor who lost out but was her choice. Only after the birth of the first child will she consent to sexual intercourse with her husband.

Within the family unit of Ouli Bangala there is a distinct division of labor. The males build houses and fences, hunt, fish, secure grass for house roofs, and weave basket containers for cotton and millet. They are prepared to fight when insults are received against either themselves or members of their families. The females haul water, prepare meals, clean the house and yard, care for the children, pound millet, make millet beer (*kito*), sell various items at the local market, and work in the fields with their husbands. During the cotton-harvest season they carry baskets of cotton to the central purchasing area. From the listing of these activities it would appear that the women are more occupied and perform more arduous work than do the men. Community members refuse to engage in activities considered to be the responsibility of the opposite sex. For example, on the first day of camp activities men hired as camp laborers refused to carry water up the bank of the Lim River, and it was necessary to recruit women for this task.

If after the union the wife does not live up to expected work standards or is surly and nagging, the husband is at liberty to send her back to her parents, who will then counsel her. Should there be valid reasons on his part for continued separation, the bride price will be returned to the husband, indicating that a divorce has occurred. The husband retains all the children.

Divorced women, even when pregnant, are not frowned upon by prospective husbands. Frequently the brothers of the girl will seek her return if she complains that her husband is lazy or mean, even though the man himself remains generally attractive in dress and demeanor. The bride price is returned to the husband, and the girl becomes available for remarriage. If the girl is pregnant as a result of the first union, her bride price becomes greater than that which was charged against the first husband. With the return of the bride price, the biological father can no longer claim his unborn child. A divorced woman who has children but who is not pregnant brings less than the original price. Unattached women are visited by un-

FIGURE 1–14. POUNDING MILLET IN OULI BANGALA

married as well as married men. In the past, when a wife caught her husband with an unattached woman, she burned the other woman's house and murdered her. More recently, the pattern has been for the neglected wife to tell everyone in her household of her husband's activity, in the hope of both ridiculing and shaming him.

While sexual freedom is permitted among male youths, attempts are made to exert controls so that the girls will remain virgins until their first marriage. Widows are not desired as marriage partners by men, because the second husbands feel they are constantly being compared to the first. Widows are thus available as sexual partners for young men. A young bride who is not a virgin attempts to keep this a secret lest the husband use this knowledge against her. He will not permit her to forget her status as a "girl of the road." Should the situation become unbearable for the unfortunate girl, she may leave the village for a larger town or city to engage in prostitution.

Men are permitted to have several wives if they have the funds for their purchase. Succeeding wives will be young, and they will receive orders from the first wife. The husband, in order to maintain harmonious relations with his wives and among the wives themselves, will invite them to share his bed in rotation, spending equal time with each of them. Since each wife has her own sleeping hut and separate kitchen, she prepares his food, as well as the food for their children, on the days that he spends with her. She does not, however, eat with him, since he prefers to eat with his friends and sons, if he has any. The wife then has her meals with the other wives.

Regularity of visitation cannot be maintained, because of the woman's menstrual cycle and because of pregnancy. During menstruation the woman must be kept isolated in her own hut; she cannot prepare food and does not do so for two weeks after cessation of the menstrual cycle. Avoidance of food preparation is carefully practiced since it is believed that partaking of this food will result in the male's vomiting for a period of a week. When the woman is six months pregnant she stops sleeping with her husband, and abstinence continues until the child is able to walk.

SOCIAL RANKING

As in other countries where rapid social and economic changes are occurring, western criteria are being used by Chadian villagers to rank individuals. Although certain prestige-conferring customs are no longer practiced, they are nevertheless still highly valued, serving as ceremonial symbols of achievement and to place the individual in the social system. The focus in this section will be on the male, since it was only in Ouarai that the study found females, expecially widows, occupying a status in the economic dimension which was competitive with the males. Otherwise, women occupy a subordinate status and are generally subservient to men. They are placed in the village structure according to their marital status.

Djimtilo

Djimtilo is a culturally homogeneous community whose members depend on the whims of environmental conditions for their livelihood. Within this framework it might be expected that a community of eighty-five households would show little in the way of social ranking. There are, however, haves and have-nots, and different levels of education and occupation which place families on various levels of the prestige scale.

In the highest echelon of the status scale are the religious and political leaders. The religious leaders (the imam and the fakirs) through their long years of Koranic training have become the diagnosticians and healers for this village. They are the wealthier persons because, in addition to having farms, they receive substantial incomes for their services. Likewise, the chief and his councilmen and their families are more prestigious than others. The influential men's possessions, particularly brightly colored pans, are an indication of their wealth, and status is gained by lending these to families whose children are getting married. Moreover, they frequently have meal and teatime guests. Visitors from other villages are treated hospitably, and the hosts who are considered most generous are highly praised.

Ouli Bangala

In Ouli Bangala there are some criteria of the old system which are still highly valued. New ones, however, have been added since the country gained its independence, which brought with it the involvement of residents in national goals and in a money economy. Also, some of the old customs which served as a basis for social ranking have been discontinued because of the influence of Protestant missionaries. Position in the status system in the old days was dependent upon wealth and property; prowess as a hunter, fisherman, or fighter; or the role of village chief, subchief, or instructor in the initiation of young boys entering manhood.

Traditionally, manly qualities are considered extremely important. A youth's behavior during his initiation rites was once the basis for the early assumption of status as a man. With the arrival of an evangelical pastor, a Sara-Kaba tribesman from Oubangui-Chari, eleven years ago, these rites were banned; their discontinuance, without replacement by another system of induction is said to have caused children to be disrespectful to their elders and to have lessened social cohesion. Although no longer practiced, the rites will be described in order to reveal why those who had been initiated were, and still are, held in high esteem.

The initiation rites began when a group of from twenty to thirty boys reached the age of ten years. The boys' fathers agreed on a date for the rites to begin, hired a drummer, and at sundown invited the boys to dance. At dawn the next day the boys were awakened, escorted into the bush, and thrown into a stream in order to clear their minds for the coming tasks. During the succeeding three years the boys learned to build homes, hunt, cultivate fields, collect wood, and speak a secret language. If food became scarce, the boys returned to the edge of the village and through the use of sign language requested their parents to leave food where it could be collected. Another way of replenishing their supply was to stalk close to the village and, with the use of a bull-roarer, frighten women and children into the houses. The initiates then stole goats, chickens, and millet. If the boys were caught, they were taken outside the village and beaten by their parents.

Another aspect of the ritual was the filing of teeth into points; this was not mandatory, but those who did not wish to participate were beaten for three days. The boys were also required periodically to spend two days and nights in the bush alone; they were expected to survive and to bring back to the camp a small animal such as a beaver or a young antelope.

The rites did not terminate with the return of the initiates to the village. The boys' first obligation was to marry the girls they had selected. Dressed in goatskin loincloths, metal ankle bracelets, and neck chains, the boys were expected to dance from 6 A.M. to noon and from 3 P.M. to 6 P.M. daily for a period of thirty days. During this period, while they might share the sleeping mat with their wives, they were not permitted to speak with them, nor were they permitted to speak to their mothers for a period of a year following their return. The only communication possible for the initiates, under penalty of being buried alive, was in their secret language with one another.

Since the independence of the country the government has stressed education, developed a road system, and outlawed revenge murders. Men who attained prestige under the old system have to share it with those who participate in the more recently developed activities. Money (with what it can purchase), level of education, and acceptance of western dress have become important. A retired French army veteran, with a $200.00 quarterly pension, is the wealthiest person in the village. Besides displaying his affluence by building houses with galvanized iron roofs and by having his three wives garbed in colorful dresses, he sponsors innumerable dances for all the members of the community. The four school teachers, all of whom are from other regions of Chad and are fluent in French, receive regular incomes; they reside in better, cleaner houses and wear western dress. The evangelical pastor also belongs to this category of higher status.

At the lower end of the status system are those who have only subsistence skills. Their lack of affluence is observable in their clothing— men on this level dress in tattered garments and women still cover their front and backsides with fresh leaves (changed daily).

Ouarai

Social ranking in Ouarai is based on several criteria. In times past, skills in hunting and fishing were highly valued. More recently, a speaking knowledge of French, indicating either some degree of education or experience in the French army, has become a symbol of prestige. In either case, the accumulation of wealth is the end result, and wealth is displayed through such items as clothing, housing, wagons, bicycles, and oxen. Persons who are considered to be wealthy sponsor village-wide feasts and lend assistance to those in need; such customs as these serve as leveling devices among members of the community.

The veterans, of whom there were seven at the time of this study, are the most affluent villagers. These persons, through their travels to urban areas in Chad and in other parts of Africa, France, and Southeast Asia, have experienced the world beyond the village. Their pensions vary, depending upon service rank at the time of retirement, but even minimally their annual incomes are far greater than those of others. Indeed, their pensions range from $240 to $1,000 per year, while the average villager lives on a subsistence level. Ex-servicemen live in rectangular homes roofed with galvanized iron sheets, own two-wheeled wagons which can be pulled by bullocks, and have numerous store-bought items in their homes. When they receive their quarterly pensions, they are obligated to sponsor a village-wide feast. This is done so that the other villagers will not slander them or make attempts to apply the *kuga*, or witchcraft.

Veterans have made innumerable attempts to introduce non-aboriginal concepts and practices. They have tried to foster the use of latrines, and they have attempted to instill the military concept of scheduling the events of the day so that there will be a minimum of quarreling and better control of children's behavior, but without much success. The only innovation accepted by the local residents has been the planting of mango trees. A veteran brought a young tree to Ouarai from Fort Archambault and, despite ridicule by other members of the community, protected it from damage by goats and made it productive. Today most families own one or more trees.

The political leaders of the village—that is, the chief, subchiefs, and the president (a civil servant representing the national government)—are also considered to have higher prestige than others. Persons in this category meet visitors and offer them hospitality. Praise is given to these individuals according to the manner in which they perform this duty.

Boum Khebir

The status system in Boum Khebir is linked closely with the tribe's chief ethical value; namely, that its members strive toward the maintenance of a stable and organized society (Pairault, 1966, pp. 283–84). The manner in which an individual fulfills his economic, social, and ceremonial roles toward this end determines the prestige which will be conferred upon him by the villagers. He must have such subsistence skills as to be able to accumulate a surplus which he will share with others and he must provide hospitality to expected and unexpected guests. The capacity for "giving his blood" to many descendants and providing for their livelihood is highly valued. It is believed that only with age does an individual accumulate and acquire the ancestral wisdom which enables him to meet the obligation to achieve high status. Those in Boum Khebir who have this status, then, are members of the power structure and are ceremonial leaders.

Faya-Largeau

In Faya-Largeau, although there are some inherent differences in cultural behavior, including status, between the Anakaza and Kamadja tribesmen, there are today possibly more similarities than differences (Chapelle, 1957). The Anakazas are nomads who spend part of the year in the lower part of Chad near Fort Lamy, where their camels and sheep are pastured. They may have rights to palm groves in Faya-Largeau which are cultivated by the Kamadjas. The Anakaza are most closely affiliated with their own social units, which are comprised of extended families. At the same time, each family considers itself autonomous, its fate being in the hands of the household head.

When slave-taking was permitted, the Anakazas used the Kamadjas to guard and water their camel herds and installed them on abandoned or virgin fields, either on the outskirts of an existing palm grove or in a new location. The Kamadjas were considered lower in status, and at present there are still some who, although no longer slaves, nevertheless serve as tenant farmers. When given their freedom the Kamadjas began to grow dates; their skills are indicated by the fact that during the date harvest season more than 10,000 nomads gather in the oasis to purchase this product (Chapelle, 1957, pp. 197–200).

RELIGION

The study of religious affiliations in the five villages revealed a diversity of stated beliefs, although not necessarily the degree of involvement in those beliefs. The religious distribution is summarized in Table 1–10.

TABLE 1–10. RELIGIOUS AFFILIATION OF HOUSEHOLD
HEADS IN THE FIVE VILLAGES

Religion	Djimtilo %	Ouli Bangala %	Ouarai %	Boum Khebir %	Faya-Largeau %
Animist-Fetishist				86.0	
Muslim	100.0		55.7	8.6	100.0
Protestant		75.3	8.6	1.1	
Catholic		24.7	35.7	3.2	
Other				1.1	
	100.0	100.0	100.0	100.0	100.0

Intensive interviews with selected informants indicated that, except for Muslims in Djimtilo and Faya-Largeau, villagers in the other communities hold strongly to their traditional belief systems. The Muslims do not, however, follow the precepts of the Koran

closely, some because of indifference and others because of igno-
rance (Chapelle, 1957, pp. 375–91). Certain aspects of behavior are
related to their traditional religious beliefs. For example, sacred
rites are held before sowing, prior to the harvest, and at the time of
fertilizing the palm trees.

All residents of Ouli Bangala hold to animistic beliefs. At the
same time, however, respondents revealed that they belonged to
either the Catholic or the Evangelical mission.

Spirits are believed to be either good or bad. They can either
protect the individual, cure him of maladies, and assure good crops
and an abundance of fish and game, or be responsible for misfortunes. This will be expanded in later sections pertaining to health
beliefs and livelihood.

The activities of the Catholic mission in Chad began in the mid-
twenties, and by 1957 an African priest had been ordained in the
Fort-Lamy apostolic prefecture (Thompson and Adloff, 1960, pp.
302–3). The missionaries in the field are largely of French extrac-
tion. In Ouli Bangala there is a retreat for priests, but none were in
residence at the time this study was made. A Catholic chapel is
located about a half-mile west of the Lim River. Of the seventy-
seven household heads interviewed, nineteen, or 24.7 percent, de-
clared themselves to be Catholics (Table 1–11).

The Protestant church in Ouli Bangala was established in 1955
with the arrival of a missionary from the Sara-Kaba tribe. Prior to
his arrival he had worked with an English missionary at Oubangui,
which is located in the southern part of the Central African Republic. The church is active, with from 130 to 140 persons attending
services on Sundays and with lesser crowds on Thursdays. In addition, the pastor performs marriage and burial ceremonies. Of the
seventy-seven persons interviewed, 75.3 percent indicated that they
were Protestants (Table 1–11). The church has been effective in
initiating social change. As an example, all persons converted to
the Protestant faith have biblical names, and the rites of initiation
for both boys and girls have been terminated because of the pastor's
belief that certain of those practices are immoral.

In Ouarai animistic beliefs are strongly adhered to despite the
activities of missionaries. Graves are not found in any circumscribed
cemetery area, but are scattered throughout the village and its
periphery. Infants are buried within the household compound.
Even a veteran of the French army is buried on the main road into
Ouarai with as yet only a flagpole flying the Chadian colors as a

TABLE 1–11. RELIGIOUS AFFILIATION IN OULI BANGALA

Religion	Total		Male		Female	
	No.	%	No.	%	No.	%
Catholic	19	24.7	16	26.7	3	17.6
Protestant	58	75.3	44	73.3	14	82.4
Total	77	100.0	60	100.0	17	100.0

marker. When the termites force the toppling of the pole a wooden grave marker will be installed. In this region of Chad only the Sara-Vare tribe uses such wooden markers.

When an Ouarai villager dies, the immediate family makes burial preparations; other relatives are notified by the use of tom-toms and, if some are located in distant cities, by telegraph. Several sheep are killed, and white millet, ground nuts, and peas are prepared for the visitors.

The body is washed by the older women. The older brother, father, or mother wraps the corpse with a white cloth, beginning with the head, and then the body is laid on its side on a bed. On the evening of the day following death the body is placed in the compound, and is kept there for two or three days or even longer so that friends and relatives from distant places can attend the service. On the day of burial, friends and relatives form a procession to the grave site. The procession is delayed as long as possible to enable the attendants to purchase additional white cloth for use as a shroud. Small pieces of the cloth, each about one meter long, are kept by the mourners; they will be made into shorts by the male mourners and into head wrappings by the females, thus serving as remembrances of the deceased.

At the grave site a small sacrifice is made for the deceased which consists of laying gourds with black or red designs next to the grave. After a large plain calabash is placed over the head, the body is lowered into the grave and the grave is filled.

Depending on the status of the deceased, the body is lowered into the grave in one of two ways. For an important person, two attendants stand on the same side of the grave and lower the body; otherwise, two individuals, one at the foot and the other at the head, lower it. After the lowering of the body and the placing of calabashes, the grave is covered first with branches and then with a mat.

The ceremonial director speaks a few words and sprinkles a handful of dirt on the mat as a signal for the others to follow suit. Finally, grave diggers shovel the remainder of the dirt into the grave and make a mound above it.

Painted calabashes (the number depending upon the status of the deceased) are then placed open side up on the grave. The departed is believed to need these in the afterworld because, being a newcomer, he must have these containers—the red ones for water and the black ones for food—when he visits others. A pot filled with millet beer is also placed on the grave.

This is the first, or small, festival. The second, more important festival is always held in June or July. It is a memorial service for all the dead and is considered to be a purification rite. Until the deceased has been through this purification, he is not allowed to associate with the dead who have already been purified. During the time between the two festivals it is believed that a boy in the afterworld is assigned to take food and water to the deceased, as no earthly person wishes to go near the malodorous corpse. The family of the deceased does, however, leave earthen pots of millet beer at his grave so that he may cleanse himself within and without, thereby ridding himself of the death odor. He is expected to share this beer with other newly dead whose relatives live too far away to attend to them. Failure to extend this courtesy may be evidenced by a cracked bowl.

The period of mourning, which begins with the death of the person, continues until the large festival, the date of which is designated by the chief in consultation with the elders. During the period of mourning the widow or widower may eat fish but not meat, and not millet that was harvested during the season in which the death occurred. The widow or widower may not remarry during this time and may not travel more than 500 meters from the village. Neighbors will stay close to the mourner to sympathize, console, and make certain that he or she does not cohabit with others during this period.

At the time of the large festival a wooden grave marker is placed on the grave. It is made of an exceptionally hard wood which can withstand the ravages of termites for years, and is carved in private away from women and children and from men and boys who have not been initiated. The placing of the marker signifies the end of the mourning period, and the mourner is now permitted to remarry. The deceased is no longer considered to be a newcomer in the after-

FIGURE 1-15. GRAVE MARKER IN OUARAI

world and is now able to receive visitors, with whom he shares food and water.

Some persons, because they disliked their spouses, do not place grave markers at the time of the memorial service. If that person is a woman, her parents may annoy her by calling her a wicked woman who killed her husband. Should the living partner marry before the large festival is held, it is believed that the new spouse will die within a two-year period.

The wooden grave marker eventually tumbles because of termites. It is not replaced, but is left on the ground until claimed by a descendant, who will make charcoal from the hard wood. The charcoal is taken to a forger who then uses it in making iron implements. When the marker tumbles it is believed that the spirit has finally left the body.

The residents of Boum Khebir, except for the few outsiders, are fetishers who comprised 86 percent of the sample in this study. Catholic and Protestant missionary activities have been limited in this area. Of the ninety-three household heads queried, 1.1 percent claimed to be Protestant, 3.2 percent stated that they belonged to the Catholic church, and 8.6 percent indicated that they were Muslims (see Table 1-10).

The traditional religion is animistic and is based on the belief that through ritualized appeals a number of spirits (genies) restore the people's harmony with nature (Pairault, 1966, pp. 258–72). The number of genies is unknown, and they are usually invisible to the human eye. It is believed that, like humans, they are born, marry, have children, and die. Terrestrial, aquatic, or aerial, the genies have an empire which surpasses that of man and they have control over life, health, rain, harvest, game, and fish.

Village Political Structure and Social Control

Chad became a republic in 1958 and was granted independence in 1960. The country is divided in thirteen prefectures administered by civil officials. The prefectures are divided into subprefectures, which in turn are divided into cantons controlled by elected chiefs whom the prefect endorses. The canton chief has power over the village chiefs within his canton. These chiefs are elected by the family heads and then are recognized by the prefect. Because of the strength of traditional customs related to the power structure at the canton and village levels, those chiefs visited were hereditary rulers, with the exception of the chief of Ouarai. Moreover, the chiefs' duties, powers, and obligations followed traditional patterns except when chiefs were acting as intercedents between the villagers and higher officials.

Djimtilo

In Djimtilo the formal political offices include the position of chief and twelve council seats, all of which are hereditary. The office of chieftainship endures as long as its occupant is effective. Should a change be desired, the council spokesman meets with the sultan at the canton level and, if the sultan agrees, a change is made by selecting one member of the council as the new chief. While customarily a seat in the council is hereditary, any member considered to be ineffective because of regular absence from meetings, or because of stupidity or general incompetence, is replaced by a new appointee. Otherwise, on the death of a councilman the vacated seat is filled by the councilman's eldest son.

Although the duties requiring council action are few, members meet daily at the chief's house, where the chief is obliged to serve tea. More formal meetings are held when the chief of the canton wishes to convey a message or when various types of infractions of local laws are committed by the residents. These sessions are held at the community house. The most common offenses in the village include fighting between wife and husband (with or without resulting death), theft, and adultery. For the first two offenses, the canton chief decides what punishment should be given. In a case involving adultery the male is fined $10.00, which is paid to the sultan.

The chief's duties are few. One of his main functions is to entertain visiting dignitaries, casual visitors, and merchants. If the visitor is a guest of others in the village, the chief still must be notified. If the foreigner has no friends or trading partners in the village, the chief offers him food and shelter.

Djimtilo's obligation to the national government is to furnish a head tax which amounts to about $4.00 per year. The village chief is responsible for its collection, and throughout the year he finds himself engaged in this activity; because the village's economic base is limited, however, he often has difficulty in making the collection. According to the chief, numerous young men have left Djimtilo for the Cameroons or Fort Lamy in order to avoid paying the tax.

Ouli Bangala

The formal political structure acknowledged in Ouli Bangala includes a chief, subchiefs (the council), a president, and an agricultural adviser. The chief's position to date has been hereditary. The incumbent has held this office for thirty years. His duties to the national government include the collection of the civic tax or head tax and the according of courtesies to visiting officials, including the serving of food and millet beer. Villagers furnish the chief with whatever is required for the entertainment of visitors.

The office of president is appointive, with the selection being made in Fort Lamy and announced through the mayor of Bessao Canton. His primary duty appears to be to maintain order. If an action considered to be a crime is committed, he, together with the chief, decides what is to be done with the accused. Some action is taken locally, while other matters are forwarded to the subprefect's office for a decision.

The agricultural adviser is stationed in Bessao. His main duties include giving instructions for planting cotton and assisting in the sale of the product in March when the fields have been picked.

The subchiefs are members of the village council. In Ouli Bangala there are three distantly related subchiefs. A senior subchief is selected by village consent, and it is his duty to function as the chief in the latter's absence and to assist in the collection of the head tax.

Another activity which the chief must oversee for national benefit is road building. Each village chief sets the time and secures the cooperation of every able-bodied man to clear the roads between villages. Each chief is held responsible for his village road and for a segment of the road between villages. Depending upon the amount of work, two weeks or more are spent in this activity shortly after the dry season begins.

Many indigenous forms of social control operate in addition to the legal methods, some of which have the backing of the village chief, whereas others are enforced through fear of supernatural sanctions. For example, during the dry season the tall grass in and around the village constitutes a fire hazard. Toward the end of the wet season each family is responsible for clearing a segment of a firebreak about thirty meters wide for a distance of 50 meters from his house. The neighboring households clear their segments, and thus the entire village is encircled. Should a family elect not to make its contribution, it will be that family's responsibility to construct a house for a neighbor should his house be destroyed by fire, as well as to pay for the burned contents.

While legal sanction against theft is repayment of twice the cost of a stolen item, belief in the supernatural is used to control theft of foodstuffs in the fields. A *kuma*, a spirit capable of causing sickness in people and represented by an orange painted staff, is placed in the fields to guard crops. Should an individual trespass, it is believed that his arm will become paralyzed and thus the thief will be detected. Most families have the *kuma* in their houses for protection; some use this spirit also as a means of poisoning, or otherwise making ill, persons who do not wish to conform to expected standards of behavior.

Punishments for unacceptable behavior give some indication of the seriousness of the offense. High on the list of infractions is adultery, which is punishable by a fine of $24.00 for males and $6.00 for the participating female. It also constitutes grounds for divorce. Murder, if provoked by an insult or an illicit liaison, was in the past acceptable without punishment. Under the present system the punishment is imprisonment, which is considered to be relatively mild. Theft has already been mentioned. Laziness and assault are considered to be minor offenses and require only reprimands by the village chief.

Ouarai

Ouarai is split politically into Ouarai I and Ouarai II. Each has its own chief, but only one is officially recognized. This cleavage of the village has roots which pre-date the independence of Chad (1960). It seems that some years ago the ruling chief left Ouarai with 400 of his followers when the villagers would not support him for the post of canton chief. An interim chief was then appointed but was murdered in 1953. The current chief is the son of this murdered man and is a veteran of the French army (a retired master sergeant). Meanwhile, in 1963, the traditional chief (who had left the village) died, and his son returned to Ouarai with forty families to take over the chieftainship, which he considered was his by right of inheritance since he came from a long line of chiefs. When the challenger found that he could not depose the incumbent, he established Ouarai II. Ouarai II was officially recognized in 1962, but higher officials have refused to recognize its chief and consider the Ouarai I chief as the only spokesman for the combined villages.

The official political positions in Ouarai include the chief, subchiefs, and the president. The chief's duties are divided between external and internal affairs. He is the intermediary between the subprefect and the villagers, meets with all visitors, and collects the head tax; he announces the village cleanup day and the time for planting; and he settles disputes or refers them to higher authorities. The president, who is a nephew of the chief and who has had commercial experience in Fort Lamy and elsewhere, works with the chief.

Boum Khebir

Traditionally, in Boum Khebir the chieftainship has been hereditary, the chief's primary responsibility being to maintain the coherence of his subjects and, through his fetishistic activities, to prevent misfortunes. If his efforts ever failed to bring about or maintain harmony, he could be replaced. For example, a long drought or an epidemic which resulted in the death of villagers could indicate that his power had begun to diminish (Pairault, 1966, pp. 273–93).

Following the independence of the country, the chief took on new duties, which include complying with orders from the subprefect's office. In 1962 the chief was imprisoned for a period of fifteen days because he did not enthusiastically support the government's program of increasing cotton production. His other duties include the supervision of road-clearing activities, delivering the head tax to the subprefect's office, serving visitors hospitably and occasionally rendering decisions in minor disagreements (Pairault, 1966, pp. 273–93).

Social control is imposed in different ways, but primarily through the maintenance of values considered to be good and proper. Certain attributes, such as deceitfulness and laziness, are considered shameful. On the other hand, a person who generously shares his wealth or who excels in some accomplishment is rewarded with increased prestige. The family head is expected to sire many children and to contribute unselfishly to the lodging, clothing, and feeding of his family. Unexpected guests are to be accorded generous hospitality. Trial by ordeal to prove the innocence or guilt of a person accused of committing a crime has been prohibited. Traditionally there were two types of ordeal: (1) taking two stones from a pot of boiling water and (2) reaching for honey in a tree where bees had made a hive. If the accused remained unharmed in either rite, he was judged innocent (Pairault, 1966, pp. 273–93).

An elaborate religious system and one's status at death also serve to control the villagers. It is believed that the dead do not actually leave their natural and familial surroundings, and the period of mourning affects not only the family circle but also the entire village. The way in which a man dies is considered to be significant; he is judged a good man if his final acts do not include urination, defecation, or entering into a trance. Those who perform these involuntary acts, or who die of some loathsome disease, are believed to have led a troubled life. Murderers, thieves, and debtors are believed to be punished in the hereafter by the supernatural (Pairault, 1966, pp. 341–51). Numerous former customs have been outlawed. Young girls are no longer permitted to have a button on the upper lip, and the wearing of clothing is required.

Faya-Largeau

The villages of Komoro-e and Garba are governed as part of the Faya-Largeau political unit. All transactions between the villages and the subprefect's office, however, are conducted by the chiefs, with perhaps the Kamadjas being less independent than the Anakazas. The Anakazas are more individual-oriented in their behavior and consider crimes as being committed against the person rather than against society (Chapelle, 1957, p. 319). The victim or victim's relatives seek vengeance as a means of carrying out justice. Occasionally the chief is asked for a decision, and the accused will be judged according to the laws of the Koran or the traditional laws of the clan. Thefts of horses and other animals and goods belonging to other tribal groups are not considered crimes.

HOUSING

House ownership and living arrangements in the household were both similar and different among the villagers in the four communities in which housing was studied. All household heads owned a house or houses, the number varying among members within each village (Table 1–12).

TABLE 1–12. COMPARISON OF HOUSE OWNERSHIP[a]

No. of Houses	Djimtilo N = 68[b]	Ouli Bangala N = 54[b]	Ouarai N = 89[b]	Boum Khebir N = 101[b]
1	36.7	40.8	48.3	74.3
2	26.5	44.5	29.2	17.8
3	19.1	7.4	12.4	4.9
4	11.8	5.5	6.7	2.0
5	5.9	1.8	3.4	1.0
	100.0	100.0	100.0	100.0

[a] No data available for Faya-Largeau.
[b] Anthropological sample.

Djimtilo

The Djimtilo houses are of two types—adobe structures with flat, compacted mud laid over logs and branch supports, and circular houses constructed of branches with thatched walls and roofs. The former are occupied by the heads of the households and, in the case of polygyny, are shared at night by different wives in rotation. Adobe houses usually have two rooms, each with a door leading to the central part of the family compound. Women and children live in one of the circular houses. Shelters without walls or with a wall on only one side are used as resting places during the day and as dining areas. Several residents own larger adobe houses which include not only living quarters but also space for animals. The distribution of heads of households by the number of houses they own is shown in Table 1–12.

Several of the houses have adjoining reed enclosures which serve as washrooms. The roofs are used to dry fish and often as places to store light-weight items, including small farm tools. The interior of an adobe house usually is bare, except for a wooden bed in which the head of the house sleeps.

Ouli Bangala

The typical house in Ouli Bangala is circular and made of adobe bricks with a thatched roof. The only opening is the doorway. Each household has one or more of these houses, depending on the size of the extended family. Ideally there are separate quarters for the head of the household, the boys, the females, and the kitchen. In practice, 40.8 percent of the households in the social science sample had only one house (Table 1–12). Rectangular houses are of recent origin, having been introduced by Chadian veterans of the French army. Several of these houses have galvanized iron roofs, a fact which distinguishes the owners as men of wealth, since the material alone is estimated to cost about $60.00. To earn this amount at the current wage rate for laborers, which is forty cents per day, would require 150 days of continuous employment.

Ouarai

Two types of houses are found in Ouarai—mud-wall houses with thatched roofs, and reed-wall houses with thatched roofs supported by log poles. Except for several rectangular ones, most of the houses are circular. Unlike the villagers of Djimtilo and Ouli Bangala, who build with adobe bricks, Ouarai residents construct their mud house walls of a method similar to that used in the making of coiled pottery. In other words, the walls are built in layers with the soft mud being positioned and patted smooth.

Single-house compounds comprised 48.3 percent of the sample studied; 29.2 percent of the sample had two houses in their compounds, and the remainder owned three-, four-, or five-house compounds. The ideal cluster would include a house for males, another for females, and a third for use as the kitchen during the rainy season; as can be seen in Table 1–12, less than one-fourth of the households approached this.

Boum Khebir

The typical structure in Boum Khebir is a circular adobe building with a woven reed roof supported by log beams. There is only one entrance, which may have a door of woven reed. The floor is hard-surfaced and extends into the courtyard. Various possessions, including stacked pots, water containers, musical instruments, baskets, firewood, and food are located around the interior walls of the house. Furniture kept outside consists of locally made beds and benches. Woven reed mats used for sleeping are placed on the floor in the evening.

Less common are the rectangular adobe structures which have plank doors and windows. These are owned by the more affluent families. Compounds may also have shade structures, storage buildings made of reeds, and storage platforms supported by five-to-six-foot poles.

Faya-Largeau

The housing area in Komoro-e in Faya-Largeau is arranged so that each household unit has adequate space. The chief and four subchiefs have their constituents living adjacent to their houses. Because the housing project had been established only a little more than a year before our research team's arrival, no trees had yet been planted, and many houses were unfinished.

Garba, the village occupied by the Anakazas, was undergoing re-planning, and the main road was cluttered with rubble from demolished walls and buildings. Here, as in Komoro-e, water is obtained from dug wells. The water table is about six feet below the surface of the earth, and many of the families have cultivated fig trees, date palms, and grape vines by planting them a few feet above the water level. Unlike the village of Komoro-e where movable tents are few, here each compound has at least one; these are dismantled during the caravan season.

EDUCATION

The national public school system of Chad was initiated in the late 1920's (Thompson and Adloff, 1960, pp. 288–90). Ten years later there were still no more than ten schools, attended by 425 pupils. Throughout the 1950's a shortage of teachers remained because of inadequate normal school facilities and because the northern tribes were opposed to having their children taught by southerners, the only ones qualified to teach. Mission schools, both Catholic and Protestant, had been established in other countries administered by the French during the late 1800's, but they did not take root in Chad until after World War II, because of the objections of the Muslim population. The Muslims were suspicious of any but Koranic schools. In view of these problems and because of a shortage of funds, schools in the outlying areas of Chad are few.

Neither Djimtilo nor Ouarai has its own government-funded school, although the children of the latter village have easy access to one located in a neighboring community. Ouli Bangala, with a four-teacher system which was established in 1960, conducts classes for 190 children through the sixth grade and was ready at the time of our study to send their first graduates to higher schools in the urban areas. In 1961 the government constructed a building in Boum Khebir and a two-teacher school was opened; although 70 children were enrolled at the time of our study, daily attendance was limited to six pupils. Generally, in all the villages only the young attend government schools; of these, by far the majority are male (see Table 1–13).

Only Koranic instruction is given in Djimtilo and Faya-Largeau. Of 158 males in Djimtilo on whom educational data were available, 15.8 percent attended classes offered by the imam. Two of 207 females in Djimtilo also received instruction. Only one person in the remaining villages aside from Faya-Largeau had gone to Koranic school— a man in his forties in Ouli Bangala.

Children in the five villages are prepared for their adult roles largely through traditional, formal, and informal methods. In Djimtilo and Ouli Bangala youngsters learn to build houses, to raise crops, and to hunt and fish by working with their elders. Likewise, the girls learn about their place in family life from their mothers and older women.

In Ouarai and Boum Khebir, in addition to instructions received from parents regarding subsistence matters, young boys learn about other desirable qualities of manhood, including survival, in the more formalized initiation rites. In Ouarai, when a boy reaches the age of seven, he joins a large group of seven-to-ten-year-olds who are expected to spend fifteen days in the bush. There are dietary

TABLE 1–13. PERCENTAGE OF SCHOOL ATTENDANCE OF MALES FIVE YEARS OLD AND OVER IN THE FIVE VILLAGES

	Djimtilo		Ouli Bangala		Ouarai		Boum Khebir		Faya-Largeau	
	Gov't	Koranic	Gov't	Koranic	Gov't	Mission	Gov't	Koranic	Gov't	Koranic
Attended	0.6	15.8	43.8	0.7	34.8	0.7	24.6	0.0	16.7	28.4
Did not attend	99.4	84.2	56.2	99.3	65.2	99.3	75.4	100.0	83.3	71.6
Total	100.0	100.0	100.0	100.0	100.0	100.0	100.0	100.0	100.0	200.0

restrictions, and cicatrices are made on the initiates' faces with a razor. In Boum Khebir, boys between eight and eighteen years of age go into the bush for a period of about four months (Pairault, 1966, pp. 222–36). During this time the initiates "die" and are "reborn" as men. They receive new names, and various rituals are performed. On their return to the village the initiates are required to hunt small game, to fish, and to help relatives in the field. Mothers are permitted to see their "newborn" sons, but are not at liberty to communicate with them directly. Finally, five months after the beginning of the rites, a hair-cutting ceremony is performed and a village-wide dance is held. The initiates' houses are burned and the boys leave for their new quarters, which are set apart from their parents'. The secret language learned in the bush is gradually replaced with the traditional tongue. Initiation rites in Ouli Bangala were discontinued upon the arrival of a Protestant missionary in 1955.

The level of education in the two Faya-Largeau villages is low. When the two villages are compared, the Kamadja group, considered to be upwardly mobile, appears to be the one which is least resistant to modern education. The Anakazas' dislike for a sedentary life has tended to preclude systematic education for their children. At the time of our study, in neither group were there adults above the age of twenty who had gone to the government school, although 13.1 percent had attended the Koranic school. Relatively few females of either tribe have had any formal education.

MEDICAL AND HEALTH SERVICES

Chad as a whole has few medical facilities, and in their absence each tribal group has its own system of diagnosis and treatment. Most illnesses are believed to be the result of witchcraft or contact with spirits, and therefore some form of ritual is required to restore the patient to health. Yet, where either a clinic or, minimally, a trained nurse is available, the villagers make use of these services and facilities.

Of the five villages studied, only Djimtilo does not have ready access to western medical facilities. Consequently, only 1.2 percent of the inhabitants had been seen by a nurse during the year preceding this study. In Ouarai, which is relatively close to Koumra, where there are both Catholic and Protestant mission hospitals, 91 percent of the respondents had been seen in the clinics. A little more than 39 percent of the Ouli Bangala household heads had received treatment at the Baibokoum clinic, while the nurse located at Boum Khebir had seen 80.2 percent of the household heads of that village in the year preceding our study. The question regarding hospital usage was not asked in Faya-Largeau.

The fairly adéquate facilities in Koumra far outrank the services available in the other villages. Although the trained staff there is small and heavily overworked, the services of physicians are available. The residents of the other villages can secure a doctor's services only by traveling long distances to large urban centers. While a hospital is located in Faya-Largeau, there was at the time of this study only one medical doctor to serve the entire population of the city; therefore, except in emergency situations, he was not available.

As in most traditional societies, the villagers have their own beliefs about the etiology of certain symptoms and debilitating conditions, as well as their preferences for certain diagnostic procedures and cures. In Djimtilo the study team encountered a twenty-five-year-old woman who had become afflicted with a form of mental illness while residing in Fort Lamy. For treatment the imam poured water over the section of the Koran called *El Kurus*, which was written in ink on a prayer board. The liquid was caught in a bowl and given to the patient to drink. Since this brought no visible improvement in her condition, the affliction was considered to be the result of forces other than that of the devil.

Illnesses in Ouli Bangala are believed to be the result of spirits lurking in and around the village. The areas close to the Lim River are considered to be particularly dangerous during the rainy season, when shadowy ghosts, probably mists, are believed to cause paralysis and vomiting accompanied by high fever. Hematuria is thought to be caused either by drinking "bad water" or, in the case of small boys, by eating goat meat or chicken, both of which are taboo until boys are married and have a child older than three years. Sorcerers are considered to be able to "witch" persons into illness or to cure them, and fetishes are placed in fields to "witch" persons who steal crops.

The Sara-Vare in Ouarai also believe that certain forms of illness and causes of death are the result of sorcery. Fear of witchcraft is perhaps greatest in Ouarai, and even guests visiting in a home might be suspected of using supernatural powers. For protection the host places a sacred ingredient called *kuga* in the food or soup and awaits the consequences; if the guest falls ill, he is considered guilty of witchcraft.

ECONOMIC ACTIVITIES

The principal subsistence base for all five villages is agriculture. No household in our study approached the $55.00 considered to be the average per capita income for Chad (National Research Council, 1966, p. 300). It may be concluded that those persons who do match or surpass the national average obtain their incomes from some other source. Livelihood is largely dependent upon home-produced goods; surplus is bartered for other products, although within each village a number of males have a second occupation which brings in cash income. Although in Faya-Largeau the principal year-round occupation of male household heads is agriculture (74.1 percent), during the caravan season the percentage drops to 29.2. Data on fields owned, the size of fields, and expenditures were not obtained for the Faya-Largeau villages.

The land base for most villagers generally is limited to one or two fields (see Table 1–14). In Boum Khebir land is assigned to individual householders by the chief of the ground (Pairault, 1966, p. 82).

TABLE 1–14. DISTRIBUTION OF FIELDS OWNED BY VILLAGERS

No. of Fields	Djimtilo No.	Djimtilo %	Ouli Bangala No.	Ouli Bangala %	Ouarai No.	Ouarai %	Boum Khebir No.	Boum Khebir %
0	4	5.9	3	5.6	4	4.5	10	10.0
1	25	36.7	18	33.3	26	29.2	33	33.0
2	25	36.7	13	24.1	35	39.4	22	22.0
3	10	14.8	6	11.1	17	19.1	12	12.0
4	4	5.9	4	7.4	5	5.6	17	17.0
5	0	—	2	3.7	1	1.1	3	3.0
6	0	—	0	—	1	1.1	3	3.0
7	0	—	4	7.4	0	—	0	—
8	0	—	1	1.8	0	—	0	—
9	0	—	0	—	0	—	0	—
10	0	—	3	5.6	0	—	0	—
Total	68	100.0	54	100.0	89	100.0	100	100.0

The size of the fields cultivated by the households is small, with most measuring two hectares (1 hectare = 2.47 acres) or less (Table 1–15). Agricultural technology is limited to the short-handled hoe, which makes it almost impossible to till more land than this. Those in our study who owned more acreage indicated

TABLE 1–15. SIZE OF FIELDS OWNED BY VILLAGERS

No. of Hectares	Djimtilo		Ouli Bangala		Ouarai		Boum Khebir	
	No. of Fields	%	No. of Fields	%	No. of Fields	%	No. of Fields	%
0	4	5.9	3	5.6	4	4.5	8	7.9
1	22	32.3	13	24.1	26	29.2	37	37.7
2	28	41.1	14	25.9	35	39.4	40	39.6
3	10	14.8	8	14.8	17	19.1	7	6.9
4	4	5.9	5	9.3	5	5.6	7	6.9
5	0	—	2	3.7	1	1.1	0	—
6	0	—	1	1.8	1	1.1	1	1.0
7	0	—	4	7.4	0	—	0	—
8	0	—	1	1.8	0	—	0	—
9	0	—	0	—	0	—	0	—
10 or more	0	—	3	5.6	0	—	0	—
Total	68	100.0	54	100.0	89	100.0	100	100.0

that they were able to manage it because of the larger size of their families.

Most vegetables and cereal crops are produced for home consumption, and, when a surplus arises, they are sold or bartered for other commodities. The single crop which is a source of cash income is cotton, with the income being used to pay the head tax required of every male eighteen years of age or older. The income from cotton was small, however, in the areas studied, particularly in Boum Khebir. That village has resisted growing cotton; only 10 percent had managed to earn more than $12.00, while 69 percent had received incomes of $4.00 or less, during the preceding year's harvest (see Table 1–16). Although Djimtilo suffers from prolonged dry periods during the rainy season which affect the crop growth, it had the highest percentage (22.3) of household heads who earned more than $20.00 during the previous year's cotton harvest. However, the highest individual earnings were in Ouarai, where 6.6 percent of the household heads brought in $48.01 or more, with one individual having earned $150.00.

Among the household heads in each village are skilled craftsmen who ply their trades on a part-time basis. Boum Khebir is the most isolated village and perhaps for this reason has a larger number of craftsmen engaged in the production of a diversity of goods. These craftsmen include potters, forgers, tailors, basket-weavers, and

TABLE 1-16. INCOME FROM COTTON HARVEST, 1966-67

Income	Djimtilo		Ouli Bangala		Ouarai		Boum Khebir	
	No.	%	No.	%	No.	%	No.	%
0	5	7.9	5	9.4	4	4.6	30	30.0
$2.00 or less	0	—	0	—	18	20.5	18	18.0
$2.01–$4.00	4	6.3	4	7.5	18	20.5	21	21.0
$4.01–$8.00	10	15.9	8	15.1	10	11.4	13	13.0
$8.01–$12.00	13	20.6	12	22.6	12	13.6	8	8.0
$12.01–$16.00	8	12.7	9	17.0	7	8.0	2	2.0
$16.01–$20.00	9	14.3	8	15.1	7	8.0	2	2.0
$20.01–$24.00	7	11.1	0	—	1	1.1	5	5.0
$24.01–$28.00	3	4.8	3	5.7	0	—	0	—
$28.01–$32.00	1	1.6	1	1.9	0	—	0	—
$32.01–$36.00	0	—	0	—	1	1.1	0	—
$36.01–$40.00	0	—	0	—	4	4.6	0	—
$40.01–$44.00	2	3.2	0	—	0	—	1	1.0
$44.01–$48.00	1	1.6	3	5.7	0	—	0	—
$48.01–$150.00	0	—	0	—	6	6.6	0	—
Total	63	100.0	53	100.0	88	100.0	100	100.0

makers of musical instruments, calabashes, and boats. The other villages have fewer individuals with the skills necessary to engage in the production of goods, possibly because they are closer to large settlements where many items can be purchased.

Other subsistence and income-producing opportunities that exist are not being exploited. In Djimtilo, Lake Chad, and the Chari River have an abundance of fish, but only a few villagers engage in fishing commercially. Despite easy access to Lake Iro, Boum Khebir residents have in recent years spent less time in fishing than before because of changing ecological factors, including an increase in the number of hippopotami and the rising level of the lake (Pairault, 1966, p. 384). The large grove of mango trees in Ouarai furnishes fruit for the residents of that village, but the surplus is not sold except by some widows who carry it to the market at Koumra.

Hunting for large wild game is an activity restricted chiefly to foreigners. The Chadians are not permitted firearms, and they use primarily the spear and long all-purpose knives for hunting small animals. However, in the spring, throughout southern Chad, fires can often be seen on the horizon. These are set to burn the dense tall grass in preparation for planting, and to flush out the animals, which then can be captured for food (Great Britain Naval Staff, 1942, p. 118).

In Ouli Bangala the natives hold community hunts for beavers, antelope, and wart hogs, as well as for rats, mice, and other small animals. Typically, the hunting party gathers in the afternoon. Some of the men scatter into a wide semicircular line and set fire to the grass, while others wait at the opening of the circle. As the fire eats into the central area, the animals run from the flames toward the opening, where the waiting hunters kill them with spears and knives. The larger animals are carried home to be divided among the members of the hunting party, while the smaller ones, including the rodents, are consumed on the spot by the hunters.

Because they live at a bare subsistence level in which most products are consumed, and because materials for building houses and making tools and ceremonial and recreational instruments are found in the vicinity of the villages, the villagers are only minimally involved in a cash economy. The amount spent by the household heads during the week preceding the interviews gives a crude measure of the spread to be found within each village and among the villagers. The more affluent generally are those persons who have sources of income from outside the villages, except in Djimtilo, where the imam and the fakirs earn lucrative incomes for services rendered to members of the community. Because of available cash, these persons are able to spend more than others, and, indeed, large

FIGURE 1-16. GRASS FIRE IN OULI BANGALA

purchases are made by them periodically. Bicycles and pots and pans with multicolored designs belong to the more affluent in Djimtilo; galvanized iron roofs, wagons, and bullocks are typical possessions of the pensioned veterans of the French army in Ouli Bangala and Ouarai. Moreover, the affluent are the individuals with more than one wife, and they are the sponsors of community-wide feasts. In Boum Khebir the display of wealth takes the form of jewelry and sponsorship of feasts.

Cash expenditures are determined not only by cash in hand but also by the availability of merchandise that can be purchased. All villages offer for sale different types of craft work, as already mentioned, and some individuals sell their skilled services as garment-makers, healers, sandal-repairers, and so on. On the other hand, there is differential access to certain goods generally found in the market system. In Djimtilo, Ouli Bangala, and Ouarai on certain days village markets are held where traders from nearby villages gather to sell their wares. Djimtilo and Ouli Bangala are also linked to larger villages by regularly scheduled buses, while Ouarai is within a few hours walking distance of a medium-sized town. Only Boum Khebir, which only very recently has permitted an Arab trader to establish his business there, is isolated from villages selling manufactured items. These factors have a bearing on the amount spent by villagers.

TABLE 1–17. EXPENDITURES IN FOUR VILLAGES DURING THE
WEEK BEFORE THE INTERVIEW

Amount	Djimtilo		Ouli Bangala		Ouarai		Boum Khebir	
	No.	%	No.	%	No.	%	No.	%
0	4	5.9	12	22.6	8	9.0	44	43.6
$1.00 or less	4	5.9	16	30.2	39	43.8	30	29.7
$1.01–$2.00	9	13.2	4	7.5	16	17.9	18	17.8
$2.01–$4.00	22	32.4	10	18.9	8	9.0	7	6.9
$4.01–$6.00	12	17.6	5	9.4	5	5.6	0	—
$6.01–$8.00	6	8.8	3	5.7	3	3.4	0	—
$8.01–$10.00	4	5.9	1	1.9	1	1.1	1	1.0
$10.01–$12.00	4	5.9	0	—	0	—	1	1.0
$12.01 or more	3	4.4	2	3.8	2	2.3	0	—
Unknown	0	—	0	—	7	7.9	0	—
Total	68	100.0	53	100.0	89	100.0	101	100.0

When the villages are compared, the data reveal that in Djimtilo the highest percentage of household heads spent the most, in Boum Khebir the least, amount of money during the week preceding the interviews (Table 1–17). A little more than 40 percent of Djimtilo household heads, 20 percent of those in Ouli Bangala and Ouarai, but only 2 percent in Boum Khebir, spent more than $4.00. As for the percentages of those who spent nothing, Boum Khebir ranked highest (43.6 percent), followed by Ouli Bangala (22.6 percent). The figures in general reveal the villagers' self-sufficiency, with commodities such as sugar, salt, tea, and other condiments constituting the bulk of purchases.

2

ENVIRONMENTAL FACTORS

Evaluations of specific environmental factors that would have possible bearing on the health of the population were made in depth in four villages: Djimtilo, Ouli Bangala, Ouarai, and Boum Khebir. The findings show that, in general, in all of these villages sanitation is inadequate and hygienic practices are lacking. However, interesting differences exist, and these are vitally important to the understanding of morbidity patterns.

WATER SUPPLY

The sources of water supply for the domestic needs of the population vary. Since the carrying of water is an arduous task, the primary concern of the people is to find the nearest available source sufficient in quantity, regardless, on the whole, of quality. In Table 2–1 the principal water sources are listed by village with the results of the coliform determinations on grab samples. A summary of the results of physical and chemical analyses is presented in Table 2–2.

Djimtilo

In Djimtilo the marsh is the most important source of water for the population because the wells are very shallow and their yields low. The coliform determinations of the water from all wells and from the four water points used along the marsh gave such high

TABLE 2–1. WATER SUPPLY SOURCES

Village	Water Source	Coliform Count per 100 ml
Djimtilo	Marsh	60,000+
	Well No. 1	250,000+
	Well No. 2	90,000+
	Well No. 3	100,000+
	Well No. 4	t.n.c.[a]
Ouli Bangala	Mbongo Creek	10,000+
	Lim River	74
	Well	19,500
Ouarai	Well No. 1	5,470
	Well No. 2	2,340
	Well No. 3	36,900
Boum Khebir	Lake Iro	1,020

[a] Too numerous to count.

numbers that they could be quantitated only by employing high dilution ratios of sterile water in each sample. Since the washing of grains for meal preparation, laundering, and bathing take place where water is drawn from the marsh, the high counts are to be expected. One of the water points also serves as a landing for dugout canoes. The very high coliform counts for the samples from the wells were due largely to the low level of water found in each well, which resulted in a heavy concentration of bacterial contaminants per unit volume. Two samples contained large amounts of iron and manganese. The pH of the well water was near neutral or above, and the hardness tests yielded values that would place the water in the "hard" class. In contrast, the marsh water was soft, had high concentrations of iron, and showed pH values in the range 6.3–6.4. All the samples had abnormally high color and turbidity values.

Ouli Bangala

Analysis of water samples from sources in Ouli Bangala showed that at the time of the survey the water of the Lim River was vastly superior in quality to that from Mbongo Creek or the well. The coliform counts were comparatively low for samples from the Lim River but high for those from the well and the creek. The Lim is a swift river of sparkling water flowing over clean sand and rocks and abounds in game fish. During the dry season, when the survey was

TABLE 2–2. PHYSICAL AND CHEMICAL ANALYSES OF WATER SAMPLES

	Djimtilo		Ouli Bangala			Ouarai	Boum Khebir
	Wells	Marsh	Mbongo Creek	Lim River	Well	Wells	Lake Iro
Temperature, °C	25	18–20	19	25	21	29–30	31
Turbidity, JTU[a]	24–175	43–55	20–35	10	290	27–250	790
pH	6.8–7.7	6.3–6.4	6.8	7.4	6.2	5.8–6.3	7.5
Nitrate Nitrogen, mg/l	2.6–10.0	0.04	4.0–6.0	3.0	4.0	0.0–0.04	8.0
Fluoride, mg/l	0.5–0.6	0.4	0.4	—[b]	—[b]	0.0–0.1	0.6
Iron, mg/l	0.2–5.5	2.0–2.4	1.8	0.2	0.8	0.2–7.8	1.3
Manganese, mg/l	0.2–1.9	0.2–0.6	0.2–0.3	0	0	0.0–0.1	0
Total hardness, CaCO$_3$, mg/l	140–245	30	50	10	10	10–125	80

[a] JTU = Jackson Turbidity Unit.
[b] No analysis made.

made, Mbongo Creek was dry except for a string of stagnant pools in the depressions of its bed. Such pools are used for many activities, including bathing, laundering, and as a source of drinking water. The high coliform counts of the well-water samples were caused by human activities around the well which resulted in the contamination of the water as it issued from the fissure in the underlying rock bed. The pH of the creek water was 6.8, that of the Lim River 7.4. The iron content was excessive in the creek water. Both the creek and well water had high turbidity and color values. However, all the samples were classified as soft.* It was reported that during the dry season a majority of the people draw water from the Lim River, often carrying it great distances, while during the rainy season most go to Mbongo Creek.

Ouarai

At the time of this study, the water supply sources for the village of Ouarai were three wells located within the village. They were owned by private individuals but were used by all the people. The wells had been dug through clay and were not cased or protected; their water level was between eighty-two and eighty-five feet (twenty-five to twenty-six meters) below ground. Two of the wells (No. 1 and No. 2) had good yields, but the third was poor and was almost dry at the time of the survey. As expected, the coliform counts for the third well were high. Well No. 1 had an exceptionally high iron content of 7.8 milligrams per liter. The pH of the water was low, ranging from 5.8 to 6.3. Color and turbidity values were excessive, the turbidity being caused by clay in suspension. The water samples from Well No. 1 and Well No. 2 were moderately hard, but the sample from Well No. 3 was soft.

Boum Khebir

In Boum Khebir the only source of water is Lake Iro. Women of the village who fetch water draw from a common water point which is approximately one kilometer from the center of the village. The samples taken from the lake all were grayish-white, opaque, and had a turbidity of 790 JTU. The coliform counts averaged 1,020 per 100 milliliters. The pH of the water was 7.5. The iron content

* Hardness classification (milligrams per liter as $CaCO_3$): 0–75, soft; 75–150, moderately hard; 150–300, hard; more than 300, very hard.

was excessive by international standards (World Health Organization, 1963), and the total hardness expressed in terms of $CaCO_3$ was moderate (80 milligrams per liter). The lake water is aerated by wave action (see Figure 2–1), and the dissolved oxygen content was measured to be 7.6 milligrams per liter.

In all four villages the fetching of water is primarily the task of women, who frequently are assisted by children but rarely by men. By and large it would seem (as is to be expected) that the number of daily trips for water corresponds inversely to the distance from the homes to the source. In Djimtilo, water is drawn by half of the

FIGURE 2–1. DRAWING WATER FROM LAKE IRO FOR DOMESTIC NEEDS

households within a distance of fifty meters, a majority of the family members making four or more trips a day. In Ouli Bangala, during the dry season most families draw water from the Lim River, a distance of only 100–150 meters for 15 percent of the population, but 400–500 meters for 33 percent, and more than 500 meters for the remaining 52 percent. Half the population makes two or three trips daily, 11 percent make four trips, while 27 percent make five or more trips a day. During the rainy season Mbongo Creek is the principal water source, and at that time 61 percent of the families can obtain creek water within a distance of 100–150 meters from their homes. In Ouarai 66 percent of the population live within a 200-meter radius of the wells. Seventeen percent of the families draw water twice a day; 34 percent, three times; 25 percent, four times; and 22 percent, five or more times. In contrast, the distance that water must be carried from Lake Iro to homes in Boum Khebir is 1,000 meters or more, and 51 percent of the households make only two trips a day; 45 percent make three trips. In Djimtilo, Ouli Bangala, and Ouarai, calabashes, burned clay pots, and enamel pans for transporting water are approximately ten to twenty liters in size, but in Boum Khebir the clay pots are larger, many with a measured capacity of thirty liters.

An estimate of per capita water consumption was made, based on the amount of water drawn. The comparative figures are given in Table 2–3. The median daily per capita water consumption for the four villages was: Djimtilo, 11 liters; Ouli Bangala, 10 liters; Ouarai, 14 liters; and Boum Khebir, 19 liters. However, these figures must be interpreted with information on general water-use practices. The people of Djimtilo are Muslims and do not brew the millet beer which is common in the other three villages. Part of the water drawn by the people in Ouli Bangala, Ouarai, and Boum Khebir goes into the making of this beer, and the users of large amounts of water are most often persons engaged in good-sized brewing operations in the village. The marsh at Djimtilo is so accessible to the village people that the washing of grain for meal preparation and of cooking and eating utensils is done there (see Figure 2–2). This is not the case in the other three villages. The use of relative amounts of water brought to the house for bathing purposes may be reflected by the provision of special places in the courtyard or near the houses for bathing. Forty-two percent of the households in Djimtilo had bathing places, 3 percent in Ouli Bangala, 87 percent in Ouarai, and 93 percent in Boum Khebir.

FIGURE 2–2. WASHING CORN MEAL IN THE MARSH IN DJIMTILO

TABLE 2–3. WATER CONSUMPTION

Consumption (liters/person/day)	Percentage Distribution			
	Djimtilo	Ouli Bangala	Ouarai	Boum Khebir
Less than 5	13	6	0	0
5–9.9	33	44	17	18
10–14.9	33	28	39	21
15–19.9	21	13	22	12
20–24.9	0	9	13	18
More than 25	0	0	9	31
Total	100	100	100	100

Excreta Disposal

Two pit latrines were noted in Djimtilo. One of these latrines is
illustrated in Figure 2–3. Latrines similar in construction were
found in Boum Khebir. The clay pot with the bottom cut open was
an added feature. More often latrines were found with two logs
laid parallel over the pit to prevent the earth from caving in. There
was no latrine in Ouli Bangala, and in the survey area of Ouarai
four pit latrines, all showing evidence of use but in a poor state of
cleanliness, were seen. In Boum Khebir twenty-nine families out of
ninety-five in the survey had latrines installed in their courtyards,

FIGURE 2–3. ONE OF TWO PIT LATRINES IN DJIMTILO

but of these only one-third could be considered reasonably clean. Odor was detectable around the latrines and flies were present.

In all of the villages surveyed, fecal deposits were readily seen immediately beyond the open areas surrounding structures used for outdoor living. In fact, it could be stated that each village was ringed with a band of fecal deposits. Also, some evidence of defecation and urination behind the houses or near courtyard walls was visible. This was said to be caused by the very young members of the families. In the village of Djimtilo thirteen of twenty-four households (54 percent) observed at random revealed positive indications of excretion near habitations. In Ouli Bangala 88 percent of the households showed positive indications of this, while in Ouarai the figure was 66 percent, in Boum Khebir 27 percent.

Although the principal defecation sites were located at the fringes of the villages, it was also common to find fecal deposits near some of the water courses. This was especially true in Djimtilo and in Ouli Bangala, although in Djimtilo more feces were found in the bush opposite the marsh than in areas along it. The people tended to defecate in sites most convenient to them and did not appear to seek out areas near water courses. At the water point on Lake Iro, which is approximately one kilometer from Boum Khebir, no evidence of feces was visible.

According to respondents, the principal cleansing materials used after defecation in these four villages are: Djimtilo, water only, water and sticks, or water and leaves (84 percent); Ouli Bangala, sticks and/or leaves (99 percent); Ouarai, sticks and/or leaves (90 percent); and Boum Khebir, sticks (87 percent). It is interesting to note that while the respondents in Djimtilo stated that water was the principal cleansing material used after defecation, considerably greater quantities of fecal deposits were observed in the bush on the side of the village opposite the marsh, where there was more cover but no readily available water.

At the time of the survey all the principal defecation sites in all four villages were dry and had little protection from the sun. Feces dried very quickly and, in some instances, were visited by dung beetles. Flies of various species were attracted to these deposits while they were fresh. Except for areas adjacent to the marsh in Djimtilo, where the soil had a pH of 6.5 and was moist and sandy-loam in texture, soil samples from principal defecation sites were slightly alkaline, dry, and generally sandy. Exposed to the direct rays of the sun, the dry, sandy soil was unfavorable for the survival of ova of soil-transmitted helminths. Where ashes from the burning of grass cover the ground, the pH of the soil at the surface was high. A typical result of soil pH tests in Ouli Bangala was 8.2 at the surface, while seven inches below the surface it was 7.0.

REFUSE

The practice of refuse disposal in the four villages is similar. Heaps were found on the ground mainly at the fringes of the village, although occasionally piles were found within the village proper. In general the heaps consisted of ashes, corn cobs, bits of reed, pieces of broken clay pots, and, occasionally, small pieces of cloth. In Ouarai, in addition to these there were peanut hulls, mango stones, and broken calabash bowls. The food habits of the people tended to indicate production of little putrescible refuse from their day-to-day living. The heaps were dry and appeared stable. Fly breeding was not evident in the heaps in any of these villages. Once the refuse is thrown onto the heaps it evidently is not handled further and is eventually blown away or scattered by animals.

VECTOR SNAILS

The natural bodies of water with which the people of Djimtilo come into contact in the course of their daily living are the marsh and the Chari River. *Bulinus truncatus rohlfsi* (Clessin), vector snails of schistosomiasis, were collected along the bank of the Chari River. A summary of snails collected during the survey is given in Table 2–4. There is no reason to believe that the marsh does not harbor vector snails also, because Leveque (1967), in an area not too distant from Djimtilo, collected *B. jousseaumei* (Dautzenberg), *B. truncatus rohlfsi* (Clessin), *B. forskalii* (Ehrenberg), *Biomphalaria pfeifferi* (Krauss), and *B. sudanica* (Martens).

In the village of Ouli Bangala the residents' contact with the Lim River and Mbongo Creek is frequent and intimate. To a lesser extent they use the water from Momia Creek, which is found near their cotton fields. In Mbongo Creek *B. pfeifferi* (Krauss) and *B. alexandrina wonsoni* (Mandahl-Barth) were collected. Of these vectors of *Schistosoma mansoni*, the latter has not previously been reported from Chad. Also collected was *Lymnaea natalensis* (Krauss), a vector of *Fasciola gigantica*, which is an animal parasite. The Lim River at Ouli Bangala is a fast-flowing, clean river with little vegetation to

TABLE 2–4. SUMMARY OF SNAILS COLLECTED IN THE REPUBLIC OF CHAD,
FEBRUARY–MAY, 1967

Body of Water	Snail Species[a]
Marsh at Djimtilo	*Lentorbis* new species
Chari River at Djimtilo	*Bulinus truncatus rohlfsi* (Clessin)
	Gabbia newmanni (Germain)
Mbongo Creek at Ouli Bangala	*Lymnaea natalensis* (Krauss)
	Biomphalaria alexandrina wonsoni (Mandahl-Barth)
	B. pfeifferi (Krauss)
Momia Creek at Ouli Bangala	*L. natalensis* (Krauss)
Petit Mandoul at Ouarai	*Lanistes ovum* (Peters)
	Gyraulus costulatus (Krauss)
	B. truncatus rohlfsi (Clessin)
	B. jousseaumei (Dautzenberg)
Marsh of Lake Iro near Boum Khebir	*Pila wernei* (Philippi)

[a] Identification was made by Dr. G. Mandahl-Barth, World Health Organization Snail Identification Center, Charlottenlund, Denmark.

protect snails; it is, therefore, an improbable habitat for these vectors. No snails were collected even after an exhaustive search along the margins of the river.

The Petit Mandoul at Ouarai is a sluggish river about three kilometers from the village and is where the children often go to swim and fish. Also, at certain times of the year a large number of people from the village go to the river to engage in mass fishing. The water is not very deep, and there is a considerable amount of aquatic vegetation, which forms ideal conditions for the support of snail life. At the time of our study, *B. truncatus rohlfsi* (Clessin) and *B. jousseaumei* (Dautzenberg), vector snails of *S. haematobium*, were collected from the vegetation along the banks.

Snails were not found in Lake Iro. The lake is fairly large and its water is agitated by wind action. The water is grayish-white in color and is characterized by a heavy suspension of colloidal clay. At the time of the survey the temperature of the lake water was found to be 31° C, which is very close to the level above which no reproduction occurs among many of the aquatic snails. Moreover, conditions existing along the banks of the lake did not appear to favor snail life. In the mud of the marsh, however, the rather large amphibious snail, *Pila wernei* (Philippi), was found.

FIGURE 2–4. GEOGRAPHICAL DISTRIBUTION OF THE INTERMEDIATE HOSTS OF SCHISTOSOMES

The geographical distribution of the intermediate hosts of schistosomes in Chad is shown in Figure 2–4. The sources of information for the map were the World Health Organization (1966), Leveque (1967), and collections from this survey.

HOUSING

Adobe, reeds, and branches are the basic materials used for the construction of houses in the four villages.

In Djimtilo one type of house is constructed of rectangular mud walls with a mud-compacted roof supported by log beams and smaller branches. The presence of termites in these structures is abundantly evident. A small window, batten door, and compacted earth floor complete the structural provisions of the house. A second type of house has a wooden superstructure and is walled and roofed with reeds. Ventilation in the mud structures is inadequate while, in general, in the reed huts it is fair to adequate. The men, who sleep in the mud houses, therefore have poorly ventilated quarters compared to those of the women and children, who sleep in the huts.

In Ouli Bangala the typical house is circular, built of sun-dried mud blocks and roofed with reeds over pole supports. These houses have neither windows nor structural provisions for keeping out biting insects. Some secondary structures made of reeds are also found. The houses in Ouarai are similar to those in Ouli Bangala.

In Boum Khebir 82 percent of the dwellings are built of adobe. Eighteen percent of the structures are made of reeds and are used mostly as secondary buildings. The reed roofs are thick, and many of the doorways are very low. The floors of the houses in Boum Khebir are far superior to those of the houses in the other three villages. They are laid out in clay so well compacted that they have the appearance of smooth stone and are extended out of the houses to form small patios for outdoor household activities. Typical house constructions in Djimtilo, Ouli Bangala, and Ouarai appear in Figures 2–5, 2–6, and 2–7.

The distribution by village of the total floor area under roof and of the sleeping space per person is shown in Tables 2–5 and 2–6 respectively. When comparing the villages it is apparent that people are the most crowded in their houses in Ouli Bangala. It is also interesting to note that Djimtilo has the greatest number of structures used for purposes other than sleeping. The ventilation in the

FIGURE 2–5. HOUSE CONSTRUCTION IN DJIMTILO

houses of Ouli Bangala is inadequate while, in Ouarai, in the mud houses it is usually fair and in the reed huts it is adequate. As many as 67 percent of the houses surveyed in Boum Khebir were judged to be inadequately ventilated.

Congestion was not a problem in the villages except for a few instances in Boum Khebir. There, about 9 percent of the houses

TABLE 2–5. SIZE OF HOUSES—PERCENTAGE DISTRIBUTION BY VILLAGE

Area under Roof (sq. meters)	Percentage Distribution			
	Djimtilo	Ouli Bangala	Ouarai	Boum Khebir
0–19	17	30	13	61
20–39	50	58	56	21
40–59	17	3	22	18
60–79	8	6	9	0
80–99	4	3	0	0
More than 99	4	0	0	0

FIGURE 2–6. A COURTYARD IN OULI BANGALA

were considered to be in congested neighborhoods and 36 percent in slightly congested areas. In all the villages the areas immediately surrounding the houses were stripped of vegetation, although there were a few large trees scattered among the houses.

The maintenance of cleanliness of houses and surrounding areas was assessed and tabulated. The comparative results are shown in Table 2–7. The low scores for Ouli Bangala and Ouarai are largely

TABLE 2–6. DISTRIBUTION OF SLEEPING SPACE PER PERSON

Space per Person (sq. meters)	Percentage Distribution			
	Djimtilo	Ouli Bangala	Ouarai	Boum Khebir
0–4.9	21.0	64	22	27
5–9.9	50.0	33	61	46
10–14.9	12.5	3	4	24
15–19.9	12.5	0	9	3
20 or more	4.0	0	4	0

FIGURE 2-7. HOUSE CONSTRUCTION IN OUARAI

TABLE 2-7. HYGIENE OF HOUSING AND SURROUNDINGS

	Percentage Distribution			
Characteristics	Djimtilo	Ouli Bangala	Ouarai	Boum Khebir
Clean house and surroundings	29	6	17	9
Clean house but dirty surroundings	25	15	0	55
Dirty house but clean surroundings	8	15	13	3
Dirty house and surroundings	38	64	70	33

TABLE 2-8. FLY INFESTATION IN HOUSES

	Percentage Distribution			
Degree of Infestation	Djimtilo	Ouli Bangala	Ouarai	Boum Khebir
Light (1–9 flies seen)	62	52	13	27
Moderate (10–50 flies seen)	38	48	87	55
Heavy (more than 50 flies)	0	0	0	18
Total	100	100	100	100

attributable to scattered refuse close to dwellings and to the animal droppings found everywhere, including inside the houses. In Boum Khebir a majority of the houses (64 percent) were in a good state of cleanliness, even though 88 percent of the areas surrounding the houses were judged far from acceptable. Hard clay floors undoubtedly contribute to the maintenance of cleanliness in the houses.

Fly infestation of houses is noted in Table 2–8. The infestation can be explained in part by the general lack of cleanliness of the houses in the villages, but it must also be viewed in the light of temperature and other climatic factors at the times of observation.

	Dates of Observation	Min. and Max. Temperature, °F
Djimtilo	February 6–20, 1967	54–101
Ouli Bangala	February 27–March 11, 1967	50–105
Ouarai	March 16–28, 1967	63–106
Boum Khebir	April 5–15, 1967	68–114

Heavy infestation in a large percentage of the houses of Boum Khebir was also due to the number of families that kept animals in their houses at night, for there is a strong association between having animals in the house and heavy fly infestation. In Djimtilo 17 percent of the households kept animals in the sleeping area, while in Ouli Bangala, Ouarai, and Boum Khebir the percentages were 6, 4, and 33 respectively.

Rodent signs were noted in 42 percent of the houses surveyed in Djimtilo, 97 percent of the homes seen in Ouli Bangala, 100 percent in Ouarai, and 70 percent in Boum Khebir. In all four villages the semidomestic, multimammate hut rat, *Mastomys natalensis*, was present. This rat has served as a link between the wild rodent reservoir of plague and the commensal rodents and man (Pollitzer, 1954). In Ouarai, in addition to the multimammate rat, a common field rat, *Arvicanthis niloticus*, was trapped inside the huts. In all instances numerous ectoparasites were collected from the trapped rodents.

Personal Hygiene

It may be said in general that people in villages close to natural bodies of water go to such water sources to bathe. They may also do their laundry at the same time. Seventy-one percent of the respondents of Djimtilo stated that they used soap in bathing. Soap was in evidence in the homes and was being sold in the village markets. In Ouli Bangala 61 percent of the households claimed to use soap. The village shop sold this item, and some use of soap among bathers was observed. Fifty-two percent of the people in Ouarai claimed to use soap, and in Boum Khebir the percentage claimed was about 30.

Information on the use of footwear was somewhat difficult to obtain. The comparative figures given in Table 2–9 were obtained through interviews and reflect what the respondents judged was the footwear usage by adult members of the households. Seventeen percent of the respondents in Djimtilo stated that they wore no shoes, while in Ouli Bangala, Ouarai, and Boum Khebir the percentages were 65, 52, and 42 respectively. The wide difference is probably due in part to the relative affluence of the people of Djimtilo, and to the contact many of them have with larger towns and cities in the area. It is also interesting to note that only 12 percent of the respondents in Djimtilo said that they wore shoes more than 50 percent of the time, while none of the respondents of Ouarai wore them more than 50 percent of the time. For Boum Khebir the figure was 3 percent, while for Ouli Bangala it was 5 percent. Those in Ouli Bangala who stated that they wore shoes all the time were members of the school teachers' families, a retired soldier, and the evangelist. Possession of footwear was easily established however, by our asking to see the shoes. Men's shoes generally were leather, while women's often were a very poor quality plastic. Children as a rule went barefoot all the time.

TABLE 2–9. USE OF FOOTWEAR BY ADULT VILLAGERS

	Percentage Distribution			
Use of Footwear	Djimtilo	Ouli Bangala	Ouarai	Boum Khebir
Never	17	65	52	42
Less than 25% of the time	46	18	44	46
25–50% of the time	25	12	4	9
50–75% of the time	12	0	0	3
All the time	0	5	0	0

In the village of Djimtilo 99 percent of the household heads stated that mosquito nets were used at night, but observations revealed that they were not available for all members of the households. The head of the household, followed by the next oldest male member, had the first right of use. In Ouli Bangala 19 percent of the households had mosquito nets, but seldom more than one per family. Fifty-seven percent of the families stated that smoke fire was used in the huts to discourage biting insects. In Ouarai 55 percent of the households owned mosquito nets, although there were not enough to provide protection for all members of the family. In Boum Khebir the percentage of households having nets was 47, with protection normally available only to the head of each household.

FOOD SANITATION

In all four villages food generally is prepared only for the meal at hand, and there are few leftovers. These are not saved except in Ouli Bangala, where leftover millet is placed in water and kept overnight; the diluted gruel is then drunk the next morning.

Most families store their staples in large clay pots usually covered with a clay dish and arranged along the walls of the houses. However, among the villagers there are some who store their food carelessly, thus inviting rodents. The presence of rodents and carelessness in food storage are closely associated.

DOMESTIC ANIMALS

The animals owned by the villagers are a reflection of affluence and, to a degree, of nutrition. Chickens head the list, followed by goats. The animals kept in the villages are listed in Table 2–10 in order of frequency.

TABLE 2–10. DOMESTIC ANIMALS IN ORDER OF FREQUENCY

Djimtilo	Ouli Bangala	Ouarai	Boum Khebir
Chickens	Chickens	Chickens	Chickens
Dogs	Goats	Goats	Goats
Goats	Sheep	Sheep	Dogs
Donkeys	Dogs	Dogs	
Cats		Bullocks	
Riding horses		Cats	

3

ARTHROPODS OF MEDICAL IMPORTANCE

GENERAL

Interesting findings concerning arthropods were made in the diverse environments characterizing the four areas of Chad where medically important insects and ticks were collected.

Djimtilo is situated along a marsh near the Chari River a few kilometers from Lake Chad. The average annual rainfall in the area is 500 millimeters, with the rainy season beginning in May and ending in September. In the dry season, areas even only slightly removed from the river are generally arid.

Ouli Bangala is in a light forest area at an elevation of approximately 420 meters above mean sea level and is within a short distance of the Lim River and Mbongo Creek. The Lim is a crystal clear mountain stream in which game fish abound. Mbongo Creek, on the other hand, is badly polluted and was not flowing at the time of our survey. The area receives from 1,200 to 1,300 millimeters of rainfall during a period of six or seven months of the year, generally between April and November. These features contribute to the extremely rich and diverse insect fauna.

Ouarai, located in the savannah, normally has from 1,100 to 1,200 millimeters of rainfall annually. The rainy season begins in May and ends in November. In the vicinity of the village flows the

The material in this chapter is based on studies carried out by Dr. James C. Hitchcock, the entomologist of the Geographic Epidemiology Unit in Chad.

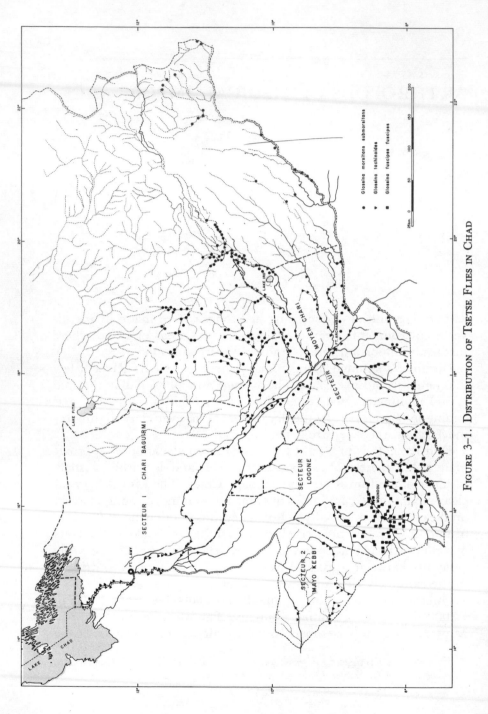

FIGURE 3–1. DISTRIBUTION OF TSETSE FLIES IN CHAD

TABLE 3–1. BREAKDOWN OF ARTHROPOD SPECIMENS AND COLLECTIONS FOR FOUR STUDY AREAS IN CHAD, FEBRUARY–APRIL, 1967

Pinned Specimens	Djimtilo		Ouli Bangala		Ouarai		Boum Khebir		Total No. of Each Specimen
	No. of Specimens	No. of Collections	No. of Specimens	No. of Collections	No. of Specimens	No. of Collections	No. of Specimens	No. of Collections	
Culicidae	644	43	217	27	436	20	216	24	1,513
Tabanidae	79	16	18	9	18	11	36	28	151
Glossinidae	104	5	15	5	—	—	5	1	124
Diptera attracted to human feces			326	16	579	21	530	24	1,435
Miscellaneous Diptera	324	57	317	58	232	32	176	38	1,049
Miscellaneous Orders	95	29	85	32	45	14	97	31	322
Total	1,246	150	978	147	1,310	98	1,060	146	4,594

Petit Mandoul, a slow-moving stream. Ouarai, like Ouli Bangala, has a large and varied insect population.

Boum Khebir, also located in the savannah and 245 kilometers north of Fort Archambault, receives from 800 to 900 millimeters of rainfall a year. Lake Iro, with its adjoining marsh, lies about one kilometer from the village. A fairly large area of the marsh is covered with water during the rainy season. Wild animals are readily seen in this region.

Collections of specimens were made in the four areas with a total of 4,594 pinned specimens (Table 3–1). There were approximately 1,500 alcohol-preserved specimens in a total of 158 collections. Altogether, forty-seven dipterous families from twenty of the world's twenty-four superfamilies were represented in the collection (Table 3–2). Of the forty-seven families, sixteen were found in all four study areas, twelve were taken from three sites, eight from only two regions, and eleven from one locality (Table 3–3). Thirty-six families were collected in Djimtilo, thirty-five in Ouli Bangala, and twenty-eight each in Ouarai and Boum Khebir. Many of the species in these families are known vectors of pathogenic agents. Of particular significance was the finding of *Simulium damnosum* (Theobald), the main vector of onchocerciasis, in Ouli Bangala. *Glossina* species, vectors of trypanosomiasis, were taken from all sites except Ouarai. The known distribution of glossinines in Chad is shown in

TABLE 3–2. BREAKDOWN BY FAMILY AND SUPERFAMILY OF THE
ORDER DIPTERA COLLECTED IN CHAD

Diptera	No. of Families Collected in Chad	No. of Families Known from the World	No. of Superfamilies Collected in Chad	No. of Superfamilies known from the World
Total	47	120	20[a]	24[a]
Nematocera	9	24	4	6
Brachycera	8	18	3	3
Cyclorrhapha	30	78	13[a]	15[a]
Aschiza	4	8	2	3
Schizophora	26	70	11[a]	12[a]
Acalyptratae	17	58	9[a]	10[a]
Calyptratae	9	12	2	2

[a] Includes unplaced families of Acalyptratae as a superfamily, although phylogenetic affinities do not necessarily exist between families of this artificial group.

Figure 3–1. *Phlebotomus langeroni orientalis,* an important vector of *Leishmania donovani,* also was taken. In addition, numerous mosquitoes that are known vectors of malaria and filariasis were collected in all areas south of the Sahara. Among the captured insects were some that play a role in the transmission of boutonneuse fever and loiasis.

TABLE 3–3. DIPTEROUS FAMILIES COLLECTED IN CHAD,
FEBRUARY–APRIL, 1967

NEMATOCERA					Acalyptratae (cont'd)			
Tipulidae	I	II	III	IV	Psilidae	II		
Psychodidae	I	II	III	IV	Otitidae	II	III	IV
Culicidae	I	II	III	IV	Platystomatidae	II		
Ceratopogonidae	I	II	III	IV	Tephritidae	I		IV
Chironomidae	I	II	III	IV	Sepsidae	I	II	IV
Simuliidae		II			Sciomyzidae	I		IV
Sciaridae		II			Lauxaniidae	I	II	
Mycetophilidae	I	II		IV	Lonchaeidae	II	III	IV
Cecidomyiidae	I	II	III		Sphaeroceridae	I II	III	IV
BRACHYCERA					Milichiidae	II	III	
Stratiomyidae	I			IV	Ephydridae	I II	III	IV
Tabanidae	I	II	III	IV	Curtonotidae	II	III	IV
Rhagionidae			III		Drosophilidae	I II	III	
Therevidae	I		III		Chloropidae	I II	III	IV
Asilidae	I	II	III	IV	Agromyzidae	I		
Bombyliidae	I	II	III	IV	Heleomyzidae	I		
Empididae	I	II		IV	Calyptratae			
Dolichopodidae	I	II	III	IV	Anthomyiidae	I		
CYCLORRHAPHA					Muscidae	I II	III	IV
ASCHIZA					Glossinidae	I II		IV
Phoridae	I	II	III		Hippoboscidae	I II		
Platypezidae	I				Nycteribiidae		III	
Pipunculidae	I	II			Calliphoridae	I II	III	IV
Syrphidae	I		III	IV	Sarcophagidae	I II	III	IV
SCHIZOPHORA					Tachinidae	I II	III	
Acalyptratae					Oestridae			IV
Diopsidae	I	II	III	IV				

KEY: I = Djimtilo (12° 50′ N, 14° 39′ E), 4–21 February 1967.
II = Ouli Bangala (7° 50′ N, 15° 52′ E), 25 February–11 March 1967.
III = Ouarai (8° 48′ N, 17° 45′ E), 14–27 March 1967.
IV = Boum Khebir (10° 10′ N, 19° 25′ E), 4–18 April 1967.

In Ouli Bangala, Ouarai, and Boum Khebir special efforts were made to collect Diptera attracted to human feces. The observations lasted long enough to permit collections of different species attracted to fecal matter as it underwent progressive decomposition and drying. The results are presented in detail in Table 3–4.

TABLE 3–4. COLLECTIONS OF DIPTERA ATTRACTED TO HUMAN FECES

	II	III	IV
NEMATOCERA			
Culicidae			
Culex univittatus		1	
Sciaridae	4		
BRACHYCERA			
Asilidae	1		
Empididae			
Drapetis aenescens Wiedemann	6		
CYCLORRHAPHA			
Acalyptratae			
Diopsidae			
Sphyracephala beccarii Rondani	1		
Otitidae			
Physiphora flavipes (Karsch)		2	
P. smaragdina (Loew)		2	9
P. africana (Hendel)		2	4
P. new species A.			1
P. new species B.			26
P. new species C.		3	17
P. new species D.		58	
Platystomatidae			
Rivellia anomala Hendel	2		
R. trigona Hendel	2		
Plagiostenopterina westermanni Hendel	18		
Elassogaster brachialis Rond	78		
Sepsidae			
Australosepsis niveipennis (Becker)			16
Sepsis lateralis Wiedemann	1		
Toxopoda nitida Macquart	7		
Lonchaeidae	2		
Milichiidae			
Phyllomyza new species	1		
Ephydridae			
Mosillus beckeri (Cresson)	5	78	35
Curtonotidae			
Curtonotum nigripalpe	3	213	
C. fuscipenne (Macquart)	1		
Calyptratae			
Muscidae			
Limnophora species	1		1
Gymnodia tonitrui (Wiedemann)	1		
Orthellia species	1		
Pyrellia scintillans Bigot			2
Atherigona species close to *haplopyga* Emden	1		
A. species close to *griseiventris* Emden		1	
A. species undetermined		4	2
Musca domestica L.	2		3

	II	III	IV
M. conducens Walker			2
M. sorbens Wiedemann	41	131	302
Calliphoridae			
Chrysomyiachloropyga F. putoria (Wiedemann)	38	4	55
C. chloropyga F. taeniata (Bigot)	3	1	11
C. marginalis (Wiedemann)	9		
Cordylobia anthropophaga (Blanchard)	1		
Hemipyrellia fernandica (Macquart)	5		
H. pulchra (Wiedemann)	10		
Tricyclea du Curran	13	1	
T. evanida Villeneuve	6	1	
T. ochracea Séguy		7	
T. species close to *ochracea* Séguy		2	
T. semicinerea Bezzi	10	4	
T. semithoracica Villeneuve	1		
Sarcophagidae			
Sarcophaga species	50	63	38
Wohlfahrtia species		1	6
Tachinidae			
Eryciini genus and species	1		
Total per Village	326	579	530

KEY: II = Ouli Bangala, III = Ouarai, IV = Boum Khebir.

Detailed Information on Selected Diptera

Psychodidae (Phlebotomini)

Phlebotomini were recovered from all areas in Chad (Table 3–5). A total of 245 specimens belonging to thirteen of the fifteen species and subspecies known to occur in Chad (Parrot and Bellon, 1952) were taken. With the exception of *Phlebotomus langeroni orientalis*, the important vector of *Leishmania donovani*, all were in the genus *Sergentomyia*.* All specimens were taken either in light traps or were attracted to light in the tents. Seven of the thirteen species and subspecies had not previously been reported from Chad. They were: *P. langeroni orientalis*, *Sergentomyia buxtoni*, *S. murphyi*, *S. africana africana*, *S. africana magna*, *S. inermis*, and *S. affinis vorax*.

* The British phlebotomini expert, Dr. D. J. Lewis, who identified the material as to species, recognized *Sergentomyia* as a generic group; consequently, this report is made in accordance with his determinations.

TABLE 3–5. PSYCHODIDAE COLLECTED IN CHAD, FEBRUARY–APRIL, 1967

Species	I	II	III	IV
Phlebotomus (Larroussius) langeroni orientalis Parrot*			III	
Sergentomyia (Sergentomyia) antennata (Newstead)				IV
S. (S.) bedfordi (Newstead)			III	
S. (S.) buxtoni (Theodor)*			III	IV
S. (S.) murphyi Lewis and McMillan*		II	III	
S. (S.) schwetzi (Adler, Theodor, and Parrot)				IV
S. (Parrotomyia) africana africana (Newstead)*		II		
S. (P.) africana magna (Sinton)*	I	II	III	IV
S. (Grassomyia) inermis (Theodor)*		II	III	IV
S. (G.) squamipleuris squamipleuris (Newstead)	I	II	III	IV
S. (Sintonius) adleri (Theodor)				IV
S. (S.) affinis vorax (Parrot) or related form*		II		
S. (S.) clydei (Sinton)		II	III	IV

```
* = species previously unrecorded in Chad.
I = Djimtilo              III = Ouarai
II = Ouli Bangala         IV = Boum Khebir
```

Since cases of kala-azar are known to occur in Chad (Parrot and Bellon, 1952), it is speculated that *P. langeroni orientalis* may be the vector there, as it is in the neighboring Sudan (Hoogstraal, 1956).

Culicidae

More than 1,500 mosquitoes were collected in Chad during our study. All were determined as to species, with the exception of three specimens of *Ficalbia* and two specimens of *Culex* (Table 3–6). Thirty-six species and varieties were recognized in seven genera, of which sixteen species and varieties constituted new records for the Republic of Chad. Of the ten species of *Anopheles* taken, all were known or suspected vectors of malaria, and seven species were taken while attempting to feed on human blood. *A. funestus*, *A. gambiae*, and *A. pharoensis* are vectors both of malaria and of *Wuchereria bancrofti*. *A. funestus*, taken in all four areas studied, was the dominant anopheline encountered. *A. pharoensis* was a persistent biter in Djimtilo, while *A. gambiae* and another malaria vector, *A. nili*, were taken only in Ouli Bangala. All of the *gambiae* and many of the *nili* specimens were captured in tents, presumably because they were attracted to human hosts. *Culex univittatus*, a known vector of West Nile virus, was the most common species encountered; like *A. funestus*, it was taken in all four study areas. *C. pipiens quinquefasciatus* was captured within tents in Djimtilo and Ouli Bangala. The recording of *A. coustani* var. *tenebrosus* at Djimtilo and of *A. rufipes* var. *ingrami* at Ouli Bangala was a first for Chad. *Ficalbia circumtestacea*, *F. uniformis*, *F. hispida*, *F. perplexens*, *F. plumosa*, and *F. splendens*, all from Djimtilo, also were new recordings for Chad. Other species previously unrecorded for this country were: four species of *Uranotaenia*, *U. alba*, *U. alboabdominalis*, *U. balfouri*, and *U. pallidocephala*; two species of *Aedeomyia*, *A. africana* and *A. furfurea;* and two species of *Culex*, *C. (N.) rubinotus* and *C. (C.) univittatus* var. *neavei*. Individual rearings of five species were undertaken: *Anopheles squamosus*, *A. wellcomei*, *Culex duttoni*, *C. poicilipes*, and *C. univittatus*.

Ten species in three genera were observed that were infested with larval water mites. These were *Anopheles coustani* var. *tenebrosus*, *A. funestus*, *A. pharoensis*, and *A. rufipes; Mansonia africana* and *M. uniformis; Culex poicilipes*, *C. univittatus*, and *C. univittatus* var. *neavei*.

Ceratopogonidae

The only biting midges taken while feeding on human bait were *Culicoides nigeriae* and *C. pallidipennis*. *C. nigeriae*, a vicious biter, was taken in abundance in Ouli Bangala along water courses and in Ouarai in camp as well as along the water course, while the single specimen of *C. pallidipennis* was taken in Boum Khebir in camp near the end of the crepuscular period.

Simulidae

Black flies were collected only in Ouli Bangala and, with the exception of one specimen, all were *Simulium damnosum*. These were captured while biting a human host in close proximity to water sources throughout the daylight and crepuscular hours; collecting rates were one black fly every six to nine minutes over one-hour and one-and-a-half-hour time periods.

Tabanidae

Nine species of tabanids, with a total of 151 specimens, were collected in Chad, and an additional species, *Tabanus biguttatus*, was found in Ouli Bangala and Ouarai (see Table 3–7). *Chrysops longicornis*, a known vector of *Loa loa*, was taken in Ouli Bangala. More than half the tabanids were *Atylotus agrestis*, and, with the

TABLE 3–6. MOSQUITO SPECIES COLLECTED IN CHAD: SUMMARY FOR FOUR AREAS, FEBRUARY–APRIL, 1967

Mosquito Species	Locality[a]	No. of Mosquitoes	Attracted to Human Bait	Tent	Light Trap	Diurnal A.M.	Diurnal P.M.	Crepuscular P.M.	Nocturnal	Reared Individual Adult	Larval Mite Ectoparasites
Anopheles coustani Laveran	II	1	x			x					
A. coustani var. tenebrosus Donitz	I	18	x	x	x	x			x		x
A. funestus Giles	I, II, III, IV	249	x	x	x	x	x	x	x		x
A. gambiae Giles	II	19	x	x	x	x		x	x		x
A. nili (Theobald)	II	56	x	x	x	x		x	x		x
A. pharoensis Theobald	I	56	x	x	x	x	x	x	x		x
A. rufipes (Gough)	III, IV	19	x	x		x			x		
A. rufipes var. ingrami Edwards	II	1								x	
A. squamosus Theobald	III	1	x		x					x	
A. wellcomei Theobald	I, III	2							x		
Ficalbia (F.) circumtestacea (Theobald)	I	1		x				x	x		
F. (F.) uniformis (Theobald)	I	1	x	x	x	x			x		
F. Mimomyia hispida (Theobald)	I	6			x			x	x		
F. (M.) perplexens Edwards	I	1			x				x		
F. (M.) plumosa (Theobald)	I	1			x				x		
F. (M.) splendens (Theobald)	I	1			x				x		
F. (M.) species A.	I	1			x				x		
F. (M.) species B.	I, II	3			x				x		
F. Etorleptiomyia mediolineata (Theobald)	I	10	x	x	x	x		x	x		
F. (E.) species A.	I	1	x	x		x			x		
F. undetermined	II	3			x				x		

Species	Sites[a]	No.								
Coquillettidia (*C.*) *metallica* (Theobald)	I, II, IV	9			x					
Mansonia mansonioides africana (Theobald)	I, II, IV	53	x	x	x	x	x	x	x	
M. (*M.*) *uniformis* (Theobald)	I, II, IV	53	x	x	x	x			x	
Uranotaenia alba Theobald	I	16		x				x		
U. alboabdominalis Theobald	I	13		x				x		
U. balfouri Theobald	I, II	14	x	x				x		
U. pallidocephala Theobald	I	2		x				x		
Aedeomyia africana Neveu-Lemaire	I, II	54	x	x		x		x		
A. furfurea (Enderlein)	III	1		x				x		
Culex lutzia tigripes Grandpré and Charmoy	II	10		x		x		x		
C. neoculex rubinotus Theobald	I	2	x	x		x		x	x	
C. (*C.*) *duttoni* Theobald	II	44	x	x		x		x		
C. (*C.*) *pipiens quinquefasciatus*	I, II	2	x	x		x	x	x	x	x
C. (*C.*) *poicilipes* Theobald	I, II, III	58	x	x		x	x	x	x	x
C. (*C.*) *univittatus* Theobald	I, II, III, IV	665	x	x		x	x	x	x	x
C. (*C.*) *univittatus* var. *neavei* Theobald	I, II, III	67	x	x	x	x	x	x	x	x
C. (*C.*) *species undetermined*	I, II	2	x	x		x		x		

[a] I = Djimtilo, II = Ouli Bangala, III = Ouarai, IV = Boum Khebir.

exception of three of this species taken in Boum Khebir, all were collected from tents in Djimtilo. Human biting by this species occurred in both areas. The second most abundant species, accounting for more than a fifth of the specimens, *T. taeniola* form *variatus* was present in the same two areas, but most were found in Boum Khebir. *T. taeniola* form *variatus* was a rather active man-biter in this area. Of the three specimens of *A. agrestis*, two were taken while attempting to feed on a human host. *T. gratus*, the most commonly encountered species in Ouli Bangala, was collected in tents at about midday and in the late afternoon. *T. chevalieri* was taken in tents and while biting human hosts near the stream early in the evening. *T. par*, a beautiful golden species, was the most abundant tabanid captured in Ouarai and was noted to be a common man-biter.

TABLE 3–7. TABANIDAE COLLECTED IN CHAD, FEBRUARY–APRIL, 1967

Species	I	II	III	IV	Total
Ancala fasciata var. *nilotica* (Austen)				1	1
Atylotus agrestis (Wiedemann)	77[a]			3[a]	80
Chrysops longicornis Macquart		1			1
Tabanus chevalieri Surcouf		4[a]			4
T. gratus Loew		10			10
T. laverani Surcouf			1		1
T. par Walker		2	17[a]		19
T. taeniola Palisot de Beauvois form *variatus* Walker	2			32[a]	34
T. sticticolis Surcouf		1			1
Total Tabanidae per Village and in Collection	79	18	18	36	151

[a] Includes at least one individual taken while biting a human host.
KEY: I = Djimtilo, II = Ouli Bangala, III = Ouarai, IV = Boum Khebir.
NOTE: *T. biguttatus* Wiedemann was observed on vegetation in Ouli Bangala and was seen on a tent flap in Ouarai.

Rhagionidae

The eight specimens of snipe flies were taken in Ouli Bangala from vegetation and detritus near water. Some species in this family commonly bite man.

Sciomyzidae

Five specimens of Sciomyzidae were collected in Chad, four in Djimtilo and one in Boum Khebir. One of the specimens was a female *Sepedon ornatifrons* Adams from Djimtilo and the other four were male *Sepedonella nana* Verbeke. The larval stage of this family is a predator of vector snails of schistosomiasis. It has been suggested, therefore, that this group could be utilized as a possible biological control agent.

Chloropidae

The geographical distribution of the eighteen species (seventy-five specimens) in ten genera of this family taken during the study is shown in Table 3–8. The collector gathered most of the specimens while sweeping vegetation, usually in close proximity to water. Two of the exceptions were found only in Boum Khebir; *Oscinella aharonii*, a "swarming gnat" of the Sudan, was captured on a tree trunk, and a specimen of *Pachylophus proximus* was found in mud. The few remaining exceptions were collected within tents, usually in the early morning hours between 7:00 and 7:45 A.M. They were: (1) all the specimens of *O. aharonii* collected in Ouarai (from 7:30 to 7:45 A.M. on two different days); (2) both specimens

TABLE 3–8. CHLOROPIDAE COLLECTED IN CHAD

	I	II	III	IV
Anatrichus erinaceus Loew		II		IV
A. new species	I			IV
Chlorops new species		II		IV
Elachiptera occipitalis (Loew)				IV
E. near *vulgaris* (Adams)				IV
E. near *scapularis* (Adams)	I			IV
E. flavofrontata (Becker)		II		IV
Hippelates new species	I			
Mepachymerus lentus (Curran)		II		IV
M. new species (or variant of *tenellus* Becker)	I			IV
Meromyza capensis Loew		II		
Oscinella aharonii Duda		II	III	IV
Pachylophus proximus Loew	I			IV
P. lugens Loew	I			IV
P. species (very close to *inornatus* Loew)	I	II	III	
P. species (*frontalis* group)		II		
Polyodaspis species				IV
Thaumatomyia new species			III	IV

KEY: I = Djimtilo, II = Ouli Bangala, III = Ouarai, IV = Boum Khebir.

of a new species of *Thaumatomyia* (in Ouarai at 7:45 A.M. and in Boum Khebir at 7:00 A.M.); and (3) a specimen of *P. proximus* in Djimtilo (at 10:00 P.M.) which had been attracted to light.

Hippoboscidae

Two species of this ectoparasitic family of Diptera were collected in Chad. *Hippobosca variegata* Megerle was taken in a tent in Djimtilo and in the U.S. Embassy bath house in Fort Lamy. *Pseudolynchia canariensis* (Macquart) was aspirated from the window of a tent in Ouli Bangala.

TICKS*

Djimtilo and Lake Chad

Eight species of ticks were collected in the Lake Chad area; five species were found in Djimtilo itself. Of these, *Hyalomma truncatum* Koch (one male) was taken crawling inside a boot while it was being worn. This species, a known vector of tick paralysis and Q fever (*Coxiella burneti*), has only occasionally been reported on man, in Nigeria and Kenya (Hoogstraal, 1956). Two species, *Hyalomma marginatum rufipes* Koch (one female) and *Amblyomma sparsum* Koch (one male), were found crawling on the leg of someone's pants. *H. marginatum rufipes* (one female) was picked up while crawling rather rapidly over open, unshaded soil. Nymphs of *H. marginatum rufipes* have been found infected with *Rickettsia conorii*, the etiological agent of boutonneuse fever (Hoogstraal, 1956). While sweeping vegetation near the marsh, *Rhipicephalus sanguineus* (Latrielle) (one male) was found; it was also taken from two host dogs (four males, five females), along with *Rhipicephalus simus* Koch (two males, two females). *R. sanguineus* is a known vector of boutonneuse fever, while *R. simus* is commonly found on man and is known to cause paralysis (Hoogstraal, 1956) and to transmit *R. conorii*.

Three additional species of ticks were collected from horses and camels in a small village near Bol in the Lake Chad area† and were added to the collection. The specimens of *Ornithodoros savignyi* Audouin (one male, three females, fifty nymphs) and *Hyalomma impeltatum* Schulze and Schlottke (two males) in this collection were

---

* All identifications were made by Dr. Harry Hoogstraal, NAMRU 2, Cairo.
† By K. K. V. Adams, a U.S. Peace Corps volunteer.

the first recorded for Central Africa. The third species was *Rhipi-cephalus evertsi evertsi* Neumann (nineteen males, twelve females) a known vector of boutonneuse fever (*R. conorii*) (Hoogstraal, 1956).

Ouli Bangala

Rhipicephalus senegalensis Koch (one female), a species found naturally infected with *Coxiella burneti* in Portuguese Guinea (Hoog-straal, 1956), was taken while crawling on the floor of a sleeping tent; another female, probably *Rhipicephalus longus* Neumann, was collected under a tent.

Ouarai

(No ticks were collected in Ouarai.)

Boum Khebir

One female of *Boophilus decoloratus* (Koch) was taken while feed-ing on a Coke's hartebeest, the species of antelope most commonly observed in the savannah surrounding Lake Iro. *B. decoloratus* is a suspected vector of Q fever in Portuguese Guinea; there is presump-tive evidence that this tick may be involved in the transmission of *Rickettsia conorii* (Hoogstraal, 1956).

4

EPIDEMIOLOGICAL FEATURES

GENERAL

An appraisal of the magnitude of public health problems in an underdeveloped country like Chad is frequently based entirely on meager existing data, which reflect gross deficiencies in the availability and distribution of health services in general and insufficient diagnostic capabilities in particular. Many diagnoses are made on the basis of clinical symptoms alone. Whenever concrete diagnostic data are available only for small and frequently non-representative population samples, there is a tendency to generalize and extrapolate. The focus of attention is drawn to such data because they can be published with confidence, while the often more prevalent or important diseases that cannot be identified without scientifically approved techniques are left in the uncomfortable pool of diagnostic anonymity. Although they are themselves subject to these restrictions, the results of the study presented in this book are based on a broad diagnostic screening program. They emphasize the difficulties of appraising public health problems in Chad when the information is based entirely on a digest of the few available statistics to which the authors had access when visiting the country (National Research Council, 1966, 2:299–307).

The less specific the capabilities for diagnosis, the broader become the categories for classifying diseases in reports made by public health administrators burdened with the planning of comprehensive health programs. A notable example is the indiscriminate use of the term "intestinal parasitism" as the numerator in prevalence rates, a use which lumps together a wide variety of helminths and protozoa with quite different life cycles and modes of transmission. Lack of sanitation, although a prerequisite for the establishment of endemic infections with the "cosmopolitan" nematodes, *Ascaris lumbricoides* and *Trichuris trichiura*, cannot be taken *ipso facto* as an indicator that such specific infestations exist in an area (World Health Organization, 1964, pp. 17–25, and Buck, Sasaki, and Anderson, 1968, pp. 64–67; see also Intestinal Parasites, pp. 163–67 below).

Another characteristic problem of developing countries, that of multiple infections by different agents in the same person, presented itself dramatically in Chad, where it was the rule rather than the exception. Little is known as yet about the complexities of interaction and their modifying influences on clinical manifestations and laboratory results, especially those measuring antibodies. Special efforts were made with the aid of numerous cross-tabulations to obtain clues to the synergistic and antagonistic influences of co-existing conditions (see Onchocerciasis and Schistosomiasis, pp. 140–50 and 150–60).

After an extensive pilot study in the major parts of Chad, which included visits to physicians working in the various areas, examinations of patients in many rural communities, and comprehensive laboratory examinations of specimens collected in the field, a tentative picture of the prevailing disease spectrum in Chad was obtained. These data, together with information furnished by Dr. Pierre Ziegler (see Table 4–1), director of the Service des Grandes Endémies and an expert on infectious diseases in Chad, were the basis for preparation of the final study protocol, which was done by adding measurements for the identification of the locally important endemic diseases to the broad, general protocol used previously (Buck, Sasaki and Anderson, 1968, pp. 105–33; Ziegler, 1967).

As shown in Chapter 5, participation in all phases of the study was high in the population samples of each of the five selected communities, with a minimum of 94.9 percent participating in physical examinations in Faya-Largeau and a maximum of 99.7 percent participating in Ouli Bangala. It is believed that this success can be attributed to two factors. The first was the vigorous support given the project by central and local government officials; the second was the availability of medical treatment for those examined. In a

TABLE 4–1. REPORTED CASES AND CASE FATALITIES OF
COMMUNICABLE DISEASES FOR 1966

Disease	No. of Cases	Deaths	
		No.	Percentage
Malaria (all forms)	101,042	149	0.1
Amebiasis	22,710	109	0.5
Schistosomiasis (hematobium)	18,824	24	0.1
Measles	9,215	141	1.5
Chickenpox	6,943	0	0
Trachoma	5,524	0	0
Infectious hepatitis	4,558	100	2.2
Pertussis	4,001	2	0.05
Grippe	3,262	0	0
Leprosy	3,177	155	4.9
Pneumococcal pneumonia	2,658	73	2.7
Otitis	2,281	0	0
Schistosomiasis (mansoni)	1,771	0	0
Tuberculosis (pulmonary)	1,252	55	4.4
Meningococcal infections	575	43	7.5
Bacillary dysentery	197	11	5.6
Leishmaniasis (tropicalis)	169	0	0
African trypanosomiasis	135	8	5.9
Typhoid fever	53	7	13.2
Poliomyelitis	34	1	2.9
Paratyphoid fever	18	2	11.1
Rabies	10	10	100.0
Diphtheria	5	0	0
Brucellosis	1	0	0
Rickettsioses	1	0	0
Total	188,416	890	0.5

community where there were many sick persons but no medical
facilities, participation in the study resembled the gathering of
patients at a large mobile outpatient clinic. This was also apparent
from the considerable influx of persons who were not part of the
sample; they were examined and treated but were not included in
the data of this report. This practice and the conducting of a census
at the beginning of the study in each village prevented dilution of
the population samples by the clandestine immigration of outsiders
into the selected families.

In addition to large regional differences in the prevalence of such
diseases as malaria, schistosomiasis, onchocerciasis, African tick-
borne typhus, trachoma, and yaws, to name only the most important endemic infections, there were interesting variations in the

prevalence of some conditions within the same village. Some of these differences, when studied in relation to ecological factors, habits, house location within the village, blood relationship, and occupational exposure, had plausible explanations (see Nutrition [pp. 102–13], Hemoglobin [pp. 116–20], Onchocerciasis [pp. 140–50], Schistosomiasis [pp. 150–60], and Rickettsioses [pp. 198–201]).

Despite the variety of diagnostic tests used in the study, many differential diagnostic questions still remain unanswered. This applies particularly to the unfortunate group of patients included in the category "Incapacitated" and may be related to some extent to the unusual frequency with which combinations of infections and pathological conditions were recognized in the same persons. An illustration is the finding made in a single specimen, a blood smear from a resident of Ouarai, in which four potentially pathogenic etiological agents were present simultaneously: *Plasmodium falciparum*, *Loa loa*, *Wuchereria bancrofti*, and *Dipetalonema perstans*.

In many instances the identification of cases of a particular condition was based on more than one measurement. This permitted comparison of the results of the different diagnostic tests for concordance. A great deal of information was obtained by interview. For some conditions it was possible to compare the statements made in health interviews with laboratory results (schistosomiasis: hematuria versus recovery of ova in urine specimens), or with findings made in physical examinations (smallpox vaccinations: histories versus presence of scars). Discrepancies between the results of the two types of measurements were then analyzed for patterns that might reveal a tendency of conditioned responses to specific interview questions that are related to cultural habits and taboos (see Schistosomiasis).

NUTRITION

Nutritional Deficiencies

The information on nutrition is based on interviews with the wives of all household heads. The interview questions permitted independent listings of the three most frequently consumed staples. Because of pronounced seasonal variations in the availability of certain basic foodstuffs, the questions were asked twice, once for the dry period and again for the rainy season. Table 4–2 lists the staple foods most frequently used by the residents of the five villages. The

TABLE 4–2. PERCENTAGE DISTRIBUTION OF STAPLE FOODS, BY SEASON

Area: Village: Staple Food	Lake Chad Djimtilo		Southwest Ouli Bangala		Central South Ouarai		Lake Iro Boum Khebir		Sahara Faya-Largeau	
	Dry Season %	Wet Season %	Dry Season %	Wet Season %	Dry Season %	Wet Season %	Dry Season %	Wet Season %	Regular Season %	Date Season %
Millet	16.6	19.5	74.0	9.9	48.2	3.6	95.6	41.7	54.4	42.2
Corn	58.7	55.2	0	0	0	9.6	0	3.3	32.2	20.0
Manioc roots	0	0	3.7	29.6	3.6	26.5	0	11.0	0	0
Manioc leaves	0	0	1.3	12.3	1.2	3.6	0	1.1	0	0
Potatoes	0	0	1.3	1.3	0	3.6	0	0	0	0
Peanuts	0	0	0	8.6	1.2	19.3	0	1.1	0	0
Beans	0	0	19.7	38.3	1.2	32.5	0	9.9	0	0
Peas	0	0	0	0	43.3	1.2	0	0	0	0
Mango	0	0	0	0	1.2	0	0	0	0	0
Rice	0	0	0	0	0	0	2.2	0	8.9	8.9
Wild roots	0	0	0	0	0	0	0	1.1	0	0
Igname (yams)	0	0	0	0	0	0	0	30.7	0	0
Dates	0	0	0	0	0	0	0	0	0	24.4
Macaroni	0	0	0	0	0	0	0	0	4.5	4.5
Fish	25.3	25.3	0	0	0	0	2.2	0	0	0
Total	100.0	100.0	100.0	100.0	99.9	99.9	100.0	99.9	100.0	100.0

percentages shown are averages of three possible entries for each season.

With the exception of Djimtilo, where fish is abundant and caught regularly in the immediate vicinity of the village, meat and other animal protein foods are not listed as staples. Generally the diet is monotonous and dependent upon the season. There are considerable regional variations in the frequency distribution of the locally most important foods. Millet is the main staple in the dry season in all villages but Djimtilo, where it is replaced by corn. A much larger diversity becomes apparent during the rainy season. This can be considered to reflect differences not only in the local availability of the various foods but also in the utilization as related to the cultural behavior and socioeconomic status of the villagers.

Manioc (cassava) roots and leaves are the foremost items in the diet of the residents of Ouli Bangala, while beans are primary in Ouarai, igname (yams) in Boum Khebir. There are no pronounced seasonal differences in the diet of residents of Djimtilo. On the other hand, in Faya-Largeau, a Saharan community unaffected by the shifting monsoon, the annual harvesting of the date palms in September and October influences the nutrition of the residents both directly and indirectly. Its direct effect on the nutrition of the local residents is the periodic abundance and availability of the fruit as a staple, as indicated in Table 4–2, whereas the indirect effect is revealed by the annual influx of caravans and merchants during the date season which brings to the community a great variety of goods, including spices and cereals.

Consumption of animal protein is probably the most sensitive indicator of the quality of nutrition in a community because of its usually close association with the economic base and cultural background of the residents. Figures 4–1 and 4–2 show for specified time intervals the cumulative percentages of households in each community which had had at least one meal of meat or fish. Only the residents in the two Arab villages had eaten meat or fish frequently. This information can be supplemented by the results shown in Table 4–3, which lists the types of meat most frequently consumed in the households. In addition to fish, the villagers of Djimtilo eat mutton, beef, and chicken. In Ouli Bangala, a living museum of pathology and a place of epidemiological curiosities, 26 percent of the wives spontaneously listed rats and other field rodents as the most frequently used meat in their families. This rather unusual statement was supported by various direct and indirect findings

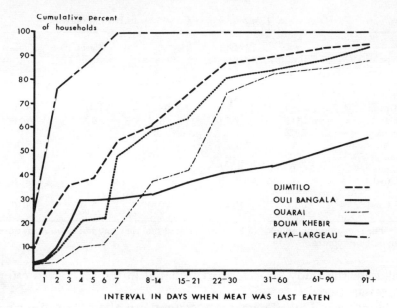

FIGURE 4–1. CUMULATIVE PERCENTAGE DISTRIBUTION OF HOUSE-
HOLDS BY TIME WHEN MEAT WAS LAST EATEN

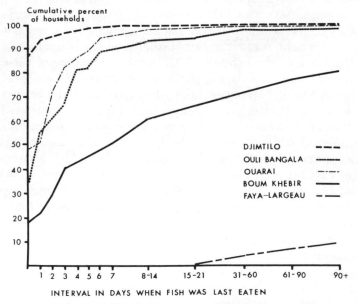

FIGURE 4–2. CUMULATIVE PERCENTAGE DISTRIBUTION OF HOUSE-
HOLDS BY TIME WHEN FISH WAS LAST EATEN

TABLE 4–3. TYPES OF MEAT CONSUMED IN HOUSEHOLDS

Type of Meat	Djimtilo %	Ouli Bangala %	Ouarai %	Boum Khebir %	Faya-Largeau %
Goat	1.3	3.8	53.4	87.9	0
Mutton	48.1	3.8	38.2	0	20.0
Beef	21.3	65.0	8.4	3.3	20.0
Chicken	29.3	0	0	0	0
Field rodent	0	26.1	0	0	0
Rabbit	0	1.3	0	0	0
Game	0	0	0	2.2	0
Camel	0	0	0	0	60.0
Total	100.0	100.0	100.0	93.4[a]	100.0

[a] The remaining households (6.6 percent) stated that they had not eaten meat during the past six months.

made in the study, as described in detail in the section Intestinal Parasites (see pp. 163–67).

Hunting in Ouli Bangala is a community affair. It is a form of battue, using fire as a means to drive the animals out of their burrows and into the spears of the hunters (for details of the "hunt," see Economic Activities, pp. 156–59). The hunt was observed by members of the research team. Larger animals are carried to the village, where the meat is divided; smaller animals, including rats, are often consumed on the spot. An indirect indicator of rat-eating and its consequences is the finding of *Capillaria* sp. (probably *hepatica*) in 5 of 381 stool specimens acquired from the residents of Ouli Bangala. This finding undoubtedly indicates spurious infections that could have resulted from the recent consumption of rat livers infected with this nematode, as in true infections ova would not be passed in the stool (Otto *et al.*, 1954). The prognosis of genuine capillariasis *quoad vitam* is uncertain (Otto *et al.*, 1954), but without further evidence from autopsies or liver biopsies one can only speculate that the infection may be one of the more important causes of death in a community where the presence of hyperendemic malaria and schistosomiasis (*mansoni*) has obscured the significance of hepatomegaly as a pathognomonic sign for any other disease in which the liver is the predilected site of infection.

Goat and mutton are the types of meat most frequently eaten in Ouarai. Goat meat is the main animal protein source in Boum Khebir, as is camel meat in Faya-Largeau. Over-all meat consumption was highest in the latter village and lowest in the former. This bipolarity in the availability of animal proteins is also apparent from the data listed in Table 4–4, which shows the percentages of families using eggs, cheese, and milk (for their children). On the basis of all information available from the study, the households of the five study communities can be ranked by the quality of their nutrition from best to worst in the following order: (1) Faya-Largeau, (2) Djimtilo, (3) Ouarai, (4) Ouli Bangala, and (5) Boum Khebir.

TABLE 4–4. PERCENTAGE OF HOUSEHOLDS CONSUMING MILK, EGGS, AND CHEESE

Type of Protein Food	Djimtilo	Ouli Bangala	Ouarai	Boum Khebir	Faya-Largeau
Eggs	24.1	14.8	27.6	5.0	2.2
Cheese	17.1	0	0	0	0
Milk (for children)	21.7	1.2	9.6	0	86.6

These basic data on nutrition, as elicited from interviews, will now be examined for their associations with the relevant physiological variables and physical signs of nutritional deficiencies which were detected in physical examinations or determined by laboratory tests. Figure 4–3 shows the regression lines of skinfold thickness on the weight/height ratio for adult males (twenty years and above) in each of the five villages. Skinfold thickness was measured at the midposterior midpoint of the left and right upper arms; the average of the two determinations was recorded. Body weight was measured in pounds, and height in inches. Weight change in adult males was found to be positively associated with subcutaneous fatness over the triceps muscle and at two thoracic areas (Albrink and Meigs, 1964; Edwards, 1950).

Under most physiological conditions it can be assumed that variations of skinfold thickness are closely associated with corresponding changes in subcutaneous fatness (Comstock, Kendrick, and Livesay, 1966). As can be seen from Figure 4–3, there were only minor variations in the positions and slopes of the regression lines for four of the five villages; only the regression line for the males of Ouli Bangala did not follow the general pattern. Although the correlation between skinfold thickness and weight/height ratio was far from perfect in all communities (as indicated by the correlation

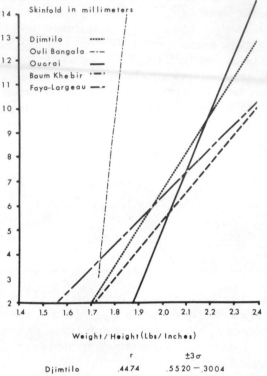

	r	±3σ
Djimtilo	.4474	.5520 − .3004
Ouli Bangala	.1873	.2600 − .1194
Ouarai	.6118	.7616 − .3910
Boum Khebir	.6247	.7531 − .4130
Faya-Largeau	.4474	.6352 − .2165

FIGURE 4–3. REGRESSION OF SKINFOLD THICKNESS
ON THE WEIGHT/HEIGHT RATIO, AND COEFFICIENTS
OF CORRELATION(r) COMPUTED FOR ADULT MALES

coefficients listed at the bottom of Figure 4–3), it was weakest in
Ouli Bangala. This finding led to the assumption that in Ouli
Bangala factors other than subcutaneous fatness must have contributed to the variations in skinfold thickness and that these factors
were unimportant in the other population samples.

As will be discussed in more detail in the section on Onchocerciasis, infections caused by *Onchocerca volvulus* were holoendemic
in Ouli Bangala but were scarce or absent in the other villages. One
of the pathognomonic signs of the disease is a characteristic wrin-
kling and thickening of the skin which is frequently referred to as

pachyderma because of its similarity to an elephant's hide. This peculiar type of dermatitis is caused by the myriads of micro-filariae of *O. volvulus* which inhabit the skin of infected persons. Because of geographical inconsistencies in the prevalence of derma-titis in hyperendemic areas of onchocerciasis classified by the per-centage of persons with microfilariae in skin snips, it was speculated that nutritional factors, especially vitamin A deficiency, play a role as determinants of this particular manifestation of the disease (Rodger, 1962).

It was technically impossible to examine all the sera collected in the field for vitamin A and carotene levels; but those from Ouli Bangala which were still available after completion of the many laboratory tests were screened for carotene concentrations by an ultramicro technique (Natelson, 1961, pp. 451–54). The carotene levels were low in all age groups, as shown in Table 4–5. A com-parison of individuals with and without onchocercal dermatitis did not reveal differences between the two groups. The mean for per-sons with positive skin snips but without dermatitis was 0.068 milligram percent and for those with dermatitis 0.067 milligram percent.

TABLE 4–5. SERUM CAROTENE LEVELS OF 142 RESIDENTS[a]
OF OULI BANGALA, BY AGE

Age (years)	No. Examined	Carotene in mg%[b]
Birth–4	27	0.065
5–9	24	0.067
10–19	34	0.069
20–29	30	0.072
30–39	20	0.073
40+	7	0.079
Total	142	0.069

[a] Includes all persons from whom a sufficient quantity of serum was still available after completion of the routine laboratory tests.
[b] Normal range = 0.05–0.2 milligram percent.

The mean values of total serum proteins, serum protein fractions as determined by electrophoresis on cellulose acetate membranes, and of serum cholesterol are listed in Table 4–6. The albumin-globulin ratio was reversed (<1.0) in all villages but the Saharan community of Faya-Largeau, where malaria was not endemic. The highest mean gamma globulin level was found in Ouli Bangala, where in addition to malaria, onchocerciasis, and infections with *S. mansoni* were hyperendemic. Serum albumin, which is associated with nutrition more closely than any of the other serum protein fractions (Scrimshaw, Taylor, and Gordon, 1959), was lowest in Ouli Bangala and highest in Faya-Largeau, where animal protein foods were most frequently available to all residents. Although cholesterol levels were low by American standards, the relatively highest mean values were found in the two Arab communities (Djimtilo and Faya-Largeau), where meat, fish, milk, and eggs were most often consumed.

TABLE 4–6. MEAN VALUES FOR TOTAL SERUM PROTEINS,
PROTEIN FRACTIONS, AND SERUM CHOLESTEROL

| | Serum Protein Fractions[a] | | | | | | | |
Village	Total Proteins gm%	Albu- min gm%	Alpha[1] gm%	Alpha[2] gm%	Beta gm%	Gamma gm%	A/G Ratio	Cho- lesterol mg%
Djimtilo	8.3	3.9	0.3	0.8	0.9	2.4	0.89	147.0
Ouli Bangala	8.5	3.6	0.3	0.8	0.8	3.0	0.73	117.3
Ouarai	8.0	3.8	0.3	0.7	0.9	2.3	0.90	113.8
Boum Khebir	8.4	3.9	0.3	0.8	0.8	2.6	0.87	111.4
Faya-Largeau	7.9	4.2	0.3	0.8	0.9	1.7	1.14	139.6

[a] Values listed are adjusted for age and sex.

The prevalence of selected signs of nutritional deficiencies is shown in Table 4–7. As can be seen, by far the highest frequency of these conditions was detected in Ouli Bangala. It is also interesting to note that only a few physical signs of nutritional deficiencies were recognized in Boum Khebir, whose residents had the lowest intake of animal proteins, according to statements made in the nutritional interviews. The interpretation of these figures must, however, take other considerations into account. The quality of the nutrition of residents of Ouli Bangala was poor, and signs of poverty were abundant; but, in addition to poor diet, this community was characterized by a higher prevalence of active, chronic infections that may have caused consumptive disease. The two conditions which were unique for Ouli Bangala were hyperendemic infections with *S. mansoni* and holoendemic onchocerciasis; infection rates, as detected in single skin snips, were already as high as 80 percent in five-to-nine-year-old children. Further analyses and comments will be presented in the appropriate sections of the book.

TABLE 4–7. PREVALENCE OF SELECTED CONDITIONS
REFLECTING NUTRITIONAL DEFICIENCIES[a]

Condition	Djimtilo %	Ouli Bangala %	Ouarai %	Boum Khebir %	Faya- Largeau %
Depigmentation of hair in children	0.3	1.8[b]	0	0.5	0
Nasolabial seborrhea	0	1.3	0	0	0
Lips					
angular lesions	1.1	0.5	0.5	0.8	2.4
cheilosis	7.4	20.3	5.8	2.9	3.4
Total conditions disregarding combinations	8.8	23.9	6.3	4.2	5.8

[a] Percentages listed are age adjusted.
[b] Includes two children with Kwashiorkor.

There is reason to believe that the nutritional histories of the residents of Boum Khebir concerning the most recent consumption of meat may have been grossly deficient. The village is located in the vicinity of the remote section of the Zakouma Wild Game Reservation, one of the few areas in the world which still has a great wealth of game animals. Because of these unique features, the area has attracted experienced hunters from all over the world who can afford the expensive hunting licenses. Hunting without a license is not permitted, and licenses are not available for permanent residents of Chad; poachers, if caught, are severely punished. Therefore, it appears quite possible that many of the local residents may have hunted frequently for their meat supply, but would not have given an affirmative answer to specific questions in the interviews for fear that this information might be revealed to government authorities.

Another comparison of the prevalence of nutritional deficiencies and of related physiological variables and pathological signs, but one restricted to children under ten years of age, is shown in Table 4–8. All indices listed point to Ouli Bangala as the community with the poorest nutritional state.

The presence of endemic goiter in various villages south of the city of Moundou along the road leading to the southern border of Chad, and also in rural communities in the vicinity of Koumra, becomes quite apparent even in visits as brief as those made during

TABLE 4–8. NUTRITIONAL DEFICIENCIES[a] AND SELECTED CLINICAL AND BIOCHEMICAL INDICES PARTIALLY DEPENDENT UPON THE NUTRITIONAL STATE OF CHILDREN UNDER TEN YEARS OF AGE

	Djimtilo (N[b] = 110)	Ouli Bangala (N = 131)	Ouarai (N = 139)	Boum Khebir (N = 134)	Faya-Largeau (N = 70)
Mean hemoglobin	11.2 gm%	10.1 gm%	11.0 gm%	10.9 gm%	12.4 gm%
Mean serum albumin	3.9 gm%	3.6 gm%	3.9 gm%	3.9 gm%	4.3 gm%
Mean serum gamma globulin	2.0 gm%	2.6 gm%	2.1 gm%	2.3 gm%	1.5 gm%
Hepatomegaly (prevalence)	31.8%	45.0%	23.4%	33.3%	8.6%
Edema (prevalence)	0.9%	3.1%	0	0.7%	0
Nutritional deficiencies (prevalence)	16.4%	33.6%	9.4%	7.5%	10.0%

[a] For details see Table 4–7.
[b] N = total number of children under ten years of age.

the pilot study. Table 4–9 shows the prevalence rates of three categories of thyroid enlargement. These figures were adjusted for age and sex by using the combined populations of all five villages as the standard for adjustment. The categories listed include moderate, diffuse enlargements of the thyroid; asymmetrical swelling with palpable nodules; and "goiter," large strumas of at least fist size. In addition to the individual and combined percentages of these conditions, the table lists the sex ratios of the prevalence rates. The usually observed preponderance of thyroid enlargement in females is apparent in our population samples and shows little variation among the villages, despite the large regional differences in the prevalence of goiter. These geographical differences were also de-

TABLE 4–9. PREVALENCE[a] OF THYROID ENLARGEMENT BY TYPE OF MANIFESTATION

Village	Moderate, Diffuse %	Nodular %	Goiter %	All Types %	Ratio Females/ Males
Djimtilo	8.4	0.3	0	8.7[b]	3.3
Ouli Bangala	8.3	2.6	0.2	11.1[b]	3.9
Ouarai	11.2	5.4	2.3	18.9[b]	3.4
Boum Khebir	3.2	0.2	0	3.4[b]	2.6
Faya-Largeau	1.9	0	0	1.9	3.0

[a] Percentages are adjusted for age and sex.
[b] Retrosternal strumas were found on routine chest roentgenograms (Table 4–37).

tected in the examination of chest roentgenograms as shown in Table 4–37. Unfortunately, no measurements of iodine were available which would have permitted an analysis of the association between the prevalence of goiter and iodine concentrations in water supplies and soil samples. It is interesting to note that the prevalence of thyroid enlargement was highest in the two areas where peanuts were eaten as staple foods. Peanuts belong to plants known to contain goitrogenic substances, which interfere with iodine absorption (Scrimshaw, 1960, p. 81).

BLOOD PRESSURE

Blood pressure was measured routinely on all persons in the population samples aged ten years or older. Because of the world-wide interest in the natural history of essential hypertension, especially in relation to hypercholesterolemia and nutrition, data on blood pressure are presented with the corresponding results of cholesterol determinations for the same persons. Table 4–10 lists mean systolic blood pressure and serum cholesterol levels by age and sex for each of the five communities studied. The number of persons examined in each age group is identical with the figures listed for participation in the physical examination included in Tables 5–2 through 5–6.

Both the systolic blood pressures and cholesterol values were low if compared with corresponding figures obtained in the United States (McDonough et al., 1965). Results of both measurements generally show slightly higher values in females. Four general age-linked tendencies can be detected: (1) both the systolic blood pressure and serum cholesterol level increase with progressing age (males in Faya-Largeau, females in Djimtilo and Boum Khebir); (2) the increase in blood pressure with age is not accompanied by a rising cholesterol value (Ouarai); (3) a higher cholesterol level in old age is not associated with a corresponding elevation of the blood pressure (males in Djimtilo, females in Faya-Largeau); and (4) neither the blood pressure nor the serum cholesterol level shows any marked increase with age (Ouli Bangala). Of the two variables, the regional differences in serum cholesterol in the two Arab communities, Djimtilo and Faya-Largeau, were on the average 30 milligram percent higher than those of the southern villages, which are inhabited by Sara and Laka tribesmen. The reason for this discrepancy between the two ethnic groups can be seen in differences in their diets. As already shown in the section on nutrition, the diet of

TABLE 4–10. SYSTOLIC BLOOD PRESSURE[a] AND SERUM CHOLESTEROL[b] BY AGE, SEX, AND REGION

Age (years)	Djimtilo		Ouli Bangala		Ouarai		Boum Khebir		Faya-Largeau	
	Syst. B.P.	Mean Cholesterol	Syst. B.P.	Mean Cholesterol	Syst. B.P.	Mean Cholesterol	Syst. B.P.	Mean Cholesterol	Syst. B.P.	Mean Cholesterol
MALES										
10–19	114.0	131.0	106.5	113.2	112.8	114.8	113.9	98.4	107.1	123.6
20–29	127.9	140.6	117.3	129.0	122.1	104.0	120.0	126.5	110.0	141.9
30–39	122.8	152.6	117.2	134.0	118.3	112.6	109.3	129.2	115.6	133.3
40–49	128.0	140.0	111.7	137.9	123.3	117.8	127.5	111.0	106.7	147.9
50+	128.6	162.8	108.4	119.2	145.5	122.7	118.7	118.2	141.9	163.8
Average	124.3	141.8	111.8	123.6	120.7	113.1	116.9	113.7	116.5	141.7
FEMALES										
10–19	117.4	147.9	105.7	103.9	116.7	106.9	120.4	103.6	101.3	134.0
20–29	120.2	154.0	115.0	122.8	118.9	129.5	122.2	119.7	102.3	139.8
30–39	126.8	163.0	119.2	129.4	118.9	121.9	127.9	118.0	110.0	159.4
40–49	136.5	167.5	123.1	129.4	126.7	124.9	127.1	124.7	124.6	165.3
50+	161.0	178.9	117.4	129.5	144.6	123.4	133.2	131.1	116.7	174.4
Average	126.6	158.9	115.3	117.7	122.4	120.6	126.1	119.8	108.5	149.9

[a] Millimeters of mercury.
[b] Milligram percent.

the residents of Djimtilo and Faya-Largeau was rich in animal protein foods, whereas meat, fish, milk, and eggs were comparatively infrequent items in the daily fare of the families in Ouli Bangala, Ouarai, and Boum Khebir. Because of these ethnogeographical group differences, the populations of the two Arab villages and of the three Sara and Laka villages were combined, and a separate analysis of association between cholesterol level and systolic blood pressure was made for each group. Figure 4–4 shows the frequency distribution curves for systolic blood pressure as observed in the combined male populations (ten years of age and older) of each ethnic group. Although the two curves are based on comparable age distributions, the regression lines of the mean cholesterol level on the systolic blood pressure value are quite different (Figure 4–5). Among the Arabs, who had a wider range of serum cholesterol levels, there was a close correlation between the two variables. On the other hand, the association was far from perfect in the Nilotic tribes, whose cholesterol levels were not only lower but also showed less variation. Whether, in addition to the recognized nutritional differences between the two groups, other factors, including ethnic

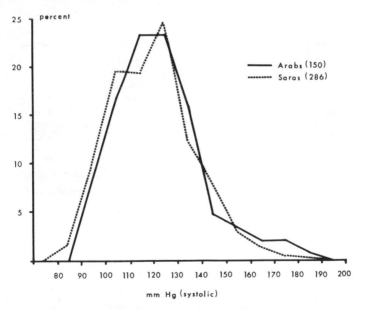

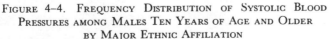

FIGURE 4–4. FREQUENCY DISTRIBUTION OF SYSTOLIC BLOOD PRESSURES AMONG MALES TEN YEARS OF AGE AND OLDER BY MAJOR ETHNIC AFFILIATION

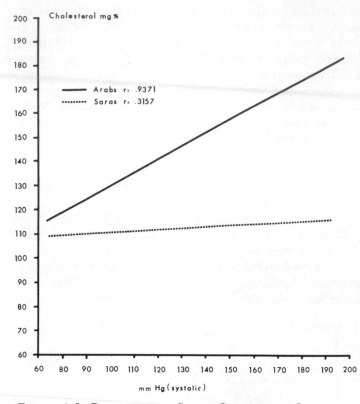

FIGURE 4–5. REGRESSION OF SERUM CHOLESTEROL LEVELS ON
SYSTOLIC BLOOD PRESSURE AND COEFFICIENT OF CORRELATION
AMONG MALES TEN YEARS OF AGE AND OLDER BY MAJOR
ETHNIC AFFILIATION

diversity, might have been directly responsible for the observed
discrepancies cannot be decided, and additional studies are needed.

HEMOGLOBIN

The information contained in this section is based on two different
screening procedures. The first was applied to study hemoglobin
concentrations with epidemiologic methods; the second was used to
learn more about the distribution of hemoglobin phenotypes in the
heterogeneous ethnic groups that were part of the population
samples.

TABLE 4–11. HEMOGLOBIN MEAN VALUES[a] BY SEX

Village	Males gm%	Females gm%
Djimtilo	13.7	12.2
Ouli Bangala	11.6	11.4
Ouarai	12.9	12.1
Boum Khebir	13.0	12.0
Faya-Largeau	13.9	13.3

[a] Values listed are age adjusted.

Table 4–11 lists the mean age-adjusted hemoglobin concentrations for individuals in each of the five communities; Figure 4–6 shows the frequency distribution curves of these values for both sexes. Both the table and the figure reveal considerable geographical differences, with Faya-Largeau at the upper end of the scale, Ouli Bangala at the lower end. Physiological sex differences in hemoglobin concentration were recognized in each of the five communities. The skewness of each of the five distribution curves resulted from the relatively large percentage of persons in each village who had anemia of varying degrees of severity. The causes of anemia in these Chadian villages are complex because of the presence of various potential factors which alone or in combination could have reduced hemoglobin levels. One of the more important determinants of anemia in Chad is endemic malaria. This is indicated by the differences in the hemoglobin levels between Faya-Largeau, where infections are sporadic, and the other four villages, where malaria is hyperendemic. Most cases of anemia were found in Ouli Bangala, where in addition to malaria other hyperendemic infections and malnutrition were most prevalent. During the dry season (when the surveys were conducted), malaria transmission is at its minimum, *Plasmodium malariae* being the predominant type of infection. The prevalence of parasitemia was highest in Ouarai (20.4 percent, of which 16.3 percent were caused by *P. malariae*, 4.1 percent by *P. falciparum*). As will be shown in the section on Malaria, 53.7 percent of the children under five years of age had parasitemia, but the figure declined rapidly and progressively to 6.1 percent in the oldest age group. This pattern of infections in Ouarai is reflected by Figure 4–7, which shows the hemoglobin concentrations by age. The amplitude between the minimum at age two and the maximum at age eighteen is 5.0 gram percent, a difference which

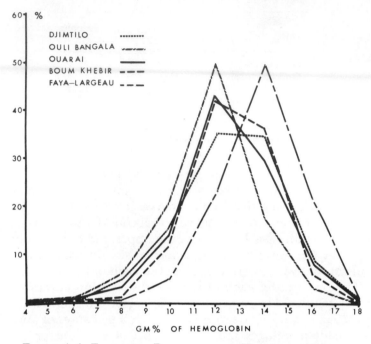

FIGURE 4–6. FREQUENCY DISTRIBUTION OF HEMOGLOBIN LEVELS

can be interpreted as the result of a coincidence of the highest prevalence of parasitemia with the physiological minimum of hemoglobin concentration.

Table 4–12 summarizes the distribution of hemoglobin phenotypes as determined by screening examinations using electrophoresis (Boyer *et al.*, 1968). The results show that the hereditary persistence of fetal hemoglobin appeared appreciably only in Djimtilo, whereas the distribution of the minor component, B_2, seemed to be more diffusely scattered. The over-all frequency of B_2 (0.007) is less than the occurrence in Maryland Negroes (0.022) and Nigerian Yoruba (0.04) (Boyer *et al.*, 1963). Such comparisons, together with assumptions concerning the admixed origin of American Negroes from African and European stocks (Boyer *et al.*, 1963), suggest that the ancestors of the present residents of Chad were not important contributors to the gene pool of American Negroes. In addition, although the numbers are admittedly small, the tendency to a negative association between B_2 and S frequencies

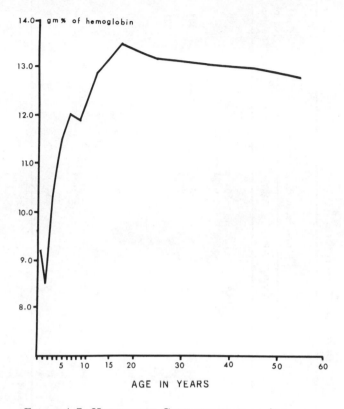

FIGURE 4–7. HEMOGLOBIN CONCENTRATION BY AGE AMONG
RESIDENTS OF OUARAI

shown in Table 4–12 supports the notion that the genes for these
hemoglobins, common in American Negroes, may have initially
arisen in different African populations (Boyer et al., 1963).

An interesting new finding made in our study was the identification of a hitherto unrecognized hemoglobin variant, hemoglobin_Chad,
in two women of Faya-Largeau (Boyer et al., 1968). It appears that
hemoglobin_Chad results from the replacement of glutamic acid by
lysine at the twenty-three position of the alpha chain of the hemoglobin molecule. The substitution responsible for this variant is
apparently benign in the heterozygous state because the affected
individuals were well and had normal hemoglobin concentrations
in their peripheral blood.

TABLE 4–12. HEMOGLOBIN TYPES IN CHAD

Place Name	Location		Predom-inant Tribe	No. of House-holds	Hemoglobin Phenotype							Total No. of Subjects
	N. Lat. ° '	E. Long. ° '			AA_2	AA_2B_2	AFA_2	ASA_2	SA_2	AC	SC	
Djimtilo	12 50	14 39	Arab-Salamat	79	207	1	12	56 (20.0%)	1	2	1	280
Ouli Bangala	7 50	15 52	Laka	77	304	5	4	50 (13.7%)	1	0	0	364
Ourai	8 48	17 45	Sara-Vare	84	286	1	0	34 (10.6%)	0	0	0	321
Boum Khebir	10 10	19 25	Goula	95	325	2	1	2 (0.6%)	0	0	0	330
Faya-Largeau	17 55	19 10	Kamadja, Anakaza	44	162	0	0	4 (2.3%)	0	5	0	173[a]
Total					1,284	9	17	146	2	7	1	1,468[a]

[a]Total includes two heterozygotes for hemoglobin Chad.

Vaccinations and Vaccination Histories

Histories of vaccinations against smallpox and yellow fever were obtained from routine questions in the health interviews. In addition, estimates of vaccination coverage were made by the registration of smallpox vaccination scars detected in physical examinations, and by the determination of antibody titers against yellow fever virus in hemagglutination inhibition tests. Because of the efficient work and well-organized campaigns of the Service des Grandes Endémies, a high percentage of the residents of all five communities included in the study had received at least one smallpox vaccination. In Djimtilo, the percentage with positive histories was 93.4. The corresponding figures in the other villages were: Ouli Bangala, 92.7 percent; Ouarai, 89.8 percent; Boum Khebir, 93.0 percent; and Faya-Largeau, 87.9 percent. By comparison, smallpox vaccination scars were recognized in 89.8 percent of the population of Djimtilo, 84.9 percent of the sample in Ouli Bangala, 78.8 percent in Ouarai, 88.2 percent in Boum Khebir, and 77.3 percent in Faya-Largeau, which had the highest proportion of seminomadic residents.

A comparison for agreement of the two estimates of vaccination coverage is shown in Table 4–13, which lists the percentage of persons with vaccination scars by age, separating those with from those without a history of previous smallpox vaccination. Generally, there was a high percentage of agreement between the two measurements. Concordance was highest among individuals who were from twenty to twenty-nine years old and lowest in the older age groups. In the interpretation of these trends various factors have to be considered. The sensitivity of physical examinations as a screening test for the detection of vaccination scars increases with age because of the presence of multiple scars in older persons who have received more than one vaccination. On the other hand, vaccination scars can be recognized more easily in children and young adults than in old persons with presbyoderma. Another factor to be considered is the inferior quality of the old vaccines as compared with the dry vaccines now in use. This could cause differences in the "take rates." Finally, inaccurate statements made in response to interview questions concerning vaccinations can be expected to occur with greater frequency in older persons because of poor memory, indifference, or ill health. The interval between receipt of the most recent vaccination and the interview was great

TABLE 4–13. AGREEMENT BETWEEN VACCINATION HISTORIES AND PRESENCE OF VACCINATION SCARS

Age (years)	Djimtilo				Ouli Bangala				Ouarai				Boum Khebir				Faya-Largeau			
	Vaccination History				Vaccination History				Vaccination History				Vaccination History				Vaccination History			
	Positive		Negative		Positive		Negative		Positive		Negative		Positive		Negative		Positive		Negative	
	No.	Scars %	No.	Scars %	No.	Scars %	No.	Scars %	No.	Scars %	No.	Scars %	No.	Scars %	No.	Scars %	No.	Scars %	No.	Scars %
Birth–9	95	88.4	15	33.3	106	84.0	24	12.5	108	77.8	31	3.2	112	92.9	23	21.7	57	73.7	13	23.1
10–19	62	88.7	4	25.0	105	92.4	4	75.0	68	95.6	4	50.0	61	93.4	1	100.0	33	87.9	4	75.0
20–29	48	97.9	2	0	68	95.6	0	0	61	96.7	1	0	51	98.0	1	100.0	29	86.2	2	100.0
30–39	74	93.2	1	0	49	95.9	0	0	36	88.9	0	0	34	91.2	1	100.0	19	100.0	4	75.0
40–49	29	86.2	0	0	24	87.5	0	0	21	81.0	1	100.0	30	100.0	0	0	21	61.9	1	100.0
50+	46	89.1	3	33.3	17	82.4	1	0	33	78.8	0	0	60	83.3	0	0	23	82.6	1	100.0
Total	354	90.7	25	28.0	369	90.2	29	20.7	327	86.5	37	10.8	348	92.5	26	30.8	182	80.8	25	52.0

for many of the older residents in our population samples. As can be seen in Table 4–14, which lists the percentage of participants in the mass vaccination campaigns of 1966–67 by age, most of the non-participants were sixty years old or over.

TABLE 4–14. PARTICIPATION IN THE MASS SMALLPOX VACCINATION CAMPAIGN OF 1966–67 AS ELICITED FROM INTERVIEWS

Age (years)	Number in Group	Vaccinated	
		Number	Percentage
Birth–9	486	454	93.4
10–19	323	283	87.6
20–29	254	212	83.5
30–39	216	185	85.6
40–49	123	108	87.8
50–59	92	77	83.7
60+	89	64	71.9
Total	1,583	1,383	87.4

It is also interesting to note that most of the adults with negative vaccination histories actually had vaccination scars. This observation is in contrast to findings made in a previous study (Buck, Sasaki, and Anderson, 1968) and could indicate the indiscriminate desire for an "injection" as the most powerful type of "medicine" in the minds of many local residents.

Vaccinations against yellow fever had been given to the populations of four of the five villages studied; no vaccinations had been given to the residents of Faya-Largeau, because of the low risk of acquiring natural infections in that desert community. Figure 4–8 shows the frequency distribution of yellow fever antibody titers for persons with positive and negative vaccination histories against yellow fever. Because of similarities in the distribution of antibody titers in both vaccinated and unvaccinated individuals of Djimtilo, Ouarai, and Boum Khebir, the data for these three communities were combined for the graphic presentation of the results. In contrast, the antibody patterns among residents of Ouli Bangala differed from those of the other communities and are shown separately in Figure 4–9. The two curves for the three combined villages indicate a close correspondence between vaccination histories and the presence of specific antibodies. The mean antibody titer in the

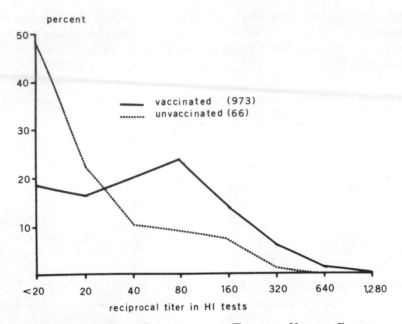

FIGURE 4–8. FREQUENCY DISTRIBUTION OF TITERS TO YELLOW FEVER IN
HEMAGGLUTINATION INHIBITION TESTS AMONG VACCINATED AND UNVAC-
CINATED RESIDENTS OF DJIMTILO, OUARAI, AND BOUM KHEBIR

vaccinated group was 1:86.2, the mean for unvaccinated persons
was 1:37.9. The difference is statistically significant (P = <0.001).
On the other hand, the response to yellow fever vaccine among the
residents of Ouli Bangala appears to be deficient when compared
with the results in the other communities, because all vaccinations
were given at about the same time, in 1966–67. The relative difference between the mean titers of vaccinated (1:64.3) and unvaccinated (1:54.3) persons in Ouli Bangala is small and statistically
insignificant (P = 0.3). In addition to inaccurate interview statements, which could have obscured the magnitude of true differences
in the antibody titers of the two groups, it is possible that more
natural infections had occurred among the unvaccinated residents
of Ouli Bangala than among those of the other three villages. These
infections would account for the relatively higher mean titer of the
unvaccinated group.

The lack of bimodality in the distribution curve and the low mean
titer among the vaccinees of Ouli Bangala can be related to other
findings made in the study. They seem to indicate a relative de-

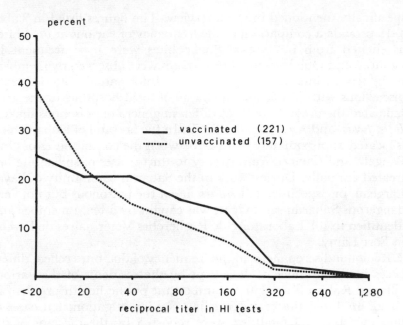

FIGURE 4–9. FREQUENCY DISTRIBUTION OF TITERS TO YELLOW FEVER IN HEMAGGLUTINATION INHIBITION TESTS AMONG VACCINATED AND UNVACCINATED RESIDENTS OF OULI BANGALA

ficiency of antibody responses to a variety of endemic infections. More detailed discussions on this subject are included in the sections on tuberculosis and other mycobacterial infections and schistosomiasis.

ANIMAL BITES

In epidemiological studies, estimates of the frequency of animal bites are of interest because they may reflect the risk of exposure to animals whose bites are either the direct or indirect cause of severe disease or injury. In addition, such estimates furnish information on the risk of exposure to certain other animals that are either vectors or reservoir hosts for the causative agents of various infectious diseases usually not directly transmitted by their bites.

The health interviews applied in this study included specific questions on the history of animal bites by snakes, dogs, rats, and scorpions. In addition to these specific questions all individuals were asked whether they had ever been bitten by other animals not specifically mentioned in the interview. The figures listed in Table 4–15 provide a comparison of the frequency of various animal bites as elicited from interviews. Snake bites were most frequent in Djimtilo and Ouli Bangala, but no cases were observed by members of the team while working in the area. Information obtained from discussions with physicians in charge of local hospitals in the area indicated the presence of three different genera of poisonous snakes: *Bitis*, *Echis*, and *Naja* (Sigales, 1967). In the hospital of Doba, which is located approximately halfway between the communities of Ouli Bangala and Ouarai, from twenty to thirty cases of snake bite are treated annually. During work in the Saharan community of Faya-Largeau, one specimen of *Cerastes vipera*, the poisonous but not very dangerous Saharan sand viper, was caught by a team member and identified in the Laboratoire de Recherches Vétérinaires de Farcha in Fort Lamy.*

Regional discrepancies in the frequency of dog bites reflect differences in the number of dogs kept by the residents of the various villages. Rabies is a relatively important public health problem in Chad. In 1966, the year preceding our investigation, ten cases of human rabies, all fatalities, were reported by the director of the Service des Grandes Endémies (Ziegler, 1967). Considering the general tendency of gross under-reporting in a country with poor

---

* During a follow-up study in Ouli Bangala in January, 1970, four different species of snakes were caught. The collection includes two poisonous snakes (*Echis carinatus*, the saw-scaled viper, and *Caudus rhombeatus*, the common night adder), and two non-poisonous species (*Boaedon fuliginosus*, the brown house snake, and *Psammophis sibilans*, the olive grass snake).

TABLE 4–15. FREQUENCY OF ANIMAL BITES, AS ELICITED FROM INTERVIEWS

Type of Animal Bite	Djimtilo (N = 373) %[a]	Ouli Bangala (N = 397) %	Ouarai (N = 362) %	Boum Khebir (N = 381) %	Faya-Largeau (N = 201) %	Total (N = 1,714) %
Snake	12.7	20.7	4.1	3.6	6.3	9.5
Dog	19.3	25.1	38.1	6.0	37.5	25.2
Wolf	0	0	0.8	0	0	0.16
Cat	0	0.9	0.3	0.2	0	0.28
Rat	11.8	4.9	6.2	0.2	0	4.6
Mouse	0	0	0	0.2	0	0.04
Scorpion	9.4	0	0.7	0	71.5	16.3

[a] Percentages are age adjusted.

medical and communication facilities, the number of reported cases appears to be high for a total population of only 3,000,000 and could reflect the importance of rabies as a public health problem.

With the exception of scorpions, the frequency of bites by the other animals listed in Table 4–15 appears to be relatively low. Scorpions were caught by the entomologist of the team in all locations but were most numerous in Faya-Largeau, where 71.5 percent of the population sample reported that they had been stung by a scorpion at least once. The fact that exposure to scorpions is widespread in Faya-Largeau is indicated by age-specific percentages that show a minimum of 38.5 percent in children under ten years of age and a maximum of 90 percent in persons over forty. Most scorpion bites in Faya-Largeau can be attributed to *Leiurus quinquestriatus*, followed in frequency by *Androctonus amoureuxi (australis)*, the large blonde desert scorpion (Vachon, 1961). Bites by the former are extremely painful and may be fatal, especially to children, old persons, and individuals in poor health.

Not listed in the table are fish bites. These were not mentioned in the interviews but were observed in two residents of Djimtilo while the team was working in the area. Both patients were treated for gangrene of the hand, which developed after they were bitten by a fish of the family Tetraodontidae while fishing in Lake Chad.

FERTILITY AND BIRTH RATES

Estimates of birth rates in this study are based on interviews with all women in the five communities who were married, separated, divorced, or widowed. In addition, all women included in the population sample were examined externally for pregnancy.

In the interviews each woman was asked to state the number of children who had been born to her within the year immediately preceding the interview, specifically the period between the national holidays (Fete Nationale de l'Indépendance) of 1966 and 1967. The national holidays are observed annually throughout the country during the week centering on the eleventh of January. Our study in Chad was carried out between January 15 and May 20, 1967. The number of births that had occurred since Independence Day, 1966, was then adjusted by a proportionate reduction which corresponded to the exact month when the investigation in a given community was carried out. The denominator for the estimated birth rate shown in Table 4–16 was obtained by a house-to-house

TABLE 4–16. ESTIMATED BIRTH AND CONCEPTION RATES IN FIVE CHADIAN VILLAGES

Village	No. of Women Interviewed	No. of Births	Estimated[a] Birth Rate	No. of Women Examined	No. of Women Pregnant (4–9 months)	Estimated[b] Conception Rate/1000 Population/Year
Djimtilo (N = 371)[c]	86	20	53.9	103	14	75.5
Ouli Bangala (N = 391)	77	30	76.7	95	9	46.0
Ouarai (N = 361)	72	27	74.7	82	9	49.9
Boum Khebir (N = 381)	76	19	49.9	82	8	42.0
Faya-Largeau (N = 197)	42	8	40.6	57	7	71.1
Total (N = 1,701)	353	104	61.1	419	47	55.3

[a] Number of births reported between national holidays of independence of 1966–67, as elicited from interviews, divided by the total population registered by our census (per 1,000 population).

[b] Expected number of pregnant women per year (two times the number of pregnancies [4–9 months] as estimated by external examination of all women between the ages of fifteen and forty-four divided by the total population registered by our census (per 1,000 population).

[c] Census population.

census and included all dwellings that fell within the boundaries of each village as drawn by the sanitary engineer of the research team (see Population Samples, pp. 236–38).

A second estimate of the birth rate was computed by extrapolating the percentage of pregnant women for one full year. The team's diagnosis of pregnancy was based on external examination only; therefore, the first three months of gestation were not recognizable. Assuming that the percentage of pregnant women can be considered to represent a cross-section of the conceptions that have and will occur in the community, extrapolation of the figures for a full year would give an exaggerated estimate of the birth rate because it assumes that all pregnancies will be full term. These rates, listed as conception rates, are shown in Table 4–16.

In 1960 the birth rate for the Republic of Chad was estimated to be 45–48 per 1,000 population (United Nations, 1967, p. 201). Of the two estimates for the combined villages shown in Table 4–16, the one based on pregnancies, even without adjustments for abortions and stillbirths, corresponds more closely to the national figures published in the *Demographic Yearbook* of the United Nations. A relative inaccuracy of interview statements can be expected because in medical histories of a predominantly illiterate population the exact time sequence of past events becomes blurred. Time is not likely to be registered as a measurable continuum, but is memorized in light of a series of unusual events in a person's lifetime as blended into the natural periodicity of seasonal activities.

A comparison of the corresponding estimates of the birth rate in each village shows a negative correlation ($r = -0.54$). This contrariety may reflect large annual variations that are related to the small size of the population samples. Two additional factors are important because their presence could have led to an exaggerated estimate of birth rates. All communities adhere to polygyny. This is reflected by an excess of females of childbearing age in all communities. For reasons unknown, this preponderance of females disappears in older age groups (see Figures 1–7, 1–10, and 1–11). Since the enumeration of persons in the survey was based on a house-to-house census, there are two possible explanations for this change. The first is that there may be a higher mortality rate among adult females; the second possibility is that single females emigrate. Both explanations are plausible because the risks associated with childbearing are more dangerous in communities without medical facilities, and divorces are much more frequent in a polygynous society, as noted in the section on Household and Family. Barrenness is a major reason for divorce and could contribute to selective changes in both the numerator and denominator which tend to increase the birth rate. It is also interesting to note that in the two areas with the highest estimated birth rates (Ouli Bangala and Ouarai) only 4.5 percent and 8.9 percent of the population was above fifty years of age, compared with 12.6 percent in Djimtilo, 16.9 percent in Boum Khebir, and 12.9 percent in Faya-Largeau.

Habitual Use of Cola Nuts and Hashish

Various locally available plant products that contain alkaloids, or other stimulating agents, are consumed frequently by the indigenous population of the villages studied. Because habitual use may cause changes in the host or be associated with factors that determine the distribution, clinical manifestations, and severity of individual diseases and infections (Buck *et al.*, 1968), specific questions concerning the habit of cola nut chewing and the use of hashish were included in the health interviews. The cola nut is easily available in many parts of Africa. The capsular fruit of a large African tree (*Cola nitida*) belonging to the chocolate family, it contains a heart-stimulating glucoside, kolanin, and between 1.5 percent and 3.5 percent caffeine.

Hashish derived from *Cannabis sativa* is used in many parts of North Africa; most frequently, "kif," as it is called locally, is smoked in a pipe. Table 4–17 summarizes the information obtained from interviews of the residents of all five villages. Cola nuts were used more frequently in Djimtilo than in any of the other communities. The habit of smoking hashish was reported by only two males in Djimtilo. Whereas, generally, more males than females stated that they had been using cola nuts, the opposite was found to be true in Djimtilo. There is no evidence from multiple cross-tabulations which indicates that the habit of cola nut chewing might be harmful to the habitual user.

Specific Infections and Infectious Diseases

Parasitic Infections

Malaria

Malaria appears to be the most significant disease of public health importance in Chad (Table 4–1). The country encompasses

TABLE 4–17. HABITUAL USE OF COLA NUTS AND HASHISH AMONG RESIDENTS OF FIVE CHADIAN VILLAGES

	Djimtilo		Ouli Bangala		Ouarai		Boum Khebir		Faya-Largeau	
	No.	% Users	No.	% Users	No.	% Users	No.	% Users	No.	% Users
Cola Nuts										
Males	156	53.8	173	13.3	168	14.9	170	2.9	71	25.4
Females	209	63.6	211	10.9	171	7.6	199	0	93	9.7
Hashish										
Males	156	1.3	173	0	168	0	170	0	71	0
Females	209	0	211	0	171	0	199	0	93	0

such contrasting areas as the Sahara, where infections occur only sporadically, and regions in the southern part of the country where malaria is hyperendemic. Sample surveys in various parts of Chad, excluding the Sahara, have shown that in children under ten years of age the range in the percentage of plasmodium-positive blood slides is between 12.5 and 80.0 percent, depending on the region. The agent most frequently found is *Plasmodium falciparum*, followed by *P. malariae* and *P. ovale*, the ratio being approximately 50:24:1 (Ziegler, 1967).

Malaria eradication has not yet begun in Chad. Thus, findings made in this study represent a true cross-section of the regional prevalence of endemic infections with *Plasmodia* at the peak of the dry season. Seasonal variations in the incidence and prevalence of clinical malaria and parasitemia are closely associated with the annual shift of the monsoon. Our study was conducted during the dry season, when the transmission of malaria is at a minimum.

Table 4–18 shows the prevalence of parasitemia by age, region and type of infection. The results are based on careful examination of thick and thin blood smears, but only one slide was available for each individual included in the study. Two species, *P. falciparum* and *P. malariae*, were found in the blood smears; infection with *P. ovale* was not detected in our population samples. In contrast to findings made during the rainy season, when most of the infections in children are caused by *P. falciparum* (Buck, Anderson, and Hewitt 1966), recovery of this plasmodium was less frequent at the time our studies were conducted. Instead, more children under the age of ten were found to have *P. malariae* in their blood smears. This discrepancy could indicate differences in the seasonal cycle of the mosquito vectors involved in the transmission of the two malaria parasites. Of the ten species of *Anopheles* collected by the entomologist, all were known or suspected vectors of malaria. Seven of these species were taken while attempting to feed on human blood. *Anopheles funestus* was the dominant anopheline encountered; it was found in all four villages south of the Sahara. *A. funestus* breeds in large bodies of water and is therefore less affected by seasonal rainfall than is *A. gambiae*, which breeds in small pools and probably is the most effective rapid transmitter of malaria in Africa from the southern edge of the Sahara to Natal. At the time of our study this important anopheline vector was collected only in Ouli Bangala.

For the interpretation of the large seasonal variations in the prevalence and predominant type of malaria, four factors will be

TABLE 4–18. PERCENTAGE WITH PLASMODIUM IN SINGLE BLOOD SMEARS

Age (years)	Djimtilo (N = 352)		Ouli Bangala (N = 395)		Ouarai (N = 363)		Boum Khebir (N = 372)		Faya-Largeau (N = 204)	
	P. falc.	P. malar.	P. falc.	P. malar.	P. falc.	P. malar.	P. falc.	P. malar.	P. falc.	P. malar.
Birth–4	3.4	8.6	1.5	1.5	13.4	40.3	1.5	23.1	0	0
5–9	0	14.6	1.6	0	8.2	19.2	1.4	24.6	0	0
10–19	0	3.2	0.9	0	4.2	11.1	3.2	16.1	0	0
20–29	0	0	1.5	0	0	11.5	0	19.2	0	0
30–39	0	0	2.0	0	0	11.1	0	8.8	0	0
40–49	0	0	4.2	0	0	9.5	6.7	10.0	0	0
50+	0	0	0	0	0	6.1	0	10.0	0	0
Average (age adjusted)	0.6	4.0	1.5	0.2	4.1	16.3	1.6	16.7	0	0

considered. The first is the already mentioned periodicity of the relative abundance of mosquito vectors, notably *A. gambiae*. The second is the temporary suppression of *P. malariae* by *P. falciparum* in areas where both malaria types are endemic and where double infections are frequent (Boyd, 1949, pp. 578–79, 701, 974). The third can be related to discrepancies in the duration of relapses that occur frequently in quartan malaria but only briefly in the tropical form of the disease. The fourth factor is differences in the persistence of parasitemia which are related to the rapid increase and decrease in the number of trophozoites of *P. falciparum* as compared with the slow build-up and disappearance from the peripheral blood of those infected with *P. malariae*.

Table 4–18 shows that the geographical differences in the prevalence of malaria are quite large. Using children from birth to nine years of age as the indicator population for estimates of the level of malaria endemicity, it appears that at the peak of the dry season differences in the prevalence of parasitemia were closely associated with the density of the vegetation in the five areas, with Ouarai having the highest percentage of children with malaria parasites in single blood smears and Faya-Largeau having the lowest.

The importance of seasonal differences in the prevalence of parasitemia and the limitations of assessing endemicity levels of malaria in a cross-sectional survey are reflected in Table 4–19, which lists the age-specific prevalence rates of splenomegaly and an index describing the average size of the enlarged (palpable) spleen. In contrast to the pronounced regional differences in parasitemia rates, the prevalence of splenomegaly was found to be similar in the four villages where malaria is endemic. The fact that the disease is of little public health importance in the Saharan town of Faya-Largeau is indicated by the negative findings in the examination of blood smears and also by the low prevalence of splenomegaly.

Following the proposal for classification of malaria endemicity by the Expert Committee on Malaria of the World Health Organization (Russell *et al.*, 1963, p. 444; Hackett, 1944), all four southern communities can be identified as belonging to hyperendemic areas because the prevalence of splenomegaly among children under ten years of age is over 50 percent and remains relatively high in adults. An important factor which might have contributed to the high prevalence of splenomegaly in three of the five communities is the presence of endemic schistosomiasis in Djimtilo, Ouli Bangala, and Ouarai (see Schistosomiasis, pp. 150–60).

TABLE 4-19. PREVALENCE OF SPLENOMEGALY AND RELATIVE SPLEEN SCORE[a] BY AGE

Age (years)	Djimtilo		Ouli Bangala		Ouarai		Boum Khebir		Faya-Largeau	
	%	Score	%	Score	%	Score	%	Score	%	Score
Birth–4	66.1	1.78	71.5	2.62	74.6	2.70	67.1	2.13	0	—
5–9	77.1	2.59	83.5	2.42	70.8	2.14	70.6	2.21	0	—
10–14	42.4	1.86	48.6	1.94	51.2	1.90	26.5	1.56	0	—
15–19	32.2	1.30	30.0	1.75	22.8	1.43	17.9	1.40	0	—
20–29	20.8	2.30	29.6	1.68	21.7	2.00	21.1	1.73	3.2	1.0
30–39	16.2	2.58	31.2	2.13	20.0	1.29	17.1	1.67	0	—
40–49	13.8	1.25	29.2	1.86	18.2	2.00	16.7	2.00	0	—
50+	16.7	1.75	38.9	2.00	18.2	2.33	11.7	1.57	4.2	1.5
Average	36.5	2.07	49.3	2.22	44.0	2.21	36.4	2.01	1.0	1.33

[a] Score is the average of the following classes: 1 = 2 cm; 2 = 2–4 cm; 3 = 4 cm to umbilicus; 4 = larger.

Trypanosomiasis (African Sleeping Disease)

Small endemic foci of human trypanosomiasis still exist in the southern part of Chad (World Health Organization, 1962; Gruvel, 1965; Ziegler, 1968; Nebout, 1969). No clinical cases of the disease were found in any of the five communities selected for study by our research team. Since practical methods for the mass screening of sera for residual antibodies to *Trypanosoma gambiense* and *T. rhodesiense* are not yet fully developed, it was not possible to examine serological patterns in the five study populations for differences in the prevalence of infections that had occurred in the past. Because of the relative public health importance of African sleeping disease in Chad, data from other sources will be used to describe its epidemiology.

It can be assumed that most human infections in Chad are caused by *T. gambiense* because the distribution of *T. rhodesiense* appears to be restricted to areas east and south of the Great Rift Valley (World Health Organization, 1962; Nebout, 1969). Three species of tsetse flies, all potential vectors of human trypanosomiasis, are found frequently in Chad, namely, *Glossina tachinoides* Westwood and *G. fuscipes fuscipes* Newstead of the *palpalis* group and *G. morsitans submorsitans* Newstead of the *morsitans* group. The distribution of tsetse flies is shown in Figure 3–1; as can be seen, their distribution follows closely the course of the major rivers and their tributaries. Table 4–20 was compiled from data included in the annual report of the director of the Service des Grandes Endémies (Ziegler, 1968). Since the administrative subdivisions (sectors) listed in the table are not always identical with the boundaries of the individual prefectures they serve, the areas of these sectors are indicated in Figure 3–1. This permits comparison between the regional density of *Glossina* and the level of endemicity of human trypanosomiasis reflected in the figures of Table 4–10. At the present time, smaller endemic foci exist only in the southernmost provinces of the Republic, namely, Logone Occidentale and Orientale, and in Moyen Chari (Nebout, 1969). The table shows that there has been a general decline in the number of newly detected cases in recent years. This can be attributed to the vigorous efforts by the physicians and nurses of the Service des Grandes Endémies to control trypanosomiasis. A comparison between the 1967 census figures listed in Table 4–20 and the average size of the population examined indicates that between 28 and 61 percent of the total population in the various

TABLE 4–20. ANNUAL INCIDENCE OF TRYPANOSOMIASIS IN NON-RANDOM POPULATION SAMPLES OF FOUR REGIONAL SECTORS OF THE SERVICE DES GRANDES ENDEMIES[a]

Year	Regional Sector[b] 1			Regional Sector 2			Regional Sector 3			Regional Sector 4		
	Population Examined	New Cases No.	per 100,000	Population Examined	New Cases No.	per 100,000	Population Examined	New Cases No.	per 100,000	Population Examined	New Cases No.	per 100,000
1958	66,163	129	195	76,325	26	34	357,945	201	56	245,888	28	11
1959	91,628	30	33	82,328	11	13	329,912	162	49	245,070	12	5
1960	193,909	72	37	93,788	5	5	252,382	305	121	217,334	20	9
1961	138,655	54	39	110,400	3	3	182,936	237	130	206,826	17	8
1962	123,602	75	61	97,931	0	0	210,070	113	54	186,357	70	38
1963	155,649	93	60	60,615	9	15	132,999	65	49	157,608	27	17
1964	145,700	48	33	104,503	2	3	200,867	35	17	209,526	9	4
1965	221,823	44	20	137,310	4	3	250,943	31	12	186,399	17	9
1966	243,990	42	17	70,801	0	0	237,321	93	39	258,865	0	0
1967	277,998	17	6	285,731	1	0.3	410,717	44	11	135,780	12	9
Average	166,114	60	36	111,973	6	5	256,609	129	50	204,965	21	10
Census 1967	339,670			399,947			615,151			333,350		

[a] Prepared from data furnished by Dr. Pierre Ziegler (1968).
[b] Subdivision of the Service des Grandes Endémies: Sector 1, Chari Baguirmi; Sector 2, Mayo Kebbi; Sector 3, Logone Occidentale and Orientale; Sector 4, Moyen Chari (see Figure 3–1).

sectors was actually examined. Since the investigations were designed entirely as case-finding surveys, the sample is biased toward inclusion of those communities in which cases had occurred or were suspected. Control of trypanosomiasis was attempted by the identification and subsequent treatment of all proved or clinically suspected cases and by mass chemoprophylaxis of the exposed population with lomidine (pentamidine).

Filarial Infections

Four different types of infections with microfilariae were recognized in three of the five population samples in Chad. They will be discussed in two subsections, the first dealing with *Wuchereria bancrofti*, *Loa loa*, and *Dipetalonema perstans*, which were identified from routinely taken blood smears, and the second devoted to a more detailed discussion of onchocerciasis, diagnosed clinically and from the examinations of skin snips.

Wuchereria bancrofti, *Loa loa*, and *Dipetalonema perstans*. Microfilariae of *W. bancrofti* were recognized in blood smears (taken between 7 A.M. and 12 M.) of the residents of both Ouli Bangala and Ouarai, but late clinical manifestations of this infection were found only in the latter village, where one man and four women had elephantiasis of one or both legs (see Table 4–21). Since all blood smears were examined in Baltimore after the completion of the entire study in Chad, the presence of pathognomonic clinical signs was the only guideline on which decisions for modifications of the standard research protocol in the field could be based. Special

TABLE 4–21. PREVALENCE[a] OF EDEMA AND ELEPHANTIASIS

Locality	Number Examined	Edema of Feet & Legs[b] %	Elephantiasis %
Djimtilo	375	4.2	0
Ouli Bangala	397	10.1	0
Ouarai	363	4.5	1.5[c]
Boum Khebir	374	3.3	0
Faya-Largeau	207	2.1	0

[a] Percentages are age and sex adjusted.
[b] Number of females per male: Djimtilo, 3.8; Ouli Bangala, 2.5; Ouarai, 3.5; Boum Khebir, 1.2; Faya-Largeau, 2.1.
[c] Number of females per male: 3.7.

collections of night blood samples for prevalence estimates of the predominantly nocturnal microfilaremia of *W. bancrofti* were scheduled for Ouarai but not for Ouli Bangala. Because of superstitions, the residents of Ouarai were afraid to walk at midnight from their houses to the medical camp, which was located amid the widely scattered graves of deceased villagers (see Religion, pp. 39–44). For this reason, special arrangements had to be made to bleed the residents near their homes. Despite these efforts, nighttime blood collections remained deficient, with only 68 percent of the sample participating.

The age-adjusted infection rates for *W. bancrofti* are shown in Table 4–22. As expected, the percentage of blood smears with microfilariae in Ouarai was higher at night than during the morning hours when they were usually taken. It is interesting to note that the sheathed microfilariae of *W. bancrofti* were also found in two urine specimens after triple concentration by a method routinely applied in the study (Buck *et al.*, 1969). No cases of elephantiasis were recognized among the residents of Ouli Bangala, where 1.2 percent had microfilariae in smears prepared from blood samples taken during the day. The conspicuously higher percentage of persons with pitting edema of the feet and lower legs in that community (Table 4–21) is related to the high prevalence of inguinal lymphadenopathy (hanging groin), which has resulted from infections with *Onchocerca volvulus*. (This infection will be discussed in the following subsection.) At the time of our study, species of *Culex pipiens quinquefasciatus*, *Anopheles gambiae*, and *A.*

TABLE 4–22. PREVALENCE[a] OF *Dipetalonema perstans*, *Loa loa*, AND *Wuchereria bancrofti* IN SINGLE BLOOD SMEARS

Locality	Number Examined	D. perstans %	L. loa %	W. bancrofti Day %	W. bancrofti Night %
Djimtilo	352	0	0	0	—[b]
Ouli Bangala	395	23.6	1.2	1.2	—[b]
Ouarai	363	59.7	8.4	4.7	9.1[c]
Boum Khebir	372	27.1	0.4	0	—[b]
Faya-Largeau	199	0	0	0	—[b]

[a] Percentages listed are age adjusted.
[b] No blood samples taken.
[c] Microfilariae of *W. bancrofti* were found in two urine specimens.

funestus (Basu and Rao, 1939), three of the most important vectors of *W. bancrofti*, were collected by the entomologist in Ouli Bangala, while *A. funestus* was found in Ouarai.

Although microfilariae of *L. loa* were found in three of the four southern villages studied, cases of loiasis (Calabar swelling or eye lesions) were not recognized. A comparison of the age-adjusted percentages of infections detected in single blood smears is presented in Table 4–22. The prevalence of infections with this parasite was lowest in children under five years of age and reached its maximum in the fourth decade of life. More males than females were infected. Specimens of the mango fly, *Chrysops silacea* and *C. dimidiata*, two main vectors of *L. loa*, were not caught at the time our study was conducted, but one specimen of *C. longicornis*, a potential vector of the agent, was taken in Ouli Bangala. The most abundant horse fly species taken in Ouarai was *Tabanus par*, a beautiful golden species not known to be involved in the life cycle of *L. loa*.

The most widely distributed and prevalent type of filariasis characterized by microfilaremia was caused by *Dipetalonema perstans*. Since typical clinical manifestations are not known to occur in this infection, our evidence is based on the recovery of morphologically characteristic microfilariae from blood smears. A comparison of the relative prevalence of infections with this nematode in Ouli Bangala, Ouarai, and Boum Khebir is shown in Table 4–22, which lists the age-adjusted percentages of positive blood smears. In each village, infection rates were closely associated with age. The minimum was observed in young children below the age of five years, and the maximum occurred in adults of forty years or more. The range was 3–58 percent in Ouli Bangala, 9–88 percent in Ouarai, and 8–63 percent in Boum Khebir. There were no significant sex differences in the percentage of infected persons.

Onchocerciasis.   Cases of onchocerciasis were recognized in three of the four southern subregions selected for study. Within these areas there were considerable variations in the prevalence of infection with *Onchocerca volvulus*. These were closely related to the distance of the houses from fast flowing streams, which provide the necessary conditions for the maintenance of the life cycle of *Simulium damnosum*, the most important vector of onchocerciasis in Africa. Contrasts in the infection rates among the populations of the six communities listed in Table 4–23 were large. In Ouli Bangala and Masidjanga, a small community situated on the southern shore of Lake Iro opposite Boum Khebir (see Figure 4–10), onchocerciasis was holoendemic, whereas in Ouarai and Boum Khebir only sporadic cases of the disease were observed. With one exception, these scattered infections were seen in males whose travel histories or occupational activities in endemic areas suggested that they had acquired their infections outside the village where they resided permanently. Onchocerciasis was not detected in Djimtilo or Faya-Largeau.

TABLE 4–23. PREVALENCE OF ONCHOCERCOMA IN ROUTINE EXAMINATIONS

| Village | Number Examined | Onchocercoma present | |
		Number	Percentage
Djimtilo	379	0	—
Ouli Bangala	398	169	42.5
Ouarai	364	4[b]	1.1
Boum Khebir	374	6[c]	1.6
Masidjanga	71[a]	33	46.5
Faya-Largeau	206	0	—

[a] A non-random sample of residents of the village of Masidjanga, canton of Boum Khebir, located on the southern shore of Lake Iro.
[b] All males with travel histories.
[c] Five males and one female with travel histories.

The wealth of information available from the routinely collected data on onchocerciasis and other endemic infections and health conditions in the same population permitted extensive analyses of the data for studies of the distribution of the infection, variations in its clinical manifestations, and possible interactions between onchocerciasis and coexisting diseases and infections. Table 4–24 shows the percentage of persons in Ouli Bangala who were infected with *O. volvulus*. The diagnosis was based on the recovery of microfilariae from skin snips that were taken routinely from the back (about two centimeters above the iliac crest) with a corneal-scleral punch biopsy instrument (Holth) (Buck *et al.*, 1969). The skin snips were transferred to welled microscope slides and examined for microfilariae. The findings were graded as follows: from one to five microfilariae, $1+$; six to ten, $2+$; eleven to twenty, $3+$; and more than twenty, $4+$.

Whereas in Ouli Bangala the entire population sample was examined as defined by a census (see Chapter 5), the investigations in Masidjanga were not originally planned but were scheduled later

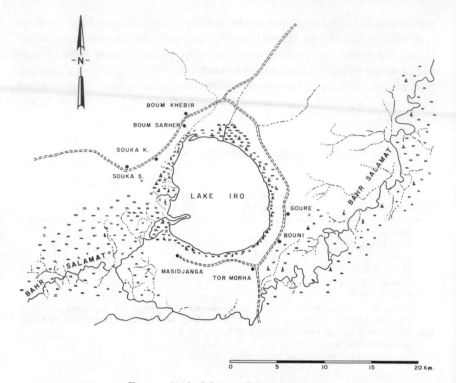

FIGURE 4–10. MAP OF LAKE IRO REGION

TABLE 4–24. AGE-SPECIFIC PREVALENCE OF INFECTIONS WITH *Onchocerca volvulus* AMONG
RESIDENTS OF OULI BANGALA BASED ON THE RECOVERY OF MICROFILARIAE

	Microfilariae of *O. volvulus*					
	Skin Snips			Urine		
		Positive			Positive	
Age (years)	No. Examined	No.	%	No. Examined	No.	%
1	0	0	—	15	0	—
1–2	19	6	31.5	20	1	5.0
3–4	27	18	66.7	24	0	—
5–9	60	49	81.7	58	4	6.9
10–19	106	92	86.8	107	17	15.9
20–29	71	66	92.9	72	9	12.5
30–39	48	46	95.8	49	10	20.5
40–49	24	23	95.8	23	1	4.3
50+	18	16	88.9	18	2	11.1
Total	373	316	84.7	386	44	11.4

as an extension of the field study. This special study was undertaken one day by several members of the research team, partly because the secretary of the canton chief of Boum Khebir indicated that clinical manifestations of onchocerciasis, including eye lesions, appeared to be numerous in Masidjanga (see Figure 4–10), and partly because it was learned that the sporadic infections among the males of Boum Khebir probably had been acquired near the southern shore of Lake Iro (the locale of Masidjanga). All villagers who were present on the day of the examination—approximately 40 percent of the population—were seen.

Because of the non-comprehensive character of this preliminary study in Masidjanga, all further results to be presented are based only on the findings made in Ouli Bangala. Table 4–25 shows the prevalence of clinical manifestations of onchocerciasis. On the precoded examination forms only one space was allotted for registering nodules, skin atrophy, or pigmentary changes; these clinical signs were recorded in that order. Therefore, whereas it was possible to compute the prevalence of onchocercoma individually, skin lesions had to be listed in a broader category with nodules. A similar deficiency in recording prevented the independent registration of inguinal lymphedema and hanging groin. The U-shaped age distribution of the prevalence of inguinal lymphadenopathies reflects the clinical observation that more children had lymphedema, whereas many of the older adults had either hanging groin or conglomerates of enlarged inguinal lymph nodes. There were no significant sex differences in the prevalence of nodules, skin lesions, inguinal lymphadenopathy, corneal opacities, or prolonged itching of the skin, the last being elicited from a question in the routine health interviews. But there was a significant difference in the percentage of males and females who had edema of the foot or leg. The excess among females was associated with pregnancy, and the sex difference became trivial when pregnant women were excluded from the comparisons. Blindness was recorded when the patient was unable to count fingers two meters from one or both eyes. More males (12.1 percent) than females (7.0 percent) were blind, but the causes of blindness were similar in both sexes.

The following ocular anomalies were present in patients in whom infection with onchocerciasis was confirmed by skin biopsy (von Noorden and Buck, 1968).

TABLE 4–25. PREVALENCE OF SOME CLINICAL MANIFESTATIONS OF ONCHOCERCIASIS IN OULI BANGALA BY AGE

Age (years)	No. Examined	Nodules		Skin Changes[a] and/or Nodules		Inguinal Lymph-edema and/or Hanging Groin		Edema of Foot and/or Leg		Blindness[b]		Corneal Opacities	
		No.	%	No.	%	No.	%	No.	%	No.	%	No.	%
Birth–9	130	23	17.7	55	42.3	28	21.5	4	3.1	0	—	9	6.9
10–19	109	36	33.0	48	44.0	24	22.0	6	5.5	7	6.4	17	15.6
20–29	68	47	69.1	56	82.4	5	7.4	16	23.5	4	5.9	13	19.1
30–39	49	32	65.3	45	91.8	9	18.4	9	18.4	9	18.4	18	36.7
40–49	24	19	79.2	21	87.5	7	29.2	2	8.3	7	29.2	8	33.3
50+	18	12	66.7	18	100.0	2	11.1	3	16.7	9	50.0	9	50.0
Total	398	169	42.5	243	61.1	75	18.8	40	10.1	36	9.0	74	18.6

[a] Includes atrophy of skin and pigmentary changes.
[b] Includes blindness of one or both eyes.

Adnexa: The ocular adnexa was essentially normal in all patients examined. Periorbital edema was absent. Ptosis, entropion,
and ectropion were not observed.

Conjunctiva: The palpebral conjunctiva was pale in all patients. Eversion of the upper lid did not reveal follicular or papillar
hypertrophy or evidence of trachomatous infection. Limbal
edema and injection of the bulbar conjunctiva were present in only
one patient, who had superficial punctate keratitis. Pigmentation
of the conjunctiva was frequent, was most dense in the limbal region,
and often extended onto the corneal epithelium. Although limbal
pigmentation was seen in patients without other ocular manifestations of onchocerciasis, it appeared to be more extensive in cases of
severe corneal involvement, in which heavy accumulations of pigment were always present adjacent to corneal lesions near the
limbus. Xerosis of the conjunctiva was not observed.

Cornea: Corneal changes were most frequent and of a characteristic morphology. The corneal epithelium was seldom involved,
although superficial stippling accompanied by intense photophobia
sometimes occurred. The disease appeared to begin at the limbus
near the 3:00 and 9:00 positions. Dense subepithelial infiltrates extended triangularly from a broad limbal base, the apex pointing
toward the center of the cornea. The central-most aspect of the
lesion consisted of densely packed gray dots located beneath Bow-
man's membrane in the anterior portion of the stroma. The appearance of the corneal opacity at this early stage has been referred to
as "snow storm zone." In more advanced cases opacification pro-
gressed toward the center of the cornea in a tongue-like fashion and
was followed by the migration of conjunctival pigment onto the
corneal epithelium. Microfilariae were found to be photosensitive,
trying to move from the illuminated to the darker parts of the anterior chamber.

Iris: The pupils reacted sluggishly to direct and indirect illumi-
nation in all subjects. Active anterior uveitis was rare, and if present
was of the granulomatous type with heavy fibrinous exudation.
Evidence of previous episodes of anterior uveitis was frequent and
consisted of extensive posterior synechiae, secclusio of occlusio
pupillae, secondary cataract, and secondary glaucoma. A pear-
shaped deformation and downward displacement of the pupil were
frequently encountered. Atrophy and heavy dark pigmentation of

the iris were seen in eyes showing evidence of previous episodes of anterior uveitis.

Lens: Cataracts occurred in patients in whom evidence of inflammatory disease of the anterior segment was observed; they had no special characteristics. Nuclear cataracts were observed in one male patient who showed no signs of ocular pathology.

Fundus: In patients in whom the posterior segment could be visualized, the fundi were normal in all but two.

When present, active or inactive anterior uveitis was always associated with other ocular manifestations of onchocerciasis, often with cataracts.

Live microfilariae were seen in the anterior chamber of eight patients, of whom seven had other ocular manifestations of onchocerciasis. In one instance intraocular microfilariae were seen without other ocular anomalies, but the skin biopsies were positive and nodules were present.

A more detailed description of ocular onchocerciasis found in Ouli Bangala has been published in a special paper (von Noorden and Buck, 1968).

A particularly interesting result of the study was the finding that 44 (11.4 percent) of 386 residents of Ouli Bangala had microfilariae of *O. volvulus* in their urine (Table 4–24). This finding was attributed both to the technique employed, that of triple concentration of complete urine specimens (Buck *et al.*, 1969), and to the severity of infections as shown in Table 4–26.*

The Lim River was the only body of water in the area where *Simulium* was caught regularly and where conditions for continued breeding were favorable. Figure 4–11 is a map of Ouli Bangala divided into four zones determined by increasing distance from the Lim River. It was expected that the risk of exposure to bites by infected black flies would become smaller the farther the individual

---

* A follow-up study of onchocerciasis was conducted in Ouli Bangala between January and February of 1970. Its results confirm the high prevalence of microfilaruria among the residents of this village. As part of the investigation, cystoscopy was performed on seventeen persons in whose urine specimens microfilariae of *O. volvulus* were found by the multiple concentration techniques mentioned. In ten of these seventeen cases, microfilariae were recovered from small urine samples collected by ureter catheterization. Living microfilariae were found in the ureter specimens of eight persons. In contrast, only dead larvae were seen in bladder urine specimens. With the exception of one woman who had lesions of schistosomiasis (*hematobium*), the cystoscopic findings were normal.

TABLE 4–26. PREVALENCE OF ONCHOCERCOMA, SKIN ATROPHY, AND
MICROFILARIAE IN THE URINE AS RELATED TO THE INTENSITY OF
SKIN INFECTION WITH *O. volvulus*, OULI BANGALA

Intensity of Skin Infection[a]	No. in Group[b]	Persons with Onchocercoma		Persons with Onchocercoma and/or Skin Atrophy		Persons with Microfilaruria	
		No.	%	No.	%	No.	%
Absent	33	3	9.1	5	15.1	2	6.1
Mild	266	142	53.4	166	62.4	34	12.8
Heavy	26	15	57.7	20	76.9	7	26.9

[a] Estimated from microfilarial counts in skin snips (mild, from one to twenty; heavy, twenty-one and over).
[b] Includes all persons five years of age and over who had skin snips, physical examinations, and urine examinations.

residences were from the Lim River, and that this variation in exposure should be reflected by decreasing infection rates from the first to the fourth area. Table 4–27 confirms this assumption and shows that the prevalence of infection with *O. volvulus* and of microfilaruria decreases as the distance of the residences from the river increases. Since all specimens of *S. damnosum* in the area were caught near the bank of the Lim while biting or attempting to bite a human host, it is probable that most infections were acquired in the immediate vicinity of the river, during the fetching of water or while fishing. This assumption is supported by Table 4–27, which shows that only the families of zone 1 used the Lim exclusively throughout the year; the majority of households in the other zones fetched their water during the rainy season from Mbongo Creek, which runs parallel to the road. Only during the dry season, when the creek became dry and muddy, did families of zones 2, 3, and 4 obtain their daily water supply from the Lim.

A chi-square test of variance for familial aggregation of microfilaruria and of all onchocercal infections gave the following results: a familial distribution of microfilaruria as uneven as the one observed could have arisen in only 0.3 percent of the samples ($P = 0.003$) if chance alone were operating. The corresponding probability for all infections of *O. volvulus* was $P = 0.06$. A more detailed description of the distribution of microfilaruria in Ouli Bangala and of epidemiological analyses for clues of its pathogenesis has been provided elsewhere (Buck *et al.*, 1969).

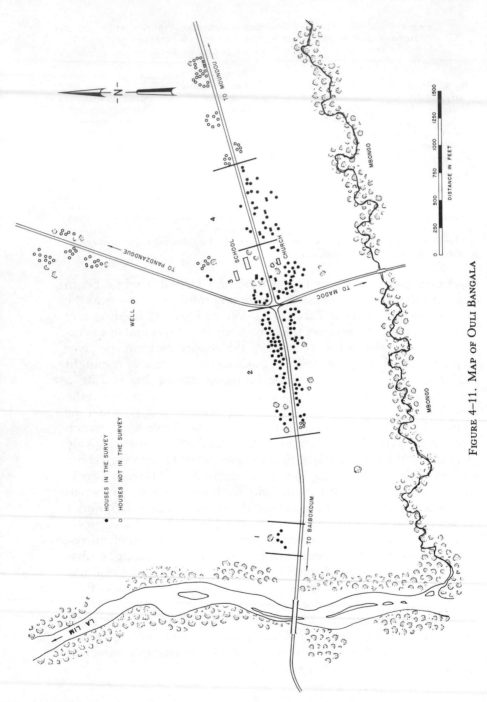

FIGURE 4-11. MAP OF OULI BANGALA

HOUSES IN THE SURVEY •
HOUSES NOT IN THE SURVEY ○

WELL ○

TO PANDZANDGUE

SCHOOL

CHURCH

TO MADOC →

TO MOUNDOU

TO BAIBOKOUM

MBONGO

MBONGO

LA LIM

DISTANCE IN FEET
0 250 500 750 1000 1250 1500

—N—

148

TABLE 4-27. PREVALENCE OF ONCHOCERCIASIS AND OF ONCHOCERCAL MICROFILARURIA BY DISTANCE OF RESIDENCES FROM LIM RIVER, OULI BANGALA

	Distance of Residences from Lim River										
	340'–620' Zone 1			1,480'–2,730' Zone 2			2,730'–3,280' Zone 3			3,370'–3,050' Zone 4		
	No. Examined	Positive		No. Examined	Positive		No. Examined	Positive		No. Examined	Positive	
		No.	%		No.	%		No.	%		No.	%
Proportion of households using Mbongo Creek as main water source during rainy season	11	0	0	58	29	50.0	21	12	57.2	18	12	66.7
Microfilariae in skin snips	35	30	85.7	197	169	85.8	88	70	79.5	66	48	72.7
Microfilaruria present	35	7	20.0	197	25	12.7	88	8	9.1	66	4	6.1

149

Other features associated with onchocerciasis in Ouli Bangala will be discussed in later sections; namely, that the pathognomonic nodules can be detected on routine chest roentgenograms (see Table 4–37); that many infected persons are anergic to tuberculin (see Tuberculosis, pp. 167–81); and that there appears to be a decreased antibody response to a variety of infections, as indicated by low HIA titers to yellow fever virus following vaccination (see Vaccinations and Vaccination Histories, pp. 121–25), and to adult and cercarial antigens of *Schistosoma mansoni* in persons infected with *S. mansoni* and *S. hematobium* (see Schistosomiasis, pp. 150–60).

Schistosomiasis

Next to malaria, schistosomiasis is the most important public health problem in Africa, where more than half of the estimated 180,000,000 cases in the world now exist (World Health Organization, 1965, p. 7). Despite the present-day knowledge of its life cycle, of snail transmission in infected water, and methods of prevention, the disease is on the increase throughout Africa. Available information from other sources (Ziegler, 1967) and findings made by the present authors indicate that the magnitude of the schistosomiasis problem in Chad is representative of the situation described for the entire continent. Nevertheless, there are considerable variations in the prevalence and type of schistosomiasis, not only among contrasting geographical areas and ethnic groups in the Republic, but also within the individual communities that were selected for detailed study. These variations can be related to differences in the risk of exposure to the snail vectors and are closely associated with the quality of the water sources that are used most frequently by the villagers. Of the three species of *Schistosoma* which affect man, two are endemic in Chad, *S. hematobium* and *S. mansoni*. A map of the geographical distribution of the intermediate snail hosts of schistosomiasis (Figure 2–4) appears on page 74.

Estimates of the prevalence of infections with *S. hematobium* and *S. mansoni* were made by four methods, namely, by examination of stool and urine specimens for ova of the trematodes with concentration techniques, and by serological tests with the adult (CF test) and cercarial (slide flocculation test) antigens of *S. mansoni*. A summary of the results for geographical comparison is given in Table 4–28. Infections with *S. hematobium* were present in all five communities but were of major importance only in Djimtilo and Ouarai, while *S. mansoni* was the predominant type of infection in Ouli Bangala. A major discrepancy in the prevalence estimates of schistosomiasis in the oasis of Faya-Largeau seems to arise when the results of this study are compared with those of another investigation (Ranque and Rioux, 1961). The French investigators reported that 77.5 percent of 214 Toubou children of unspecified ages had clinical hematuria. The Toubous live near the date palm plantations on the outskirts of Faya-Largeau. The area is characterized by numerous stagnant ponds and irrigation ditches in which *Bulinus truncatus*, an important vector snail of *S. hematobium*, was found frequently. By contrast, our own studies in Faya-Largeau were carried out among the Anakaza and Kamadja people whose daily water needs were supplied by conveniently located dug wells, and who were therefore much less exposed to the cercariae of *S. hematobium* than were the Toubous, who had to fetch surface water.

The relative importance of micro-epidemiological contrasts, even within small communities, is also evident from findings made in Ouli Bangala (Table 4–29). As in Faya-Largeau, the differences in the prevalence of schistosomiasis were closely associated with the quality of the most accessible water supply. The zonal subdivisions of residences in Ouli Bangala listed in Table 4–29 correspond to those shown in Figure 4–11. Whereas the clean, highly oxygenated, and fast-flowing water of the Lim River provided ideal conditions for the breeding of *Simulium*, it was an unfavorable habitat for vector snails of schistosomiasis. This is reflected by a higher prevalence of onchocerciasis and a lower rate of infection with *S. mansoni* among those villagers who used the Lim exclusively for their daily water needs. On the other hand, residents of Ouli Bangala whose houses were located at greater distances from the Lim River preferred Mbongo Creek (see Figure 4–11) as their main water source. *Biomphalaria alexandrina wonsoni* and *B. pfeifferi*, both vector snails of *S. mansoni*, were easily collected from the creek but were never taken from the Lim. As a result of these differences in exposure, schistosomiasis was more frequent, onchocerciasis less prevalent and severe, among the villagers residing in zones 2–4.

The highest percentage of urine specimens with ova of *S. hematobium* was found in ten-to-fourteen-year-old children. Thereafter the prevalence of confirmed infections decreased continuously with progressing age. This pattern is considered typical for endemic schistosomiasis, but the decline in prevalence after the age of twenty is more pronounced in infections with *S. hematobium* than in those

TABLE 4–28. Percentage[a] of Residents with Ova of *S. hematobium* and *S. mansoni* in Single Urine and Stool Specimens, and Prevalence of Serological Reactions in Slide Flocculation and Complement Fixation Tests with Cercarial and Adult Antigens of *S. mansoni*

Locality	No. Examined		Ova Present		Serological Reactions		
	Urine	Stool	*S. hematobium* %	*S. mansoni* %	SF Reactive[b] %	CF Reactive[b] %	SF/CF
Djimtilo	362	368	26.0	0.8	60.9	46.5[c]	1.3
Ouli Bangala	387	381	6.2	43.7	74.4	38.2[c]	1.9
Ouarai	351	352	31.4	0.9	81.0	59.8[c]	1.4
Boum Khebir	358	356	0.3	1.0	40.5	24.3[c]	1.7
Faya-Largeau	163	191	1.8	0	33.1	8.2[c]	4.0

[a] Percentages are age and sex adjusted.
[b] Weak reactions included.
[c] Anticomplementary sera: Djimtilo, 26.7; Ouli Bangala, 10.4; Ouarai, 9.1; Boum Khebir, 27.2; and Faya-Largeau, 1.1.

TABLE 4-29. PREVALENCE OF INFECTION WITH *S. mansoni* AND *S. hematobium* IN RESIDENTS OF OULI BANGALA BY DISTANCE FROM LIM RIVER, AND USE OF ALTERNATE WATER SUPPLY

Distance of Residence from Lim River	No. Examined	*S. hematobium* Ova Present			*S. mansoni* Ova Present			Estimated Proportion of Households Using Mbongo Creek as Main Water Source During Rainy Season
		No.	%	Adjusted %[a]	No.	%	Adjusted %[a]	
340'– 620' (zone 1)	34	2	5.9	9.3	5	14.7	13.0	0
1,480'–2,730' (zone 2)	197	12	6.1	5.9	94	48.7	48.4	50.0
2,730'–3,280' (zone 3)	87	7	8.0	7.1	41	47.0	47.5	59.2
3,370'–4,050' (zone 4)	66	4	6.3	6.1	27	42.8	45.8	66.7

[a] Percentages are adjusted for age.

153

with *S. mansoni* (Farooq *et al.*, 1966). Figure 4–12 shows that a similar tendency can be found when the number of the excreted eggs is plotted as a function of age. The numbers listed were estimated from egg counts and adjusted to the exact volume of the urine specimen. The averages computed for individual age groups included only those persons who had positive specimens. The age distribution of the prevalence of proved schistosomiasis in both villages with endemic foci of *S. hematobium* is almost congruent with the two curves shown in Figure 4–12. It is reasonable to assume that the sensitivity of urine examination as a screening test for the detection of infections with *S. hematobium* is to some degree dependent upon the number of excreted eggs because higher egg counts tend to increase the probability of their recovery in single specimens. It is realized that the estimates shown in Figure 4–12 may be too low, since the specimens were taken without consideration of quantitative diurnal variations of egg excretion. The maximum output of ova in the urine was found to occur between 12:00 and 2:00 P.M. (World Health Organization, 1967), whereas our specimens were acquired in the early morning hours. A certain degree of standardization was achieved by instructing the individuals in the samples to empty their bladders completely into special containers that were distributed the night before the examination was scheduled.

As already mentioned, infections with *S. mansoni*, although present in all four villages south of the Sahara, were of major importance only in Ouli Bangala, where 7 percent of the residents also had ova of *S. hematobium* in their urine. Double infections occurred in 3.4 percent of the village population. The distribution of these infections was random; thirteen, or 7.8 percent, of the twenty-eight cases of urinary bilharziasis occurred in persons who also had ova of *S. mansoni* in their stools; and fifteen, or 6.5 percent, of the cases were found in villagers whose stools were negative. In contrast to the strong variations in the prevalence of *S. mansoni* infections within the village, intraregional differences in the infection rates of *S. hematobium* were trivial. In endemic areas of schistosomiasis the decline in the percentage of ova recovered from the excreta of persons above the age of twenty was found to be less pronounced in infections with *S. mansoni* than in infections with *S. hematobium* (Farooq *et al.*, 1966). Although the age pattern in Ouli Bangala showed the typical increase of infection rates up to the fifteenth year, no decrease was observed thereafter. It is speculated that this tendency could be related to certain deficiencies in antibody responses to a variety

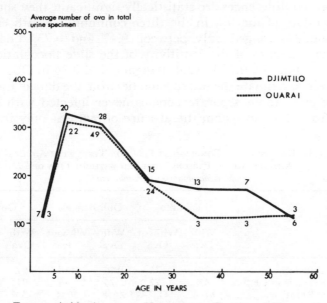

FIGURE 4–12. AVERAGE NUMBER OF OVA OF *Schistosoma hematobium* IN SINGLE URINE SPECIMENS BY AGE

of infections, including schistosomiasis, as already mentioned in the section on Onchocerciasis.

A summary of the results of the slide flocculation and the complement fixation tests for schistosomiasis is shown in Table 4–28. Interpretation of the results of the CF test is hampered by the fact that between 9 and 27 percent of the sera collected had to be excluded because of anticomplementary activity (see Chapter 5). A perusal of the table shows that there is only a relatively weak association between the prevalence of ova and that of reactions in the serological tests. The observed discrepancies between the results of the CF and SF tests are related to their inherent sensitivities and specificities and are modified further by coexisting infections and general health conditions in each community which may or may not affect the individual capacities of either test.

Table 4–30 lists the relative percentages of serological reactions among persons with and without ova of either *S. mansoni* or *S. hematobium*, or both. As can be seen, reactions in the CF tests were more frequent among the confirmed cases than in the group with parasitologically negative stool and urine examinations. Although the observed differences are statistically significant, they show that the sensitivity of the test in the three communities with endemic schistosomiasis ranged only between 0.47 and 0.73. The corresponding estimates of the sensitivity of the slide flocculation tests are 0.8 in Djimtilo, 0.77 in Ouli Bangala, and 0.86 in Ouarai. It is impossible to estimate the test specificities from the data of the study, because one cannot separate persons never infected with schistosomes from those in whom the absence of ova was only transient.

TABLE 4–30. REACTIVITY IN COMPLEMENT FIXATION TEST[a] WITH ADULT *S. mansoni* ANTIGEN AMONG PERSONS WITH AND WITHOUT OVA OF *S. hematobium* AND *S. mansoni*[b]

	Djimtilo		Ouli Bangala		Ouarai	
	With Ova	Without Ova	With Ova	Without Ova	With Ova	Without Ova
Number Tested	70	175	156	158	97	198
Number Reactive in CF Test	43	72	73	48	71	108
Percentage Reactive	61.4	41.1	46.8	30.4	73.2	54.2
Chi^2 of Difference	8.3		8.9		9.5	
P of Difference	<0.01		<0.01		<0.01	

[a] Anticomplementary sera: 84 in Djimtilo; 41 in Ouli Bangala; 31 in Ouarai.
[b] Includes all persons from whom stool, urine, and serum samples were available; 156 individuals had to be excluded because their sera were anticomplementary.

The prevalence of CF test reactions in the areas with endemic schistosomiasis was lowest in Ouli Bangala, where the prevalence of ova was highest. This finding suggests the presence of peculiar host factors among the residents of Ouli Bangala which might have been responsible for relative deficiencies in the serological reactions.

Table 4–31 shows the statistical significance of interregional differences in the prevalence of serological reactions among persons with confirmed bilharziasis. Variations in the prevalence of ova among residents of endemic areas are closely associated with age because age determines the risk of exposure to the cercariae of the trematodes and relates to the progressive formation of fibrous tissue in the organs involved and to the degree of immunity acquired (World Health Organization, 1967). Therefore, the data in Table 4–31 are presented for two age categories, that is, birth to nineteen years and twenty years and older. The statistical significance of the differences in the prevalence of reactions in CF tests between Ouli

TABLE 4–31. STATISTICAL SIGNIFICANCE OF DIFFERENCES IN THE FREQUENCY OF REACTIONS IN COMPLEMENT FIXATION AND SLIDE FLOCCULATION TESTS WITH *S. mansoni* ANTIGENS BETWEEN CONFIRMED CASES OF SCHISTOSOMIASIS IN OULI BANGALA AND DJIMTILO, AND IN OULI BANGALA AND OUARAI

Age (years)	Differences in CF Reactions						Differences in SF Reactions					
	Djimtilo *vs* Ouli Bangala			Ouarai *vs* Ouli Bangala			Djimtilo *vs* Ouli Bangala			Ouarai *vs* Ouli Bangala		
	Chi²	df	P	Chi²	df	P	Chi²	df	P	Chi²	df	P
Birth–19	6.63	1	0.01	13.7	1	0.001	0.07	1	0.9	0.03	1	0.9
20+	0.01	1	0.9	3.9	1	0.05	0.382	1	0.5	10.03	1	0.002
Total	6.64	2	0.05	17.6	2	0.001	0.452	2	0.8	10.06	2	0.01

Bangala and Djimtilo or between Ouli Bangala and Ouarai was stronger in the younger age group; the opposite was observed for reactions in slide flocculation tests, where the discrepancies were greater in the adult group. From the table it appears that the relative unresponsiveness was more pronounced in the CF tests than in the SF tests.

Enlargement of the liver and spleen is a typical sign of chronic schistosomiasis but occurs more frequently in infections with *S. mansoni* than in those with *S. hematobium*. In the three communities with endemic bilharziasis, malaria was also hyperendemic. Therefore, hepatosplenomegaly could have developed as a result of either disease, alone or in combination. The prevalence rates of hepatomegaly and splenomegaly among various age groups in the four communities with endemic malaria are given in Table 4–32. The percentage of persons who had enlarged spleens or livers was highest in Ouli Bangala; of the two indices, the excess in the prevalence of hepatomegaly was generally much greater in all age groups. The following interpretations of the figures are offered. The age pattern of splenomegaly in all villages is consistent with the spleen rates of malaria in hyperendemic areas. The age-specific prevalence of hepatomegaly is U-shaped, with the first mode in the youngest group and the second in the oldest group. This bimodality is considered to reflect the actions of different disease determinants, namely, pathological liver changes from malaria in children and cirrhosis of mixed etiologies in older residents. The reason for the preponderance of hepatomegaly in Ouli Bangala could be related to the high prevalence of chronic infections with *S. mansoni* in that village, while *S. hematobium* was the predominant type of infection in the other villages. The relatively higher rate of splenomegaly in Ouli Bangala could be interpreted as being related to cirrhotic changes that have resulted from chronic schistosomiasis of the liver.

Occasionally, estimates of the prevalence of schistosomiasis are based on specific questions in health interviews. One of the pathognomonic signs in *hematobium* infections is hematuria. It is assumed that this rather dramatic sign will be recognized by the patient whenever it occurs. A validation of interview methods as a screening test to detect schistosomiasis (*hematobium*) is shown in Table 4–33. Interview statements concerning the presence of hematuria were available from all individuals from whom a urine specimen for parasitological examination was acquired. Therefore, it became possible to compare the results of the urine examinations for the

TABLE 4–32. PREVALENCE[a] OF HEPATOMEGALY(L) AND SPLENOMEGALY(S) AND THEIR RELATIVE RATIO BY AGE

Age (years)	Djimtilo (N = 376)			Ouli Bangala (N = 393)			Ouarai (N = 361)			Boum Khebir (N = 371)		
	L	S	L/S	L	S	L/S	L	S	L/S	L	S	L/S
Birth–4	30.6	66.1	0.46	47.9	71.5	0.67	28.4	74.6	0.38	43.3	67.1	0.65
5–9	33.3	77.1	0.43	41.8	83.5	0.50	19.4	70.8	0.27	23.5	70.6	0.33
10–14	38.2	42.4	0.90	32.9	48.6	0.68	19.5	51.2	0.38	6.3	26.5	0.24
15–19	3.2	32.2	0.10	12.5	30.0	0.42	10.0	22.8	0.44	3.7	17.9	0.21
20–29	8.0	20.8	0.38	34.3	29.6	1.16	13.3	21.7	0.61	9.6	21.1	0.45
30–39	10.8	16.2	0.67	58.2	31.2	1.87	22.9	20.0	1.15	14.3	17.1	0.83
40+	15.6	15.6	1.00	35.7	33.3	1.07	38.2	18.2	2.10	14.4	13.3	1.08
Average	19.4	36.5	0.53	38.4	49.3	0.78	22.5	44.0	0.51	19.1	36.4	0.52

[a] Listed in percentages.

TABLE 4–33. ASSOCIATION BETWEEN PRESENCE OF HEMATURIA, AS ELICITED
FROM INTERVIEWS, AND RECOVERY OF OVA OF *S. hematobium*
IN SINGLE URINE SPECIMENS, BY SEX

	Djimtilo		Ouarai	
	Males %	Females %	Males %	Females %
Prevalence of hematuria of one or more days duration at time of interview	16.3	3.3	29.0	6.5
Presence of ova of *S. hematobium* in urine specimen	28.2	23.9	35.4	29.0
Ratio (% ova ÷ % hematuria)	1.73	7.24	1.22	4.46

presence of ova of *S. hematobium* with answers to the interview question concerning the presence of hematuria.

As can be seen from Table 4–33, there are great sex differences in the percentage of persons who stated that they had hematuria. This discrepancy between the sexes is not associated with similar variations in the prevalence of ova of *S. hematobium* in urine specimens. The ratio (percentage of ova in urine divided by prevalence of hematuria) shows the magnitude of the differences between men and women. An explanation for this disparity could be a significant sex difference in the recognition of hematuria by men and women. Reasons for this discrepancy might be menstruation, urination habits, and, last but not least, a culture-associated modesty or fear on the part of women to report vaginal bleeding.

Trichinosis

Of the 1,691 sera collected, 1,592, or 94.1 percent, were examined in card tests for trichinosis (Anderson, Sadun, and Schoenbechler, 1963; Schultz, Kagan, and Warner, 1967). Relatively little is known as yet about the frequency and distribution of this infection in human and animal populations of Africa. Nelson, Guggisberg, and Mukundi (1963) reported that infections with *Trichinella spiralis* were prevalent in man and animals in East Africa. Larvae of the parasite were found in man, the bush pig (*Potamochoerus porcus*), leopard, jackal, lion, serval cat, spotted hyena, striped hyena, and domestic dog. In their investigations in Kenya these authors found that all human infections were traceable to meals containing flesh of the bush pig. They also reported a very low infection rate with *T. spiralis* in rats, domestic pigs, and the wart hog (*Phacochoerus aethiopicus*).

From food histories and other observations made in our study, it appeared that parts of the populations of the four southern villages ran the risk of acquiring infections with *T. spiralis*. In Ouli Bangala and Boum Khebir, consumption of rats was quite common in some families, whereas the meat of wild pigs was eaten occasionally by residents of all four communities south of the Sahara. Observations made in the study indicated that, except in Faya-Largeau, meat was always in short supply and was the most valued item in the diet of the villagers. One might speculate that this permanent craving for meat has made the residents less fastidious in their selection of animal protein sources, and that some of them may have eaten the flesh of carnivorous animals usually not considered fit for human consumption.

Table 4–34 shows the results of the serological tests for trichinosis in all five villages studied. The crude prevalence rates of reactions were highest in the bush village of Ouarai, where wild pigs were abundant, and in Ouli Bangala, where 25 percent of the households indicated that they had eaten rats. By contrast, the serum of only one resident of Faya-Largeau was found to be reactive in the test. While these regional differences can be explained by corresponding variations in the risk of exposure to animals that are known to serve as reservoir hosts of *T. spiralis*, it is difficult to interpret the age trends of the serological reactions. In all four southern communities the highest prevalence of reactions was observed in young children or teenagers. This was followed by a gradual decrease not only in the prevalence but also in the intensity of the reactions, as shown in the last column of the table. This tendency suggests non-specific interaction by host factors that are present more frequently in children than in adults. An analysis for association between the results of the charcoal card flocculation test for trichinosis and those of similar types of tests that employ cholesterol or lecithin (VDRL, slide flocculation tests with *S. mansoni* antigens) was inconclusive. A lack of association was observed when the results of the complement fixation tests with *Entamoeba histolytica* antigens were compared with those of the card tests for trichinosis. The results of the former test showed an age pattern similar to that observed for trichinosis. It is therefore impossible to decide whether the findings indicate true infection with *T. spiralis* or whether the serological reactions

TABLE 4–34. PREVALENCE AND DEGREE OF REACTIONS IN TRICHINOSIS CARD TESTS

Age (years)	Djimtilo		Ouli Bangala		Ouarai		Boum Khebir		Faya-Largeau		Total[a]		
	No. Examined	% Reactive	No. Examined	% Reactive	No. Examined	% Reactive	No. Examined	% Reactive	No. Examined	% Reactive	No. Examined	% Reactive	% Reactivity[b] Score
Birth–9	81	3.8	113	11.5	110	10.9	112	4.5	55	0	471	7.3	1.34
10–19	65	4.6	109	6.5	68	13.2	60	1.7	36	0	338	6.3	1.22
20–29	51	2.0	67	3.0	57	7.0	52	1.9	33	3.0	260	3.7	1.20
30–39	76	0	50	6.0	34	2.9	35	2.8	23	0	218	2.2	1.20
40–49	27	3.7	24	4.2	21	4.8	30	0	22	0	124	2.0	1.13
50+	47	2.1	18	0	31	3.2	61	1.6	24	0	181	1.6	1.00
Total	347	2.6	381	6.8	321	8.7	350	2.6	193	0.5	1,592	4.6	1.21

[a] Sex ratio (males per female) among reactors: 0.6.
[b] Reactions were graded as 1+, 2+, 3+, and 4+.

were non-specific because of certain unidentified host conditions that have caused some sera to react with the relatively crude antigen employed in the card test.

Intestinal Parasites

Indiscriminate defecation habits, lack of hygiene in handling or preserving food, use of unprotected and contaminated water supplies for household needs, and crowding of sleeping places were peculiarities common to all villages in the sample. These factors are known as essential determinants of endemic infections with the soil-transmitted helminths, especially *Ascaris lumbricoides* and *Trichuris trichiura*, which have a world-wide distribution. Infection rates with these two nematodes are often used as indicators of the quality of sanitation in an area (Spruyt *et al.*, 1967). It was therefore anticipated that the careful examination of stool specimens from all five study areas would yield a high percentage of stools in which the eggs of *Ascaris* and *Trichuris* had been excreted. This prediction proved to be wrong, as is evident from the results shown in Table 4–35.

A great variety of parasitic infections was found among the residents of the study communities, but the two "cosmopolitan" nematodes, *A. lumbricoides* and *T. trichiura*, were conspicuous by their absence. The fact that poor hygiene alone cannot be taken *ipso facto* as proof of the existence of endemic infections with roundworm or whipworm was also determined in some of the rural communities of Peru, where similar studies were conducted by Buck, Sasaki, and Anderson (1968). Systematic analyses for clues to factors that determine the distribution of ascariasis and trichuriasis in rural areas of developing countries will be made at a later time when more data from contrasting communities of various countries become available for comparison.

From the information available on Chad, the following observations appear relevant to speculations as to why eggs of *A. lumbricoides* and *T. trichiura* were not found. The main defecation sites were at the fringes of each village. Regardless of their religious affiliation, a majority of the residents of all communities used either water, sticks, or leaves as the principal cleansing material after defecation. At the peak of the dry season (when the study was conducted) the most frequently used defecation sites in the villages were dry and had little protection from the sun. Exposure to the direct heat of

TABLE 4–35. PREVALENCE[a] OF INTESTINAL PARASITES AMONG POPULATION OF FIVE VILLAGES IN THE REPUBLIC OF CHAD

Village	No. Examined	Nematodes[b]					Cestodes		Protozoa								
									E. histolytica								
		Ascaris	Trichuris	Hookworm	Strongyloides	Capillaria sp.	Taenia	H. nana	Small Cysts	Large Cysts	Ratio (large/small)	E. coli	I. butschlii	E. nana	G. lamblia	C. mesnili
Djimtilo	368	0	0	0.9	0.3	0	0	0	11.1	5.0	0.45	56.5	5.7	25.3	3.3	5.4
Ouli Bangala	381	0	0.5	9.4	1.3	1.3	0.3	0.3	10.6	7.2	0.68	70.6	2.6	22.0	3.9	1.6
Ouarai	352	0	0	13.2	1.1	0	1.7	0.3	9.5	8.3	0.87	63.9	0.9	15.9	2.6	2.0
Boum Khebir	356	0	0	6.1	0	1.1	0.8	1.4	6.1	13.1	2.15	43.5	3.7	16.8	6.5	12.1
Faya-Largeau	191	0	0.5	0	0	0	1.0	4.2	9.5	27.9	2.94	65.4	2.1	15.2	7.3	12.0

[a] Percentages listed are age adjusted.
[b] Eggs of Enterobius vermicularis were found in 41, or 2.5 percent, of 1,621 urine specimens and in 18, or 1.1 percent, of 1,649 stool specimens.

the sun is extremely detrimental to the eggs of the two nematodes. Fecal deposits were observed to dry very quickly; frequently they were visited by dung beetles, and while fresh they attracted numerous species of flies (see Chapters 2 and 3). With few exceptions, the soil of the defecation sites was alkaline, dry, and generally sandy. Where ashes from the repeated burning of vegetation in plantation areas covered the ground, the pH of the soil was as high as 8.2 at the surface, while only 7.0 a few inches deeper.

The environmental factors mentioned are all unfavorable to the survival and development of *Ascaris* and *Trichuris* eggs, but they do not explain why the more sensitive larvae of hookworm and *Strongyloides stercoralis* developed to the infective stage while the thick-shelled and more resistant eggs of *Ascaris* were never found in the sample. Two factors were recognized which would have little effect on the prevalence of hookworm or *Strongyloides* infections but which might prevent ascariasis and trichuriasis in rural areas. The first is the lack of low-growing garden vegetables in the diet of the villagers; the second is the observation that night soil was never used as a fertilizer of fields or gardens.

With the exception of Faya-Largeau in the Sahara, hookworm eggs were found in varying percentages of stool specimens from the residents of the villages (Table 4–35). They were most frequent in Ouarai, where trees and a thick cover of underbrush provide conditions that are favorable for the development of hookworm larvae. Differences in exposure risks related to host factors were not detected; shoes were seldom worn by the residents of any of the five communities included in the study. The interesting observation that five persons in Ouli Bangala and four in Boum Khebir had eggs of *Capillaria* (tentatively identified as *hepatica*) in their stool specimens has already been mentioned in the section on nutrition. It was speculated that these eggs indicated the presence of spurious infections with this common nematode of rats, since in true infections they would not have been excreted in the stool. It was assumed that the eggs were contained in the livers of infected rodents that had recently been consumed by the residents having positive stool specimens. From nutritional histories it was known that 26 percent of the households in Ouli Bangala ate rats so frequently that they considered them to be a major source of animal protein in their diet. Corresponding statements about rat eating were not obtained from the residents of Boum Khebir. Further studies of capillariasis in Chad are planned for the near future.

Infestation with tapeworms was recognized in all villages except Djimtilo. Stool examination is a relatively insensitive method for the detection of *Taenia* because many patients excrete no eggs, but pass gravid proglottids in their feces. Therefore, the estimates of the prevalence of taeniasis listed in Table 4–35 are too low. From the morphology of the eggs in stool specimens it cannot be decided whether the persons were infected with *T. saginata* or *T. solium*. The fact that no pigs were kept by the residents of any of the five villages suggests that they were infected with the beef tapeworm, although the possibility of sporadic infections with *T. solium* from wild pigs cannot be ruled out. Only a few stools were positive for eggs of the dwarf tapeworm, *Hymenolepis nana*. The highest prevalence was found in Faya-Largeau, where the peak (13.5 percent) occurred in the age group of children from five to nine years old.

From discussions with physicians in various parts of Chad, it became evident that amoebiasis represented a major public health problem. A review of hospital records indicated that extra-intestinal manifestations of the infection, especially amoebic liver abscess, were uncommonly frequent. The highest percentage of carriers of cysts of *Entamoeba histolytica* was found in Faya-Largeau. Cysts of the parasite were not only more frequent in this Saharan community but most were of the large type, which is indicative of a more virulent subspecies of the amoeba. A comparison for regional differences in the prevalence of diarrhea within the twenty-four-hour period preceding the health interview revealed the following variations:

Village	Crude Prevalence
Djimtilo	6.3%
Ouli Bangala	31.1
Ouarai	16.3
Boum Khebir	8.6
Faya-Largeau	34.5

Since *E. histolytica* is only one of the various agents that have to be considered in the differential diagnosis of diarrhea, the coincidence of the maxima of the prevalence of diarrhea and the recovery of cysts of *E. histolytica* is merely suggestive. The observation gains importance when the results of bacteriological stool examinations among children are included in the etiological considerations. Faya-Largeau had the lowest percentage of isolations of pathogenic and facultatively pathogenic enterobacteria, but the highest prevalence of cysts of *E. histolytica*. In Ouli Bangala, where complaints of diarrhea were almost as frequent as they were in Faya-Largeau, the recovery rate of amoebic cysts was similar to the rates found in the other three southern villages, while isolations of *Shigella* and *Salmonella* were more frequent there than in any of the other communities (see Enteric Bacteria, pp. 195–97).

Indirect evidence of amoebiasis is available from the results of complement fixation tests with *E. histolytica* antigens as shown in Table 4–36. Although the reactions in the CF test were more frequent in Faya-Largeau than in the other villages studied, it is also apparent from the results that concordance between the prevalence of amoebic cysts in stool specimens and reactions in the CF test is poor. Of particular interest is the obvious deficiency of reactions in Ouli Bangala.

The distribution of infections with the other protozoa listed in Table 4–35 did not reveal any peculiarities, with the exception of *Chilomastix mesnili*, where an unexplained preponderance of infection among women (two women for every man infected) was observed in all five communities.

Bacterial Diseases and Infections

Tuberculosis and Other Mycobacterial Infections

Tuberculosis. Estimates of the prevalence of diseases and infections described in this section are based on the results of different screening methods. They include tuberculin skin tests with the purified protein derivative of the human tuberculin bacillus (PPD-S) and a similarly prepared antigen of *Mycobacterium gause* (PPD-G), an antigenically broad representative of the group of ubiquitous mycobacteria that may cause ulcers or mild or inapparent infections in man, yet produce skin hypersensitivity of the delayed type. The hypersensitivity acquired by infection with an atypical mycobacterium is responsible for cross-reactions to the human-type tuberculin and may obscure the interpretation of the results of skin tests with this antigen. Differential testing with two antigens, PPD-S and PPD-G, has proved to be of value in distinguishing between homologous and heterologous skin reactions to tuberculin (Edwards and Palmer, 1958; World Health Organization, 1955; Wijsmuller, 1963).

TABLE 4–36. PREVALENCE OF REACTIONS IN COMPLEMENT FIXATION TESTS WITH E. histolytica ANTIGEN BY AGE

Age (years)	Djimtilo		Ouli Bangala		Ouarai		Boum Khebir		Faya-Largeau		Total	
	No.	% Reactive	No.	% Reactive	No.	% Reactive	No.	% Reactive	No.	% Reactive	No.	% Reactive
Birth–4	34	52.9	53	9.4	44	15.9	41	31.7	17	23.5	189	24.9
5–9	42	30.9	60	11.6	70	34.3	61	16.4	40	50.0	273	27.1
10–19	60	31.6	107	4.8	70	17.1	50	4.0	35	51.4	322	17.4
20–29	43	39.5	64	0	56	10.7	39	7.7	33	51.5	235	18.3
30–39	60	35.0	44	9.1	35	11.5	23	8.6	23	17.3	185	18.9
40–49	25	32.0	21	0	19	0	20	0	22	31.8	107	14.0
50+	37	45.9	14	0	29	6.8	44	4.5	24	20.9	148	17.6
Total	301	37.5	363	5.8	323	17.0	278	11.6	194	38.7	1,459	20.3

In addition to the skin tests, all residents were examined for clinical evidence of leprosy and for the presence of ulcers. Individuals who had ulcers were then compared to a suitable control group for differences in the prevalence of skin reactions to either type of tuberculin. Chest roentgenograms were taken of all individuals who were older than six years. These were examined for signs of active or inactive tuberculosis, as well as for other abnormal conditions of the lungs, heart, bony thorax, and soft tissue. Because of the relatively great importance of pulmonary tuberculosis in Chad, the summary tabulation of radiological diagnoses is included in this section as Table 4–37. The results contained in the table will be referred to in other sections of the book, whenever the particular disease under discussion has manifestations that are detectable on chest roentgenograms and can be subjected to epidemiological analyses (see Nutrition [Thyroid Enlargement], Onchocerciasis, Treponematoses, and Histoplasmosis).

From the pilot study it was learned that among the five study communities Boum Khebir probably had the highest prevalence of leprosy. For this reason a special study on the prevalence of acid-fast bacilli was conducted in that village. These bacilli were recovered from tissue specimens that were obtained by routine punch biopsy of the earlobe (Kar, Elliston, and Taylor, 1964).

The age-specific percentages of reactions to PPD-S and PPD-G are shown in Tables 4–38 and 4–39. Because sex differences were trivial, the data are presented for the entire population. In all five communities, reactions to PPD-G were more prevalent than those to PPD-S, but for each antigen there were large regional differences. The highest percentage of reactions to the human-type tuberculin was found among the residents of Faya-Largeau, who also had the highest prevalence of tuberculous lesions in chest roentgenograms (Table 4–37). In contrast, there appeared to be a striking deficiency in the frequency of tuberculin reactions among the villagers of Ouli Bangala, whose radiological diagnoses indicated that the prevalence of pulmonary tuberculosis was higher there than in Djimtilo, Ouarai, and Boum Khebir. This discrepancy becomes even more apparent when the reactor status of the five residents with radiologically suspected pulmonary tuberculosis is taken into consideration. Three of these persons were found to be non-reactive in tuberculin skin tests with both antigens and included one individual in whose sputum numerous acid-fact bacilli were detected. The apparent deficiencies in the prevalence of skin reactions to PPD-S and

TABLE 4–37. DIAGNOSES FROM ROUTINE CHEST ROENTGENOGRAMS

Diagnosis	Percentage[a] with Given Condition				
	Djimtilo (N = 215)	Ouli Bangala (N = 169)	Ouarai (N = 237)	Boum Khebir (N = 237)	Faya-Largeau (N = 154)
Heart					
General enlargement	4.2	3.0	12.1	6.4	0
Enlargement of left side	2.3	0	1.6	1.3	1.6
Mitral configuration	0	0	0	0	0
Aorta					
Elongation	9.8	6.6	7.2	4.8	3.5
Widening and elongation	0.5	0.9	2.0	0.3	0.6
Tuberculosis	1.9	3.0	1.6	2.0	5.7
Other pulmonary findings					
Hilar/mediastinal lymph node enlargement	3.3	3.1	4.9	0.6	1.4
Calcification	7.4	19.7	15.3	18.5	9.3
Scarring	1.9	1.3	0.4	1.2	3.6
Atelectasis	0	0	0	0	0
Infiltrate	1.4	3.0	2.7	1.1	2.4
Tumor	0	0.4	0	0	0.3
Pleura					
Thickening	0	0.8	1.2	0.3	0.3
Calcification	0	0	0	0.4	0
Fluid	0	0	0	0	1.4
Fibrothorax	0	0	0	0	0
Bony Thorax					
Congenital abnormalities	0.5[b]	0	0	0.7[c]	0.3[d]
Rib fracture	0	0	0	0.4	1.1
Compression of vertebra	0	0	0	0	0
Scoliosis	0	0	0	0.2	0.3
Kyphosis	0.5	0	0	0	0
Kyphoscoliosis	0	0	0	0	0
Soft Tissue					
Calcification	0.5	0	0	0.2	0
Retrosternal struma	0.5	1.3	6.3	0.3	0
Situs inversus	0.5	0	0	0	0
Nodules (onchocercoma)	0	5.1	0	0	0

[a] Percentages listed are age adjusted.
[b] Hypoplastic first rib (one person).
[c] Cervical rib (two persons).
[d] Cervical rib (one person).

PPD-G in Ouli Bangala suggested that a considerable percentage of the residents might have been anergic to these antigens because other conditions interfered with the mechanisms responsible for delayed hypersensitivity. Conditions which may lead to the phenomenon of tuberculin-negative tuberculosis include cachexia, measles, old age, and other hitherto unexplained factors (Mascher, 1951). Pepys (1955), who examined the relationship of non-specific and specific factors in the tuberculin reaction, states that pregnancy, some febrile and infectious disorders, and cachexia due to malnutrition can lead to a partial or total inhibition of the tuberculin reaction. Furculow, Emge, and Bunnell (1948) showed that the depression of skin sensitivity to tuberculin was associated with critical illness, regardless of the etiology and that the anergy became more pronounced in old age. Analyses for clues to the identity of host factors that may have been responsible for the non-specific suppression of tuberculin skin reactions among the residents of Ouli Bangala will be discussed briefly in this section; the results of a more detailed study will be published elsewhere.

The age-specific percentages of reactions to PPD-S and PPD-G listed in Tables 4–38 and 4–39 show the typical increase by age up to fifty years and a more or less pronounced decrease thereafter. Little is known as yet about the factors associated with old age that are responsible for the drop in the prevalence of delayed-type skin reactions in a general population. From the data presented in Tables 4–38 and 4–39 it appears that the association of "aging" with anergy to tuberculin occurs much earlier in the lives of the residents of Ouli Bangala than among those of the other four communities. As has already been discussed in the section on Onchocerciasis, the feature that distinguished Ouli Bangala from the other villages was the presence of holoendemic onchocerciasis in that community. It is therefore interesting to note that some investigators have found similarities between the histopathological architecture of the skin of persons infected with *O. volvulus* and certain physiological changes that occur in old age (Hoeppli and Gunders, 1962).

The merely descriptive prevalence data of the two previously discussed tables do not indicate whether the sizes of the tuberculin skin reactions were relatively larger for PPD-S or for PPD-G. In order to obtain clues to the prevalence of "true" infections with the tubercle bacillus, reactions to the human-type tuberculin (PPD-S) were subdivided into those that were either larger or smaller than

TABLE 4-38. PREVALENCE OF REACTIONS[a] IN TUBERCULIN TESTS WITH PPD-S

Age (years)	Djimtilo		Ouli Bangala		Ouarai		Boum Khebir		Faya-Largeau	
	No. Tested	% Reactors	No. Tested	% Reactors	No. Tested	% Reactors	No. Tested	% Reactors	No. Tested	% Reactors
Birth–4	45	22.2	45	4.4	50	10.0	50	10.0	13	30.8
5–9	46	43.5	58	1.7	72	11.1	67	28.4	32	40.6
10–19	66	56.1	102	10.8	67	34.3	62	50.0	35	62.9
20–29	50	64.0	58	29.3	60	38.3	52	42.2	23	73.9
30–39	73	78.1	44	20.5	35	48.6	34	26.5	21	76.2
40–49	29	72.4	19	15.8	22	68.2	30	43.3	20	75.0
50+	49	55.1	17	23.5	32	37.5	58	19.0	18	77.8
Total	358	57.0	343	13.7	338	30.5	353	31.2	162	62.3

[a] Induration sizes of five or more millimeters in diameter are called reactions.

TABLE 4-39. PREVALENCE OF REACTIONS[a] IN TUBERCULIN TESTS WITH PPD-G

Age (years)	Djimtilo		Ouli Bangala		Ouarai		Boum Khebir		Faya-Largeau	
	No. Tested	% Reactors	No. Tested	% Reactors	No. Tested	% Reactors	No. Tested	% Reactors	No. Tested	% Reactors
Birth–4	45	48.9	45	11.1	50	20.0	50	26.0	13	38.5
5–9	46	69.6	57	14.0	72	34.7	67	74.6	32	50.0
10–19	65	75.4	102	30.4	67	64.2	62	85.5	35	74.3
20–29	50	90.0	58	43.1	60	58.3	52	86.4	23	87.0
30–39	73	89.0	44	36.4	35	71.4	34	91.1	21	90.5
40–49	28	89.3	19	31.6	22	81.8	30	86.6	20	90.0
50+	49	75.5	17	35.3	32	53.1	58	70.7	18	72.2
Total	356	77.2	342	28.4	338	51.2	353	73.4	162	72.2

[a] Induration sizes of five or more millimeters in diameter are called reactions.

173

the observed induration sizes for PPD-G. The frequency distribution of reaction sizes to PPD-S is shown separately for each of the five villages in Figures 4–13 through 4–17. The black area of each bar indicates the reactions in which responses to PPD-S were larger than those to PPD-G (homologous reactions), whereas the dotted area denotes the reverse reactor status (heterologous reactions).

The figures show that more tuberculous infections had occurred among the residents of Faya-Largeau (Figure 4–17), which also had the highest percentage of persons with radiological evidence of

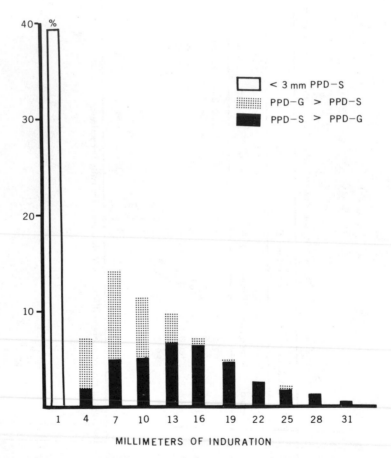

FIGURE 4–13. FREQUENCY DISTRIBUTION OF REACTION SIZES IN
TUBERCULIN SKIN TESTS WITH PPD-S AND CROSS REACTIONS
TO PPD-G, DJIMTILO

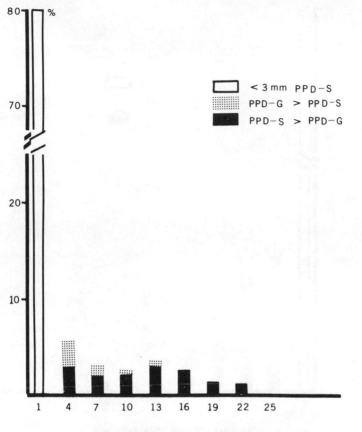

MILLIMETERS OF INDURATION

FIGURE 4–14. FREQUENCY DISTRIBUTION OF REACTION SIZES IN
TUBERCULIN SKIN TESTS WITH PPD-S AND CROSS REACTIONS
TO PPD-G, OULI BANGALA

pulmonary tuberculosis. Next in order was the population of
Djimtilo (Figure 4–13). In both of these Arab communities the
distribution curves were bimodal, even without correction for the
relative size of the two tuberculin reactions. In contrast, the distribution of the PPD-S reactions in the three remaining southern
villages would not have permitted a clear-cut separation of the
infected and non-infected population groups without subclassifying
the reactions into presumably homologous and heterologous responses, because of the preponderance of infections with atypical

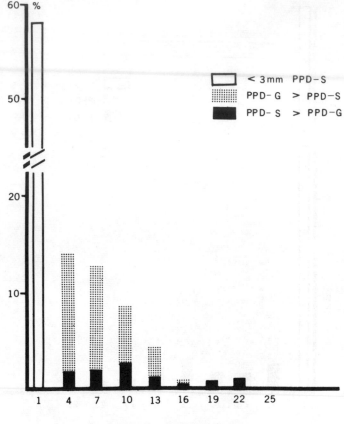

FIGURE 4–15. FREQUENCY DISTRIBUTION OF REACTION SIZES IN
TUBERCULIN SKIN TESTS WITH PPD-S AND CROSS REACTIONS
TO PPD-G, OUARAI

mycobacteria. The deficiency in the frequency of tuberculin reactions among the villagers of Ouli Bangala (Figure 4–14) is also
evident from a comparison of the figures. The results suggest that
the suppression has affected disproportionately more of the weaker
skin reactions (up to ten millimeters induration size) than the
stronger ones.

The broad information available from our study permitted the
selection of multiple variables that appeared relevant for further
analyses of the association between host factors and skin reactivity

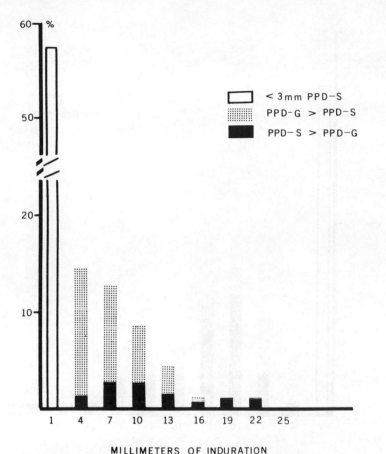

FIGURE 4–16. FREQUENCY DISTRIBUTION OF REACTION SIZES IN
TUBERCULIN SKIN TESTS WITH PPD-S AND CROSS REACTIONS
TO PPD-G, BOUM KHEBIR

to tuberculin. In the section on nutrition it was shown that there
was a relatively close association between skinfold thickness and the
weight/height ratio in all study communities but Ouli Bangala,
where the correlation was weak. It was concluded that in the latter
village variations in skinfold thickness were heavily dependent upon
the high prevalence of onchocercal dermatitis, and that this interference had led to a distortion of the normal pattern. It was also
noted that the elevation of serum gamma globulin was relatively
greater in Ouli Bangala than in the other four communities.

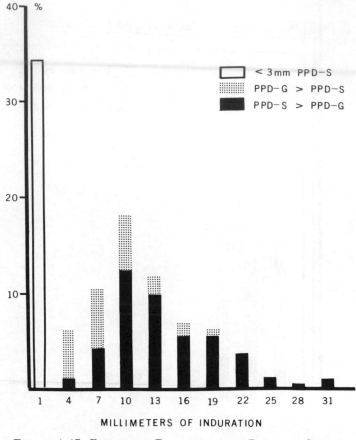

FIGURE 4–17. FREQUENCY DISTRIBUTION OF REACTION SIZES IN
TUBERCULIN SKIN TESTS WITH PPD-S AND CROSS REACTIONS
TO PPG-D, FAYA-LARGEAU

Hypergammaglobulinemia is found frequently in patients with
sarcoidosis (McCuiston and Hudgins, 1960), Hodgkin's disease
(Schier *et al.*, 1956), and lepromatous leprosy (Lechat, 1961). In all
of these diseases suppression of delayed-type hypersensitivity reactions is known to occur frequently (Buck, 1961). Cachexia and
malnutrition are other conditions known to inhibit the tuberculin
reaction (Pepys, 1955).

The various factors listed above were considered in multiple
analyses for association with the reactor status to tuberculin (PPD-S

and PPD-G). From other investigations, like those cited above, it is known that the suppression of skin reactions is non-specific in character. For this reason the reactions to PPD-S and PPD-G were combined in the cross-tabulations of data; any person with a tuberculin reaction of five or more millimeters of induration to either or both tuberculins was called a reactor.

All comparisons were made between subgroups of persons who were over fifteen years of age. At that age the infection rate for onchocerciasis had become stable (90+ percent), and growth-related variations in body weight, height, and skinfold thickness were minimal. Figure 4–18 shows the frequency distribution of serum gamma globulins for reactors and non-reactors. As can be

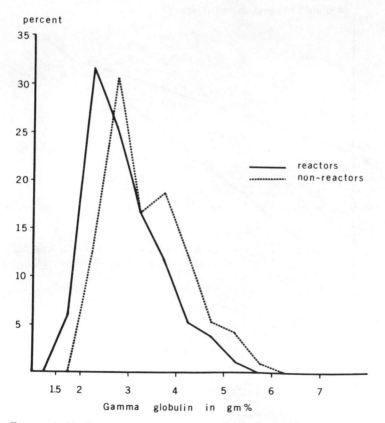

FIGURE 4–18. FREQUENCY DISTRIBUTION OF SERUM GAMMA GLOBULIN LEVELS AMONG REACTORS AND NON-REACTORS TO TUBERCULIN (PPD-S AND PPD-G COMBINED), OULI BANGALA

seen, the non-reactors had higher gamma globulin levels than the reactors.

Figure 4–19 presents the regression lines of skinfold thickness on the weight/height ratio for the two reaction classes. Because of significant sex differences in skinfold thickness, body weight, and height after the age of puberty, the analyses were made separately for each sex. Since the results of these analyses are similar, only the data for the males are presented in Figure 4–19. The results indicate that the non-reactors had relatively thicker skinfolds for corresponding weight/height ratios than did the reactors to tuberculin. This discrepancy is more pronounced for low weight/height ratios.

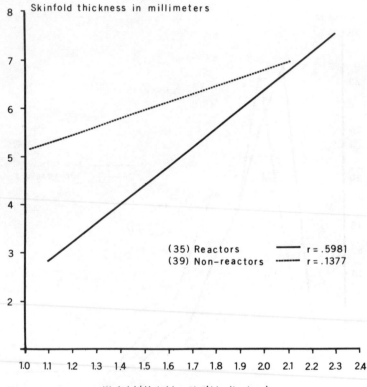

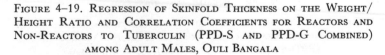

FIGURE 4–19. REGRESSION OF SKINFOLD THICKNESS ON THE WEIGHT/ HEIGHT RATIO AND CORRELATION COEFFICIENTS FOR REACTORS AND NON-REACTORS TO TUBERCULIN (PPD-S AND PPD-G COMBINED) AMONG ADULT MALES, OULI BANGALA

Generally, the magnitude of the variations in height of adult males in Ouli Bangala was much smaller that that of variations in weight. Therefore, a low weight/height ratio indicated an underweight condition rather than tallness and slenderness.

A comparative analysis for the relative significance of differences in the reaction status of individuals with hypergammaglobulinemia, low weight/height ratio, presence of onchocercal dermatitis (clinical diagnosis), and pachyderma (skinfold thickness) was made by a combined Chi-square test of 2 × 2 contingency tables (Cochran, 1954). The results are shown in Tables 4–40 and 4–41. The group means for the variables examined in the table were computed separately for each sex. The relative deviation of the individual measurement from the corresponding mean was indicated as + (above) and − (below). Thereafter the two sexes were combined and the entire group was examined for differences in the prevalence of skin reaction which were associated with specified host factors. The tables show that a low weight/height ratio, relative hypergammaglobulinemia, and excess skinfold thickness in persons who were underweight and had a clinical diagnosis of onchocercal dermatitis were closely associated with the non-reactor status. The statistical significance of the difference in prevalence of tuberculin reactions is indicated for each factor by a Chi-square and P Value.

The two main reasons for being underweight were chronic malnutrition and consumptive disease. In order to determine the relative importance of each of these factors in causing the suppression of delayed skin reactions, data obtained from nutritional histories were utilized. A comparison of individuals whose weight/height ratios were either above or below the mean shows large differences in the interval between the interview and the last meal at which meat or fish was eaten. The difference between the two groups was 2.5 days (P = 0.02) for fish and 30.7 days (P = 0.07) for meat. These data support the interpretation that underweight was at least partially caused by malnutrition. The probability that chronic, systemic, and severe infection of the skin could also determine the reactor status of an individual is suggested by the results of microfilarial counts (*O. volvulus*) from skin snips. These results show that the percentage (age adjusted) of reactions to PPD-S and PPD-G decreases as worm densities increase. Further studies to elucidate this interesting problem are scheduled for the near future.

Skin Ulcers. Ulcers, defined in this study as any open skin lesion with a diameter of at least two centimeters, were found with varying

TABLE 4–40. The Statistical Significance of Differences in the Prevalence of Reactions to PPD-S and PPD-G in Relation to Weight/Height Ratio, Skinfold Thickness, and Presence of Onchocercal Dermatitis, and the Subdivision of the Chi-Square into Components (2 × 8 Table)

Weight/Height Ratio	Skinfold Thickness	Onchocercal Dermatitis	Degrees of Freedom	Sum of Squares	Chi-Square	P
Below mean	Below mean	Present vs absent	1	0.0305	0.124	0.8
Below mean	Above mean	Present vs absent	1	1.1856	4.809	0.03
Above mean	Below mean	Present vs absent	1	0.1917	0.777	0.4
Above mean	Above mean	Present vs absent	1	0.1143	0.464	0.5
Below mean	Above mean vs below mean		1	0.3920	1.590	0.2
Above mean	Above mean vs below mean		1	0.0189	0.077	0.9
Above mean vs below mean			1	5.7639	23.377	<0.001
		Total	7	7.6969	31.218	<0.001

182

TABLE 4–41. THE STATISTICAL SIGNIFICANCE OF DIFFERENCES OF REACTIONS TO PPD-S AND PPD-G IN RELATION TO SERUM GAMMA GLOBULIN AND WEIGHT/HEIGHT RATIO, AND THE SUBDIVISION OF THE CHI-SQUARE INTO COMPONENTS (2 × 4 TABLE)

Gamma Globulin Level	Weight/Height Ratio	Degrees of Freedom	Sum of Squares	Chi-Square	P
Above mean	Above mean *vs* below mean	1	1.8954	7.652	0.006
Below mean	Above mean *vs* below mean	1	1.4050	5.672	0.02
Above mean *vs* below mean		1	2.0160	8.139	0.004
	Total	3	5.3164	21.463	<0.001

183

frequency in the five Chadian villages. The highest prevalence was observed in Ouli Bangala, where 13.1 percent of the residents had these lesions; the lowest was seen in Ouarai, where 1.9 percent of the population sample had ulcers. A subdivision into broader etiological categories was made possible by the residents' medical histories. Three classes were established, namely, post-traumatic ulcers, ulcers associated with pyoderma, and a third group for which the etiology was unknown. When this classification was used to make geographical comparisons, it appeared that most of the ulcers of unknown etiology occurred among the residents of the four southern villages. In Ouli Bangala many persons had ulcers of the pyoderma type. These were associated with skin lesions produced by *O. volvulus*, especially with filarial scabies (*gâle filarienne*).

Mycobacteria have recently been recovered from large ulcers of Africans. Subsequently, *Mycobacterium ulcerans* was identified as the etiological agent of these lesions in widely separated areas of Uganda and the Congo (Connor and Fletcher Lunn, 1965 and 1966). These findings made it appear worthwhile to study the association between the prevalence of skin reactions to PPD-S and that of reactions to PPD-G among persons with and without ulcers. Because of gross deficiencies in skin reactivity to these tuberculins in Ouli Bangala, the comparisons were restricted to the populations of Djimtilo, Ouarai, and Boum Khebir, where most ulcers of unidentified etiology were seen. Table 4–42 shows the age-specific prevalence of skin reactions to PPD-S and PPD-G among the combined populations of the three villages and among ulcer patients. For both types of antigen more reactions were observed in individ-

TABLE 4–42. PREVALENCE OF TUBERCULIN REACTIONS IN THE GENERAL POPULATION[a] AND AMONG PATIENTS WITH CHRONIC ULCERS

Age (years)	General Population			Ulcer Patients		
	No. Tested	Percentage PPD-S Reactors	Percentage PPD-G Reactors	No. Tested	Percentage PPD-S Reactors	Percentage PPD-G Reactors
Birth–9	330	20.3	46.0	9	55.6	88.9
10–49	580	51.7	79.3	10	60.0	90.0
50+	139	36.0	68.3	5	20.0	60.0
Total	1,049	39.7	67.4	24	54.2	87.5

[a] Included are the total population samples of Djimtilo, Ouarai, and Boum Khebir.

uals who had ulcers than in the general population, but only the difference for PPD-G reactions was statistically significant (P = 0.04). The data indicate that the discrepancy in the percentage of tuberculin reactions was largest in children.

The results suggest that ulcers promote the establishment of infections with certain mycobacteria, either by providing conditions that are favorable to the saprophytic growth of the agents in lesions or by active infection through tissue invasion. It is assumed that the subsequent development of specific skin hypersensitivity may result from both types of infection.

Leprosy. Leprosy is a disease of major public health importance in Chad (see Table 4–1). The highest concentration of cases was found in the southern part of Chad, below eleven degrees north latitude. The peculiar geographical distribution of leprosy in the Republic is also evident from our study. The disease was recognized in seven (1.7 percent) residents of Ouli Bangala, in one (0.4 percent) of Ouarai, and in five (1.5 percent) of Boum Khebir. Of these thirteen cases, five were classified as tuberculoid and eight as lepromatous forms of the disease. The excess of lepromatous leprosy cases suggests that the prevalence estimates for leprosy may be too low; the difficulty lies in recognizing the milder tuberculoid form of the disease in population samples where abnormal skin conditions of varied etiology abound. Although only 5 of the 374 residents of Boum Khebir were found to have leprosy, 94 cases had been registered in the dispensary which serves the entire canton. The over-all prevalence of leprosy in the subprefecture of Kyabe, to which Boum Khebir belongs, was 2.19 percent, only slightly higher than that in our sample (Ziegler, 1967).

At the time the team worked in Boum Khebir, a research associate of the Department of International Health of the Johns Hopkins School of Hygiene and Public Health was assigned to the group to attempt isolations of mycobacteria from skin biopsies. These were taken from the ear lobes of all persons in the sample. The specimens were then examined for mycobacteria by a concentration method described by Kar, Elliston, and Taylor (1964). In 19, or 5.1 percent of the 372 specimens examined, acid-fast bacilli were recovered. A study of the distribution of these 19 cases revealed that 8, or 42.1 percent, were children under eight years of age, and that of the 11 adults 8 were females and 3 males. None of the cases belonged to a family in which a member had clinically recognized leprosy. With the exception of 2 individuals who were members of the same household, the cases were found scattered in different families. One case was a seven-year-old boy in whose specimen fifty acid-fast bacilli were found on a single slide. The possibility that the unknown mycobacterial agent is one capable of inducing a hypersensitivity reaction to PPD-G is reflected by the findings from the skin tests. With the exception of three children who were less than six years old, all persons with mycobacteria in their ear lobes reacted to PPD-G (84.2 percent). The largest reaction size to the Gause antigen in this group of residents was observed in the boy who had numerous bacilli in his tissue specimen. The induration size of his skin reaction was twenty-two millimeters in diameter.

Whether persons from whom acid-fast bacilli are recovered can be regarded as healthy carriers of leprosy bacilli or whether the findings are merely indicative of a more ubiquitous infection with unclassified mycobacteria of little or no pathogenicity cannot be determined at this time. Recent studies by Nishimura *et al.* (1965) suggest that the presence of acid-fast bacilli in the skin may be merely coincidental, because they recovered acid-fast bacilli from a high percentage of healthy persons who had had no contact with leprosy patients.

Treponematoses

Of the human treponematoses, three are known to occur in Chad: venereal syphilis, endemic syphilis, and yaws. Venereal syphilis has been reported from all major areas of the country; foci of endemic syphilis have been recognized in the northern and northeastern sections of the Republic, namely, in the prefectures of Kanem, Batha, Biltine, and Ouaddai. Endemic yaws, once an important public health problem in Chad, has been brought under control in most areas, but residual foci exist in the prefectures of Salamat, Mayo-Kebbi, Moyen-Chari, and Chari Baguirmi. During our pilot study, six communities were selected for investigation. They included a town (Guéréda, in the prefecture of Biltine) with cases of endemic syphilis, another (Boum Khebir) in which yaws was known to occur, and four villages (Djimtilo, Ouli Bangala, Ouarai, and Faya-Largeau) where sporadic cases of venereal syphilis could be expected. Unfortunately, the increased guerrilla activities in the northeast of Chad made it impossible for the team to revisit Guéréda. While it has been possible by mass treatment campaigns to reduce considerably the level of endemicity of yaws, complete eradication of the disease is difficult, for two reasons. The first is the inaccessibility of the areas where yaws is endemic; the second is the high degree of absenteeism which prevailed when mass treatment was given to the residents in endemic areas by mobile teams of the Service des Grandes Endémies (Ziegler, 1967).

Estimates of the prevalence of infections with treponemes were made by the Venereal Disease Research Laboratory Slide Flocculation Test (VDRL), the Fluorescent Treponemal Antibody-Absorption Test (FTA-ABS), and by physical examinations for clinical signs of syphilis and yaws. Since only a cursory examination of the genitals was acceptable to most persons in the samples, it is realized that the prevalence estimates of genital lesions in syphilis and yaws may be deficient. Primary lesions of syphilis were recognized in one male resident of Djimtilo and in one of Ouli Bangala. In both communities, cases of gonorrhea also were diagnosed (see Skin Diseases and Conditions, pp. 223–25). Of the clinical signs that have a relatively high pathognomonic significance for yaws, the following were found in the population samples: gangosa, juxta-articular nodes, and saber shin. The highest prevalence was observed in Boum Khebir, where six, or 1.7 percent, of the residents had such abnormalities. In Ouli Bangala one person had gangosa and another saber shin. In Djimtilo two persons were tentatively diagnosed as having late yaws or syphilis (one with gangosa, one with saber shin). No clinical evidence of yaws was found among the inhabitants of Ouarai and Faya-Largeau.

Figures 4–20 and 4–21 show the age-specific percentages of reactions in the FTA-ABS and VDRL tests for all five communities. The highest prevalence in both tests was found in Boum Khebir, where yaws had been hyperendemic until 1961–63, when mass treatment with penicillin was given to residents of all ages. Since infections with *Treponema pertenue* in endemic areas are usually acquired in childhood, it could be expected that the removal of infectious cases by the treatment campaigns would have an effect on the serological profile of the population. This is reflected by the low prevalence of FTA reactions among children under ten years of age. The fact that the eradication of yaws has not yet been achieved in the area is also evident from the curve for Boum Khebir; the sera of some of the children who were born after the mass treatment campaign were reactive in the FTA tests. A comparison of Figures 4–20 and 4–21 shows that reactives were generally more prevalent

in the FTA test than in the VDRL test, with the exception of
children under ten years of age, where the situation was reversed.
These findings can be interpreted by means of differences in the
diagnostic capacities of the two tests. The VDRL test is less specific

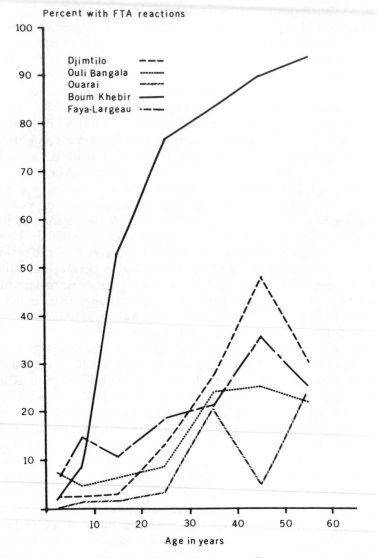

FIGURE 4–20. PREVALENCE OF SEROLOGIC REACTIONS IN THE
FLUORESCENT TREPONEMAL ANTIBODY-ABSORPTION TEST BY AGE

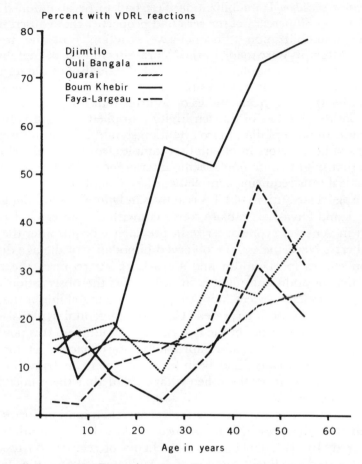

FIGURE 4–21. PREVALENCE OF SEROLOGIC REACTIONS IN THE
VENEREAL DISEASE RESEARCH LABORATORY SLIDE
FLOCCULATION TEST BY AGE

for treponematoses; false positive reactions may result from a
variety of active infections that occur more frequently in children
than in adults. On the other hand, the observed preponderance of
reactions to the FTA test in the adult population can be explained
by a longer persistence of antibodies to *T. pallidum* in treated and
untreated persons with treponematoses, compared to the longevity
of the antilipids that are detected by the VDRL test.

The original plans for studying the sero-epidemiology of yaws
thoroughly by including systematic examinations of all sera in the

Treponema pallidum Immobilization Test had to be abandoned because almost 80 percent of the sera had properties that caused non-specific immobilization ("inconclusive reaction") of the treponemes. Attempts were made by the Neurath technique of euglobulin precipitation (see Chapter 5) to improve the quality of the sera for the TPI test. While it was possible to test the majority of the sera, it became apparent from studies of controls that the procedure led to a considerable loss of test sensitivity if applied to small volumes of serum. In our opinion, more attention should be paid to investigations of host factors in population samples from underdeveloped areas that might cause non-specific interference with the results of serological tests requiring complement (see Chapter 5).

The age distributions of FTA reactives in Djimtilo, Ouli Bangala, Ouarai, and Faya-Largeau are consistent with the pattern normally found in venereal syphilis; a rise in prevalence begins after the age of puberty. Nevertheless, the observed bimodality of the age distribution curves for Djimtilo and Faya-Largeau requires the consideration of additional factors in order that the observation that serological reactions were more frequent in young children than in adolescents may be interpreted. Cases of congenital syphilis were not recognized in either of the two Arab communities. It is possible that infections with certain saprophytic spirochaetes, as, for example, *T. microdentium*, had been more prevalent in Djimtilo and Faya-Largeau than in the other villages, and that these infections caused cross-reactions in the FTA test.

The protocol of standardized physical examination forms required that the presence or absence of skin depigmentations be registered. In accordance with the schema of registration used in previous studies (Buck, Sasaki, and Anderson, 1968), the depigmentations were further subclassified into leucoderma with and without scarring, as well as according to whether they were larger or smaller than two by two centimeters in diameter. Depigmentations of the skin are known as sequelae of syphilis and yaws and also are found frequently in onchocerciasis. Therefore, their occurrence was examined for associations with seroreactivity in the FTA-ABS test and with proved onchocerciasis. The results are presented in Table 4–43. Leucoderma without scarring in the residents of Djimtilo and Boum Khebir was significantly associated with positive reactions in the FTA tests; skin depigmentations in the population of Ouli Bangala were closely correlated with onchocerciasis.

TABLE 4–43. PREVALENCE OF SKIN DEPIGMENTATIONS, BY SIZE AND SCARRING

Type of Depigmentation	Percentage[a] with Condition				
	Djimtilo (N = 376)	Ouli Bangala (N = 394)	Ouarai (N = 364)	Boum Khebir (N = 374)	Faya-Largeau (N = 204)
With scarring	17.8	35.5	38.3	13.0	19.7
Without scarring < 2 X 2 cm	7.0[b]	7.9[c]	4.7	3.0[d]	2.9
Without scarring > 2 X 2 cm	0.4[b]	7.4[c]	0.8	1.2[d]	0.5

[a] Percentages listed are age adjusted.
[b] Significantly associated with reactions in FTA-ABS tests (P = 0.01).
[c] Significantly associated with onchocerciasis (P = < 0.01).
[d] Significantly associated with reactions in FTA-ABS tests (P = 0.04).

The results of a similar analysis of the association between FTA reactions and the presence of ulcers were inconclusive.

Elongation and widening of the aorta were detected on chest roentgenograms of various individuals in the population samples. All radiological diagnoses were made independently by specialists who had no knowledge of other findings made in the study. Although generally considered non-specific as a pathognomonic sign of syphilitic mesaortitis, the presence of tortuous aorta in African peasants could be indicative of cardiovascular syphilis, since high blood pressure and hypercholesterolemia were quite uncommon in these population samples. A comparison of individuals with and without radiological evidence of elongation or widening of the aorta for differences in the prevalence of FTA reactions revealed a significant association between the two conditions among the residents of Ouli Bangala, but not in the other four villages. This association is described in Table 4–44. The prevalence of FTA reactions among persons with specified pathological signs of the aorta was much higher than that among those who had a normal aorta. The relative risk (adjusted for age) of having a positive FTA test was 4.1 times higher for persons with widening or elongation of the aorta than for the group without these abnormalities. The results suggest that a significant proportion of the persons for whom radiological findings revealed an abnormal aorta had mesaortitis syphilitica.

TABLE 4–44. ASSOCIATION BETWEEN REACTOR STATUS IN FTA ABSORPTION TESTS AND PATHOLOGY OF AORTA
IN ROUTINE CHEST ROENTGENOGRAMS, OULI BANGALA

Age (years)	No. X-ray Exams	Radiological Diagnosis										Total FTA-ABS Reactive	
		Aorta Normal			Aorta Elongated			Aorta Tortuous					
		No. in Group	FTA-ABS Reactive		No. in Group	FTA-ABS Reactive		No. in Group	FTA-ABS Reactive				
			No.	%		No.	%		No.	%		No.	%
10–19	43	42	2	4.8	1	0	—	0	0	—		2	4.7
20–29	48	47	3	6.4	1	0	—	0	0	—		3	6.3
30–39	32	25	4	16.0	5	2	40.0	2	2	100.0		8	25.0
40–49	20	17	3	17.6	3	3	100.0	0	0	—		6	30.0
50+	14	11	1	9.1	3	2	66.7	0	0	—		3	21.4
Total	157	142	13	9.2	13	7	53.8	2	2	100.0		22	14.0

Plague

All sera were examined in complement fixation tests with *Pasteurella pestis* antigen, but 140 specimens had to be excluded from the epidemiological analyses because of anticomplementary activity. Seven, or 0.5 percent, of the 1,466 sera were found to be reactive in the tests. Of these seven cases, one (43 y male) was a resident of Djimtilo, another (7 y male) lived in Ouli Bangala, three were male residents of Ouarai (3 y, 12 y, 43 y), one was an eight-year-old boy from Boum Khebir, and the seventh was a seven-year-old girl from Faya-Largeau. There was no evidence from the medical histories to suggest that any one of these persons had suffered from bubonic plague. No information was available from the studies which would have permitted a relating of the serological findings to case histories that were consistent with tularemia or with diseases caused by other pasteurellae, such as *P. pseudotuberculosis* or *P. multocida*.

Brucellosis

The prevalence of residual antibodies from past infections with *Brucella melitensis* or *B. abortus* was estimated from the results of card tests for brucellosis (see Chapter 5). A total of 11, or 0.7 percent, of the 1,609 sera examined were found to be reactive in the test. Of these, one case was found in each of the population samples of Ouli Bangala, Ouarai, Boum Khebir, and Faya-Largeau, but seven persons in Djimtilo had reactive sera. For this reason the age distribution of reactors in Djimtilo is shown in Table 4–45. Four of the

TABLE 4–45. AGE DISTRIBUTION OF REACTIONS IN
BRUCELLOSIS CARD TEST, DJIMTILO

Age (years)	Number Examined	Reactive	
		Number	Percentage
Birth–4	37	0	—
5–9	44	0	—
10–19	65	1	1.5
20–29	51	2	3.9
30–39	76	1	1.3
40–49	27	0	—
50+	47	3	6.3
Total	347	7	2.0

TABLE 4-46. GEOGRAPHICAL DISTRIBUTION OF SEROLOGICAL REACTIONS IN SLIDE
AGGLUTINATION TESTS WITH FOUR ANTIGEN POOLS OF *Leptospira* SEROTYPES

Antigen	Djimtilo (N = 341)		Ouli Bangala (N = 368)		Ourai (N = 280)		Boum Khebir (N = 334)		Faya-Largeau (N = 188)	
	No.	%	No.	%	No.	%	No.	%	No.	%
Pool 1										
L. ballum	1	0.3	9	2.4	2	0.7	2	0.6	0	—
L. canicola										
L. icterohaemor-rhagiae										
Pool 2										
L. bataviae	1	0.3	0	—	1	0.4	2	0.6	0	—
L. grippotyphosa										
L. pyrogenes										
Pool 3										
L. autumnalis	2	0.6	1	0.3	3	1.1	1	0.3	0	—
L. pomona										
L. sejroe										
Pool 4										
L. australis	0	—	1	0.3	0	—	1	0.3	0	—
L. hyos										
L. mini, georgia										
Total	4	1.2	11	3.0	6	2.2	6	1.8	0	—

seven individuals were women and three were men; there was no evidence of a familial aggregation of the reactors. The geographical arrangement of the cases by household in the five communities parallels the distribution of the number of domestic animals, which can serve as reservoirs for *Brucella*.

Leptospirosis

A summary of the results of slide macro-agglutination tests for leptospirosis is shown in Table 4–46. *Leptospira* infections were more frequent in Ouli Bangala, where rat eating was quite common, than in the other four communities. No antibodies to leptospirae were detected in the population sample of Faya-Largeau. When compared with many of the other diseases and infections described in this report, the epidemiological importance of leptospirosis appears to be relatively low in Chad.

Enteric Bacteria

Rectal swabs for bacteriological examinations of slow- or non-lactose-fermenting enteric bacteria were taken in the five study villages from all children who were under ten years of age. A summary for regional comparisons of the findings is shown in Table 4–47. Specimens producing colonies on MacConkey or SS agar which did not have the typical appearance of *Escherichia coli* were found in eighty-two, or 14.4 percent, of the children examined. These were identified according to species. Furthermore, the somatic (O) and flagellar (H) antigen groups of all slow- and non-lactose-fermenting colonies of *E. coli* were determined when possible. Among the isolates was a new serotype of *Salmonella* (6,7:k:17) from a four-year-old child in Ouli Bangala. The notes to Table 4–47 contain a complete list of the pathogenic or facultatively pathogenic agents that were recovered in Chad.

For clues to the pathogenicity of individual bacteria, the prevalence of diarrhea in each group of children from which a specific genus was recovered by rectal swabs was compared to that of the total sample of children in the study. The results are listed in Table 4–48. As can be seen, there were statistically significant differences for children who harbored *Shigella* and *Aeromonas*. Of the latter group, all but one of the isolates were *A. shigelloides*. It is realized that the number of cases is too small to provide conclusive

TABLE 4–47. PREVALENCE OF PATHOGENIC AND FACULTATIVELY PATHOGENIC
ENTEROBACTERIA ISOLATED FROM RECTAL SWABS OF
CHILDREN UNDER TEN YEARS OF AGE

	Percentage of Isolated Enterobacteria					
Enterobacterial Group Isolated	Djimtilo (N = 108)	Ouli Bangala (N = (137)	Ouarai (N = 133)	Boum Khebir (N = 135)	Faya- Largeau (N = 55)	No. of Isola- tions
Salmonella	0	1.5ᵃ	0.8ᵇ	0	0	3
Shigella	1.9ᶜ	1.5ᵈ	0.8ᵉ	0	0	5
Bethesda	0	0	0	0	0	0
Arizona	0	0	0.8	0	0	1ᶠ
Providence	0.9	1.5	0	0.7	0	4ᵍ
Edwardsiella	1.9	0	0.8	3.0	0	7ʰ
Alkalescens-Dispar	0.9	0	0	0	0	1ⁱ
Alcaligenes	0.9	0	0	0	0	1ʲ
Aeromonas	4.5	0.7	2.3	0.7	0	10ᵏ
Slow- or non-lactose fermenting Escherichia	5.6	9.5	13.5	0	23.6	50ˡ
Total	16.6	14.7	19.0	4.4	23.6	82

ᵃ One new *Salmonella* serotype 6,7:k:17, and one *S. kingston*.
ᵇ *S. chandans*.
ᶜ One *Shigella boÿdii* and one *Sh. dysenteriae*.
ᵈ Two *Sh. dysenteriae*.
ᵉ One *Sh. boydii*.
ᶠ *Arizona* sp.
ᵍ Three *Providence alcalifaciens* and one *P. stuartii*.
ʰ *Edwardsiella tarda*.
ⁱ *Alkalescens-Dispar* sp.
ʲ *Alcaligenes* sp.
ᵏ Nine *Aeromonas shigelloides* and one *A. hydrophila*.
ˡ Sixteen *Escherichia coli* O Group undetermined, non-motile; five *E. coli* O Group
50, non-motile; four *E. coli* O Group 0119, non-motile; three *E. coli* O Group 25,
non-motile; two *E. coli* O Group 4:H5; two *E. coli* O Group 145:H4; and one each
of the following: O Group 1:H7; O Group X3, non-motile; O Group 4:H40; O Group
5, non-motile; O Group 16:H6; O Group 39:H48; O Group 60, non-motile; O Group
73:H18; O Group 81, non-motile; O Group 99, non-motile; O Group 115:H undetermined; O Group 123, non-motile; O Group 131:H21; O Group 132:H undetermined;
O undetermined:H10; O undetermined:H11; O undetermined:H4; and O undeter-
mined:H28.
Identifications were either made or confirmed by the Enteric Bacteriology Unit,
National Communicable Disease Center, Atlanta, Georgia.

evidence that the two groups of agents had caused diarrhea. The
over-all prevalence of diarrhea among children on examination day
was 25.4 percent. Removal of all cases with isolations of known or
suspected pathogens still leaves a large majority of children with

diarrhea for which the etiology remains unknown. It is emphasized that, unlike the more static prevalence of intestinal parasites, the percentages of isolations of enterobacteria cannot be used to generalize about regional differences by projecting the figures into the future or the past. Seasonal and interspersed local epidemics may change the isolation rates abruptly and shift the highest prevalence from one village to another.

TABLE 4–48. PREVALENCE OF DIARRHEA ON EXAMINATION DAY AMONG CHILDREN WITH ISOLATIONS OF PATHOGENIC AND FACULTATIVELY PATHOGENIC BACILLI FROM RECTAL SWABS

All Children from Birth to Nine Years of Age	Total No.	With Diarrhea		Chi-Square of Difference (all children vs groups with isolates)	P
		No.	%		
	568	144	25.4		
With *Salmonella*	3	2	66.7	2.68	0.12
With *Shigella*	5	4	80.0	7.73	0.01
With *Arizona*	1	1			
With *Providence*	4	0	—		
With *Edwardsiella*	7	2	28.6	0.04	0.8
With *Alkalescens-Dispar*	1	1			
With *Alcaligenes*	1	0	—		
With *Aeromonas*	10	6	60.0	6.14	0.02
With slow- or non-lactose-fermenting *Escherichia*	50	17	34.0	1.78	0.2
With isolates of any "atypical" enteric bacilli	82	33	40.2	8.02	<0.01

Meningococcal Meningitis

In the African countries north of the equator and south of the Sahara, the incidence of cerebrospinal meningitis has remained high for many years. Annual outbreaks of the disease in Chad have been reported regularly since 1955, with major epidemics occurring in

1955, 1957, and 1967 (Ziegler, 1968), the year in which our study was conducted. The over-all fatality rate among the 13,506 meningitis patients diagnosed since 1955 is 13.2 percent (Ziegler, 1968). Table 4–49 shows the geographical distribution (by prefecture) of the cases in the last epidemic. Three of the areas listed were represented by communities included in our study. Two patients with meningitis, a seven-year-old girl and a forty-two-year-old man, were treated with penicillin and sulfadiazine by a physician of our team during his stay in Ouli Bangala; both recovered. There are pronounced seasonal variations in the incidence of meningococcal meningitis in Chad (see Figure 4–22). The peak usually occurs in March, the month our team worked in Ouli Bangala; the incidence of the disease drops sharply with the onset of the rainy season.

TABLE 4–49. GEOGRAPHICAL DISTRIBUTION OF REPORTED CASES OF
EPIDEMIC MENINGITIS IN CHAD, 1967, AND CASE FATALITY RATES[a]

Prefecture	Representation of Area by Study Community	Number of Cases Reported	Percentage of Total	Case Fatality Rate (%)
Ouaddai		193	29.4	18.1
La Tjandilé		140	21.3	19.3
Logone Occidental	Ouli Bangala	101	15.4	23.8
Biltine		92	14.0	6.5
Guéra		68	10.4	42.6
Mayo-Kebbi		23	3.5	8.7
Salamat		20	2.9	5.0
Logone Oriental		7	1.1	14.3
Moyen Chari	Boum Khebir Ouarai	7	1.1	14.3
Chari Baguirmi	Djimtilo	6	0.9	50.0
Total		657	100.0	19.6

[a] Prepared from data furnished by Dr. Pierre Ziegler, director of the Service des Grandes Endémies, Fort Lamy (1968).

Rickettsioses

All sera available from the study were screened for antibodies in CF tests with group-specific antigens of *Rickettsia prowazecki*, *R. mooseri*, *R. rickettsii*, and *Coxiella burneti* (see Chapter 5). Reactions

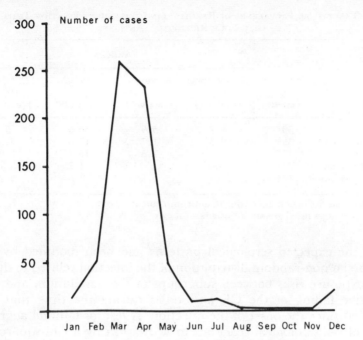

FIGURE 4–22. MONTHLY INCIDENCE OF CEREBROSPINAL MENIN-
GITIS IN CHAD, 1967

to the antigens in these tests were detected in varying frequencies among the residents of the five study areas; these findings are summarized in Table 4–50. In Djimtilo, Ouli Bangala, and Ouarai the sera of many persons contained antibodies to *R. rickettsii*. This is interpreted as an indication of past infection with *R. conorii* or a closely related agent that reacts with the group-specific antigen of *R. rickettsii*.

At the time of our study no clinical cases of boutonneuse fever were observed. The geographical distribution of antibodies to tick-borne *Rickettsiae* corresponds well with findings made by the entomologist. Most of the ticks that are known or suspected vectors of boutonneuse fever were found in Djimtilo. The collection included *Rhipicephalus sanguineus*, *R. simus*, *R. evertsi evertsi*, *Hyalomma truncatum*, *H. marginatum rufipes*, *H. impeltatum*, and *Amblyomma sparsum*. The prevalence of CF reactions to *R. rickettsii* in the general populations of Djimtilo, Ouli Bangala, and Ouarai showed little variation among different age groups. This observation suggested

TABLE 4–50. PREVALENCE OF REACTIONS IN COMPLEMENT FIXATION TESTS
WITH FOUR RICKETTSIAL ANTIGENS

| | | Antigen | | | |
| | | R. prowazecki (% reactive[b]) | R. mooseri (% reactive[b]) | R. rickettsii (% reactive[b]) | C. burneti (% reactive[b]) |
Village	No. Tested[a]				
Djimtilo	301	4.7	5.9	33.9	0
Ouli Bangala	363	0.3	1.7	17.9	3.3
Ouarai	323	0	2.5	16.4	1.9
Boum Khebir	278	0	0	2.2	0.7
Faya-Largeau	194	0	0.5	0.5	6.2

[a] Deficiency of denominator due to anticomplementary sera.
[b] Percentages listed are age adjusted.

that the expected serological patterns had been modified by two
factors: a non-random distribution of the infection related to different exposure risks between subgroups of the population, and progressive fading of the CF antibodies during the time that had
elapsed since the onset of the infection. A test for familial aggregation of the serological reactions to R. rickettsii by a Chi-square test
of variance (Cochran, 1954) showed that a familial distribution of
cases as uneven as the one observed in Djimtilo could have arisen
in less than 1 percent of the samples (P = 0.01) if chance alone had
been operating. The corresponding probability for the familial
clustering of cases in Ouli Bangala was P = 0.03. In contrast, the
distribution of antibodies among the residents of Ouarai was not
significantly different from what would be expected in a random
allocation of cases.

Antibodies indicative of a history of epidemic typhus were detected in fourteen residents of Djimtilo and in one of Ouli Bangala.
The cases in Djimtilo were concentrated in only four families. A
test for familial aggregation by the method described above was
statistically significant (P = 0.001).

In contrast to the findings for epidemic typhus, the CF test reactions to R. mooseri were distributed in a random fashion in the
four communities where residual antibodies of murine typhus were
detected.

Past episodes of Q fever, as indicated by the serological reactions
in CF tests with Coxiella burneti antigen, appeared to have occurred
more frequently in the Saharan community of Faya-Largeau than

in the other four villages. Of the twelve individuals whose sera were reactive in the test, seven were children and five adults; of these, all but one were females. Camels were kept by all families in which a member had antibodies to *C. burneti*. At least seven of the twelve cases occurred in households that were engaged in annual caravan travel.

Virus Diseases and Infections

Smallpox

With the exception of a thirty-nine-year-old male resident of Faya-Largeau who had typical pockmarks, no residual scars from smallpox were detected among persons included in the five population samples. Smallpox vaccination scars were found in 84 percent of all persons examined, while 93.4 percent replied in the health interview that they had been vaccinated. As a result of vigorous campaigns on the part of vaccination teams of the Service des Grandes Endémies, recently assisted by AID, the annual incidence of smallpox in Chad had dropped from 2,789 reported cases in 1952 ($\pm$ 9.3/10,000) to 86 ($\pm$ 0.3/10,000) in 1967 (Ziegler, 1968). Vaccination coverage is still deficient in the inaccessible eastern and northern parts of Chad and among the widely scattered small hamlets in the Lake Chad region. In the 1967 outbreak the source of the infection could be traced to six primary cases in three different areas. All of these were travelers, including pilgrims to Mecca, who had passed the western border of Chad without being checked by public health officers. While good vaccination coverage in Fort Lamy and Moussoro prevented the development of secondary cases in these two cities, a small epidemic erupted in some of the hamlets of the Lake Chad region from a single primary case.

Measles

The high prevalence and fatality rates of measles among young children make the disease a major public health problem in Chad (Ziegler, 1968). Vaccination campaigns with attenuated rubeola virus have been carried out since 1965. However, at the time of our study the vaccination coverage in the population group at risk (six-month-to-six-year-old children) was still incomplete, partly because of the newness of the program and partly because of difficulties in reaching large parts of the population who lived in remote or politically unstable areas.

Outbreaks of measles in Chad show marked seasonal variations, the highest incidence being recorded between March and May, the three hottest months of the year. Although our studies in four of the five villages were conducted during the time of the anticipated annual maximum of rubeola, no cases were observed by the team physicians. Estimates of the degree of immunity in the population samples were made from the results of complement fixation tests with measles antigen. In order to distinguish between naturally acquired and vaccination-induced antibodies, children under six years of age were separated as a special group because they had been the target population of the vaccination campaigns. The results of the complement fixation tests are shown in Table 4–51. According to records available from the central office of the Service des Grandes Endémies, rubeola vaccinations given prior to our study included the children of the four southern villages, but not those of Faya-Largeau. No information was available that would permit an estimation of vaccination coverage among children in the four communities. A regional comparison among the five villages for differences in the cumulative prevalence of naturally acquired antibodies was made by excluding children under ten years of age, since the presence of specific antibodies in this group could indicate both true infections and antibody responses to vaccinations. The age-adjusted percentages of reactions in the complement fixation tests with measles antigen can be ranked as follows: Djimtilo, 58.7 percent; Ouli Bangala, 43.0 percent; Ouarai, 40.2 percent; Faya-Largeau, 27.4 percent; and Boum Khebir, 23.4 percent. The prevalence of serological reactions that indicate a history of measles is closely associated ($r = 0.9628$) with the eastern longitudinal locations of the five villages: Djimtilo, 14°39′; Ouli Bangala, 15°52′; Ouarai, 17°45′; Faya-Largeau, 19°10′; and Boum Khebir, 19°25′. In order to interpret this finding, one has also to consider the relative inaccessibility of these places to major population centers. A ranking of the villages by degree of isolation from major traffic routes would be similar to the ranking of percentages of reactions to the complement fixation test.

The age patterns in the five villages show a prevalence maximum in children, followed by an even decline with progressing age. This tendency is probably related to the lifetime of the specific antibody detected in the complement fixation test (Davis *et al.*, 1968, p. 1210). It appears that, as the interval between the occurrence of the disease and the date the serum sample is obtained increases,

TABLE 4–51. PREVALENCE[a] OF REACTIONS[b] IN COMPLEMENT FIXATION TESTS WITH MEASLES ANTIGEN BY AGE

Age (years)	Djimtilo			Ouli Bangala			Ouarai			Boum Khebir			Faya-Largeau		
	No. Examined	Reactive No.	%	No. Examined	Reactive No.	%	No. Examined	Reactive No.	%	No. Examined	Reactive No.	%	No. Examined	Reactive No.	%
Birth–6	56	35	62.5	76	24	31.6	70	20	28.6	67	9	13.4	36	15	41.7
7–9	20	16	80.0	37	17	45.9	44	18	40.9	35	18	51.4	21	10	47.6
10–19	60	37	61.7	107	55	51.4	70	37	52.9	50	22	44.0	35	15	42.9
20–29	43	29	67.4	64	25	39.1	56	31	55.4	39	8	20.5	33	11	33.3
30–39	60	38	63.3	44	16	36.4	35	11	31.4	23	2	8.6	23	3	13.0
40–49	25	11	44.0	21	8	38.1	19	4	21.1	20	2	10.0	22	3	13.6
50+	37	16	43.2	14	6	42.8	30	4	13.3	44	5	11.4	24	3	12.5
Total	301	182	60.5	363	151	41.6	324	125	38.6	278	66	23.7	194	60	30.9

[a] Deficiencies in denominator due to anticomplementary sera.
[b] Weak reactions included.

fewer individuals will have antibody concentrations that are high enough to be detected by the test. On the other hand, one would have to postulate that the disappearance of complement-fixing antibodies does not indicate a loss of naturally acquired immunity during childhood.

Infectious Hepatitis

From observations made during our four field trips in Chad and from discussions with local physicians in Fort Lamy, Moundou, Fort Archambault, and Abéché it appeared that the incidence of infectious hepatitis is high among non-indigenous, temporary residents of the major cities of the country. Recognizing how difficult it was to make the differential diagnosis of jaundice among natives of Chad, where liver ailments of various etiologies abound, the Service des Grandes Endémies had reported 5,451 cases of infectious hepatitis, with 179 fatalities, in 1967.

Estimating the prevalence of hepatitis in a cross-sectional survey of Chadian villages is difficult for two major reasons. The first is the problem of detecting icterus in dark-skinned individuals, especially when a high prevalence of exterior eye diseases and yellowing of the sclerae further reduce the recognizability of jaundice. The second is the already mentioned difficulty in making the differential diagnosis of hepatitis in residents of areas where hyperendemic malaria, chronic schistosomiasis, capillariasis, and nutritional deficiencies may cause subacute and chronic liver disease. This is reflected in the figures shown in Table 4–52, which lists the percentage of persons who had mentioned episodes of jaundice in their medical histories. A similar lack of specificity exists for hepatomegaly if it is used as a pathognomonic sign of hepatitis in a screening program in Africa. As already shown in Table 4–32, enlargement of the liver was so frequent among the residents of the four southern villages studied that hepatomegaly in certain age groups was the rule rather than the exception.

The more objective methods of determining the level of bilirubin, and that of serum glutamic oxaloacetic (SGOT) or pyruvic (SGPT) transaminase as an indicator of parenchymal damage, are also less specific in serological screening tests for hepatitis than they would be in the population of a highly developed country. An example is shown in Table 4–53, which lists the mean values of these three variables for the population of Ouli Bangala.

TABLE 4–52. PERCENTAGE WITH HISTORY OF JAUNDICE AS ELICITED FROM INERVIEWS

Age (years)	Djimtilo		Ouli Bangala		Ouarai		Boum Khebir		Faya-Largeau	
	No. in Group	% with Jaundice	No. in Group	% with Jaundice	No. in Group	% with Jaundice	No. in Group	% with Jaundice	No. in Group	% with Jaundice
Birth–9	108	4.6	130	7.0	140	32.8	139	2.2	70	0
10–19	64	3.1	110	16.4	71	26.8	63	4.8	34	2.9
20–29	48	0	67	13.6	61	41.0	51	3.9	31	6.5
30–39	76	7.9	51	15.7	36	36.1	35	2.9	21	9.5
40–49	29	13.8	24	4.1	21	33.3	30	3.3	22	0
50+	48	16.7	17	11.8	33	27.3	63	3.2	24	4.2
Total	373	6.7	399	11.8	362	32.8	381	3.1	202	3.0

TABLE 4–53. DISTRIBUTION OF SERUM BILIRUBIN AND TRANSAMINASE
LEVELS (SGOT AND SGPT) AMONG RESIDENTS OF OULI BANGALA

Total Bilirubin			SGOT			SGPT		
Range in mg%	No.	%	Range in Units	No.	%	Range in Units	No.	%
0.5	2	0.6	1–19	227	74.8	1–19	257	85.4
0.5–0.99	37	12.5	20–29	29	9.6	20–29	23	7.6
1.0–1.49	145	48.8	30–39	12	4.0	30–39	9	3.0
1.5–1.99	88	29.6	40–49	16	5.3	40–49	6	2.0
2.0–2.45	15	5.1	50–74	7	2.3	50–74	5	1.7
+2.5	10	3.4	75–99	7	2.3	75–99	1	0.3
			100+	5	1.7	100+	0	0
Total	297	100.0		303	100.0		301	100.0

While the clinical records of hospitals and practicing physicians
in the major cities of Chad leave no doubt that infectious hepatitis
is a serious threat to susceptible persons, reliable measurements of
its incidence and prevalence, as well as of levels of acquired immunity from inapparent infections, must be postponed until specific
methods by which antibodies to hepatitis viruses can be determined are made available.

Trachoma

Of the infectious eye diseases that frequently cause blindness,
two are endemic in Chad, trachoma and onchocerciasis. In our
study, external eye examinations were conducted routinely, but
scrapings from the conjunctiva and examinations for inclusion
bodies were not made. Listed in Table 4–54 for regional comparisons are selected clinical indices of varying degrees of specificity for
trachoma. A characteristic manifestation of established trachoma is
the invasion of the upper limbus by superficial branching vessels.
The upper cornea is the site of pannus involvement because of the
predominant infection in the upper lid. The percentages listed in
Table 4–54 indicate that trachoma is much more frequent at the
southern edge of and in the Sahara than in southern Chad, where
Ouli Bangala, Ouarai, and Boum Khebir are located. Similar but
less pronounced geographical differences exist for entropion, a
typical manifestation of cicatricial trachoma, and for conjunctivitis
in general. The natural cause of the disease is reflected by a perusal

of the age-specific percentages of conjunctivitis, entropion, and pannus shown in Table 4–55. While the prevalence of conjunctivitis declines with progressing age, that of pannus and entropion increases.

TABLE 4–54. PREVALENCE OF SELECTED CLINICAL MANIFESTATIONS
RELATED TO TRACHOMA

Manifestation	Djimtilo %	Ouli Bangala %	Ouarai %	Boum Khebir %	Faya-Largeau %
Conjunctivitis	23.5	3.5	8.9	7.5	17.6
Superior pannus	15.3	0.3	0.6	0.3	16.9
Entropion	8.5	0	1.7	0	1.5
Blindness					
One eye	1.8	5.8	0.8	2.4	3.7
Complete	2.4	3.3	1.4	1.3	4.1
Total	4.2	9.1	2.2	3.7	7.8

TABLE 4–55. PREVALENCE OF CONJUNCTIVITIS, SUPERIOR PANNUS,
AND ENTROPION BY AGE, DJIMTILO

Age (years)	No. Examined	Conjunctivitis No.	Conjunctivitis %	Superior Pannus No.	Superior Pannus %	Entropion No.	Entropion %
Birth–4	62	33	53.2	2	3.2	0	0
5–9	48	22	45.8	8	16.7	0	0
10–14	34	8	23.5	1	2.9	2	5.9
15–19	32	8	25.0	4	12.5	1	3.1
20–29	50	5	10.0	6	12.0	4	8.0
30–39	75	7	9.3	16	21.3	7	9.3
40–49	29	0	0	8	27.6	3	10.3
50–59	27	3	11.1	6	22.2	8	29.6
60+	22	3	13.6	6	27.3	7	31.8
Total	379	89	23.5	57	15.0	32	8.4

The importance of trachoma as a cause of blindness is less evident from the data in Table 4–54. Of the two endemic eye diseases in our samples, onchocerciasis (in Ouli Bangala) was recognized as a more important cause of blindness than the type of endemic trachoma found in the two Arab communities of Djimtilo and Faya-Largeau.

Arbovirus Infections

No serological surveys of arbovirus infections had been carried out in Chad prior to this study. All sera collected by our team were examined by the hemagglutination inhibition (HI) test against the following arboviruses: Group A—Chikungunya, Semliki Forest, and Sindbis; Group B—Yellow Fever, Dengue II, Uganda S, West Nile, and Zika; others—Bunyamwera and Germiston. Selection of these antigens was made by Dr. Winston Price, director of the Kenneth F. Maxcy Laboratories of The Johns Hopkins University School of Hygiene and Public Health. The choice was based on reports from other African countries where the geographical distribution of arbovirus infections was known and which had environmental conditions similar to those found in Chad.

A regional comparison of the results of the HI tests is shown in Table 4–56. Judged by prevalence alone, the following, or antigenically closely related viruses, appeared to be of epidemiological importance in the country in at least one of the five villages: Chikungunya, Yellow Fever, West Nile, Zika, Uganda S, and Germiston. In contrast, relatively few reactions to the virus antigens of Sindbis and Bunyamwera were observed. Representative samples of sera with HI titers of 1:40 or more to any of the viruses included in the study were also examined in neutralization tests for a more specific serological diagnosis. A perusal of the data in Table 4–56 shows that Group A arbovirus infections were important in the four communities south of the Sahara, but not in the oasis of Largeau. In contrast, many residents of the desert town had antibodies to viruses of the Arbo-B Group, although the over-all prevalence was generally lower there than in the southern villages.

A more detailed presentation of the data is given in Figure 4–23, which shows the prevalence of HI reactions by age and location for each of the six selected arboviruses. As can be seen, infections with Chikungunya, West Nile, and Zika viruses were holoendemic in at least one of the southern communities. The age at which the entire population was infected with these viruses varied from place to place; in general, infections occurred at an earlier age among the residents of Boum Khebir than they did among those of the other communities.

The high prevalence of reactions in HI tests with Yellow Fever antigen is the result of mass vaccination with 17D Yellow Fever vaccine (see Vaccinations and Vaccination Histories). Neverthe-

TABLE 4–56. PREVALENCE OF REACTIONS (1:40 OR MORE) IN HEMAGGLUTINATION INHIBITION TESTS FOR SELECTED ARBOVIRUSES

| | Percentage[a] with Titers of 1:40 or More in HI Tests | | | | |
Arboviruses	Djimtilo (N = 353)	Ouli Bangala (N = 382)	Ouarai (N = 338)	Boum Khebir (N = 351)	Faya-Largeau (N = 194)
Arbo-A Group					
Chikungunya	55.6	74.6	60.2	76.3	2.1
Semliki Forest	15.1	16.5	11.3	16.0	—
Sindbis	5.2	—	6.3	2.6	2.1
Arbo-B Group					
Yellow Fever	61.1	47.9	56.4	69.8	40.2
Dengue II	25.6	9.9	12.4	30.5	8.4
Uganda S	31.2	15.6	8.1	38.7	15.6
West Nile	67.1	39.4	65.7	78.2	53.6
Zika	50.1	31.5	68.6	54.4	16.0
Bunyamwera	8.1	6.9	6.9	12.4	—
Germiston	28.0	10.3	8.5	51.7	0.5

[a] Percentages listed are age adjusted.

less, even among persons with negative vaccination histories, there were between 20 and 40 percent who had reactive sera. This finding is not substantiated by reports of clinical cases of the disease.

Neutralization tests were performed on selected sera from each village. In hemagglutination tests all of these sera had titers of 1:40 or more to at least two virus antigens of the same antigenic group. In testing each serum sixteen white mice were used, four each for serum dilutions of 1:2, 1:8, 1:32, and 1:128. Listed in Table 4–57 are the number and percentage of sera with neutralizing antibodies that had protected at least 50 percent of the animals.

The selection of sera for neutralization tests with viruses of Group A was based on two criteria. The first was the presence in HI tests of antibodies to the two antigenically related Chikungunya and Semliki Forest viruses; the second was the demonstration of antibodies to Sindbis antigens in the screening test. The results are presented in Table 4–57. They show that neutralizing antibodies were recovered for both Chikungunya and Semliki Forest viruses. The greater frequency of the former probably reflects the generally higher prevalence of infection with this virus as indicated in Table 4–56. Of the few sera that gave reactions in HI tests with Sindbis antigen, between 22 and 60 percent also had protective antibodies

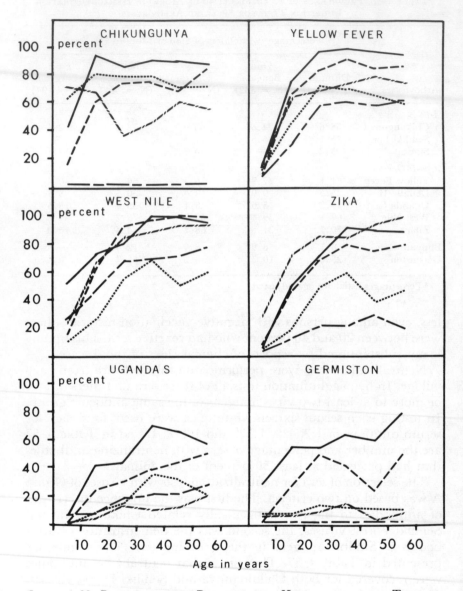

FIGURE 4–23. PREVALENCE OF REACTIONS IN HEMAGGLUTINATION TESTS TO
ARBOVIRUSES BY AGE

------ Djimtilo	——— Boum Khebir
·········· Ouli Bangala	– – – Faya-Largeau
–·–·–· Ouarai	

TABLE 4–57. RESULTS OF NEUTRALIZATION TESTS OF SELECTED SERA WITH ANTIBODY TITERS OF 1:40 OR MORE TO AT LEAST TWO ANTIGENICALLY RELATED VIRUSES IN HEMAGGLUTINATION INHIBITION TESTS

Virus	Djimtilo			Ouli Bangala			Ouarai			Boum Khebir			Faya-Largeau		
	No. Tested	With Protection No.	%	No. Tested	With Protection No.	%	No. Tested	With Protection No.	%	No. Tested	With Protection No.	%	No. Tested	With Protection No.	%
Group A															
Chikungunya	20	12	60.0	12	11	91.7	18	9	50.0	17	12	70.5	6	3	50.0
Semliki Forest	20	4	20.0	12	3	25.0	18	5	27.8	17	3	17.6	6	0	—
Sindbis	9	2	22.2	9	3	33.3	0			6	3	50.0	5	3	60.0
Group B															
West Nile	0			0			20	1	5.0	18	2	11.1	17	1	5.9
Zika	0			0			20	10	50.0	18	11	61.1	18	1	5.6
Yellow Fever	0			0			20	3	15.0	18	6	33.3	18	4	22.2
Uganda S	0			0			20	3	15.0	18	2	11.1	18	1	5.6
Dengue II	0			0			20	3	—	18	0	—	17	0	—
Bunyamwera	10	8	80.0	10	10	100.0	9	8	88.9	10	9	90.0	0		
Germiston	10	9	90.0	10	10	100.0	9	8	88.9	10	8	80.0	0		

in the neutralization tests. This finding supports the assumption that true infections with Sindbis, or an antigenically closely related virus, had occurred sporadically in the population samples.

The selection of sera for neutralization tests to viruses of Group B was made specifically for the serological differential diagnosis of yellow fever. Therefore, only sera from persons with negative vaccination histories but with HI titers of 1:40 or more to yellow fever antigen were included in the examinations. The results presented in Table 4–57 show that only a few had neutralizing antibodies, but that most had protected the animals against infections with Zika virus. Nevertheless, the results are still inconclusive because they can neither confirm nor refute the assumption that sporadic cases of yellow fever may have occurred in Ouarai, Boum Khebir, and Faya-Largeau. It is possible, of course, that some of the persons with negative vaccination histories had made inaccurate statements in the health interviews from which the information was elicited.

Most of the ten sera that were selected because they gave reactions in HI tests with both Bunyamwera and Germiston virus antigens also had neutralizing antibodies to these two viruses. This finding supports the assumption that natural infection with these two agents has occurred in Chad.

Fungal Infections

The findings presented in this section were obtained by two methods: physical examinations for the presence of tinea capitis, tinea corporis, and tinea versicolor; and skin tests with histoplasmin. While all persons included in the population samples were examined by a physician, only the residents of Boum Khebir and Faya-Largeau were given skin tests.

Dermatomycoses

The prevalence of three skin mycoses in each of the five villages is presented in Table 4–58. In all five communities the highest percentage with tinea capitis was found in children between five and fifteen years of age. Although more males than females were affected, this difference was not significant statistically. The geographical distribution of tinea versicolor was associated with the climatic characteristics of the communities studied. The prevalence was lowest in the dry desert climate of Faya-Largeau and highest in Ouarai, where the typical tropical conditions of high temperature, humidity, and lush vegetation were most pronounced. The over-all prevalence of tinea corporis was relatively low in all areas, but it was highest in Ouli Bangala, where sanitary conditions were poorest.

TABLE 4–58. PREVALENCE OF DERMATOMYCOSES

	Djimtilo (N = 379)	Ouli Bangala (N = 399)	Ouarai (N = 364)	Boum Khebir (N = 374)	Faya-Largeau (N = 207)
Tinea capitis	6.9	19.1	7.7	5.5	11.5
Tinea corporis	2.0	3.9	0.6	0.6	0
Tinea versicolor	20.2	13.8	41.0	27.2	5.4

a Percentages listed are age adjusted.

Histoplasmosis

Infections with *Histoplasma* are known to occur in Africa (Stolt, 1954; Merveille, Andebond, and Cecaldi 1954; Edwards *et al.*, 1956), but the knowledge is still fragmentary. It also is not clear whether histoplasmosis in Africans is predominantly caused by *H. capsulatum* or by *H. duboisii*, which has recently been isolated from soil samples (Ajello, 1968). The latter agent is immunologically indistinguishable from *H. capsulatum* but has different morphological characteristics (Kaufman and Blumer, 1968). Whereas of the 162 residents tested in Faya-Largeau only two males had skin reactions with induration sizes of five or more millimeters, 38.4 percent of the residents in Boum Khebir were classified as reactors. Thus, only the results of the latter village are presented in Table 4–59.

The prevalence of histoplasmin reactions reached a peak of 71.4 percent in the age group of fifteen-to-nineteen-year-old adolescents and declined thereafter. For clues to the medical significance of these findings the prevalence of reactions to histoplasmin and the frequency distribution of induration sizes among the thirty-five persons with radiological diagnoses of intrapulmonary calcifications, a characteristic late manifestation of histoplasmosis, were compared with those of the general population of the same age composition. Among the individuals with calcifications, 57.1 percent were reactors, as compared to 41.6 percent in the controls. The

TABLE 4–59. PREVALENCE OF REACTIONS IN SKIN TESTS WITH
HISTOPLASMIN BY AGE, BOUM KHEBIR

| Age (years) | No. Tested | Reactors[a] | |
		No.	%
Birth–4	50	8	16.0
5–9	66	24	36.4
10–14	34	18	52.9
15–19	28	20	71.4
20–29	52	27	51.8
30–39	34	14	41.2
40–49	30	10	33.3
50+	58	14	24.1
Total	352	135	38.4

[a] Induration sizes of five or more millimeters in diameter.

difference is on the borderline of statistical significance (P = 0.07). The frequency distribution of the reaction sizes for each group is shown in Figure 4–24. The differences between the two curves support the assumption that *H. capsulatum* or *H. duboisii* might have been the causative agent for some of the pulmonary lesions detected on chest roentgenograms. Unfortunately, various soil samples collected in the area for attempts to isolate *Histoplasma* were inadequate. Therefore, the interesting epidemiological question of the regional importance of *H. capsulatum* and *H. duboisii* must remain open.

Diseases and Conditions of Varied or Undetermined Etiology

Incapacitations

The prevalence of disabling conditions and of temporarily incapacitating illnesses was estimated by two methods: first by notation during physical examinations, and second through specific information elicited from health interviews of all persons who were at least ten years old. The results of the physical examinations are listed in Table 4–60 and show that in each of the five communities impaired vision was the most frequent type of disability. In four of the five villages partial or complete blindness accounted for more than half of all incapacitations registered. The highest prevalence of eye disease and all other disabling conditions was found among the residents of Ouli Bangala.

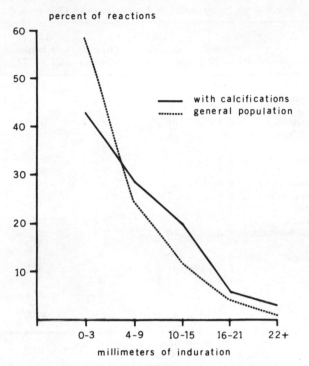

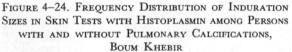

FIGURE 4–24. FREQUENCY DISTRIBUTION OF INDURATION
SIZES IN SKIN TESTS WITH HISTOPLASMIN AMONG PERSONS
WITH AND WITHOUT PULMONARY CALCIFICATIONS,
BOUM KHEBIR

The number of workdays lost because of illness and the percentage of residents who had been ill during the month preceding the
interview are shown in Table 4–61. Contrary to the expectation that
disabling illness would be reported more frequently in communities
where the prevalence of incapacitating conditions was high, an
almost paradoxical correlation was observed when comparing the
results shown in Tables 4–60 and 4–61 (r = −0.2917). In order to
learn more about the possible reasons for this discrepancy, the kinds
of disabling illnesses reported were compared for regional differences. Table 4–62 shows that a high percentage of the complaints
were indicative of acute and subacute diseases. It is also interesting
to note that the sex ratio of persons who had reported incapacitating
illness (Table 4–62) was negatively associated with the corresponding total percentages of ill persons in most villages (Table 6–61)

TABLE 4–60. PREVALENCE[a] OF INCAPACITATING CONDITIONS[b]

Condition	Djimtilo (N = 379)	Ouli Bangala (N = 395)	Ouarai (N = 363)	Boum Khebir (N = 373)	Faya-Largeau (N = 206)
Impaired vision	9.6	13.1	6.1	5.8	7.8
Impaired hearing	0.8	0	0.2	0	0
Deaf mutism	0	0.2	0	0	0.4
Loss of fingers, toes	0.4	1.7	0.8	0.4	0
Loss of hand, foot	0	1.1	0.4	0	0
Loss of arm, leg	0	0	0	0	0
Malformation of hand	0.3	0	0	0.5	0
foot	0.5	0	0.7	0.6	0
Severe kyphoscoliosis	0.3	0.2	0	0	0
Severe contractures	1.0	3.4	1.4	0	0.8
Elephantiasis, severe edema	0	0	3.2	0.6	0
Neurological disorders	0.2	0.5	0.2	0	0
Mental disorders	0[c]	0	0.2	0	0
Severe dyspnea	0.2	0.3	0	0	0
Cachexia	0.5	1.2	0.6	0	0.6
Large ulcers	1.6	3.5	0	0	0.5
Tumors	0.8	0.3	0	0	0
Total	16.2	25.5	13.8	7.9	10.1

[a] Percentages listed are age adjusted.
[b] Disregarding multiple conditions in the same persons.
[c] One patient seen was not part of the population sample.

($r = -0.6$). In other words, the prevalence of these illnesses was generally lower when males and females were equally represented in the sample of subjectively ill persons than when there was an excess of women.

From these and other observations made in the field it appears that the gross deformities and conditions listed in Table 4–60 undoubtedly reduce the work capacity of the persons afflicted; however, the people adapt to this state and find new and useful functions in the daily subsistence activities of their families. Only when new diseases or exacerbations interrupt their daily work routine do they complain about "incapacitating illness." One experience during the pilot study may serve as an illustration of the humble acceptance of a chronic disease as an inevitable event. When the twelve elders of a southern village, of whom five had severely impaired vision, were asked to describe the health problems of their community, they mentioned many diseases but did not include eye problems. After being asked specifically about the possible im-

TABLE 4-61. WORKDAYS LOST BECAUSE OF ILLNESS DURING MONTH PRECEDING INTERVIEW

Age (years)	Djimtilo			Ouli Bangala			Ouarai			Boum Khebir			Faya-Largeau		
	No.	% Ill	Person-days of Illness[a]/Month	No.	% Ill	Person-days of Illness/Month	No.	% Ill	Person-days of Illness/Month	No.	% Ill	Person-days of Illness/Month	No.	% Ill	Person-days of Illness/Month
10–19	64	12.5	1.0	110	10.9	0.5	71	8.5	0.3	66	6.1	0.4	14	35.7	1.6
20–29	47	23.4	2.9	66	7.6	1.1	60	13.3	0.8	50	12.0	1.0	24	33.3	2.5
30+	152	27.6	3.5	90	14.4	2.0	90	20.0	1.9	129	12.4	2.0	42	31.0	3.3
Total	263	23.2	2.8	266	11.3	1.1	221	14.5	1.1	245	10.6	1.4	80	32.5	2.7
Age-Adjusted Total			2.60			1.34			1.16			1.29			2.60

[a] Represents the sum of lost workdays divided by the total number of persons in each age group.

TABLE 4–62. REASONS FOR INCAPACITATION DURING MONTH PRECEDING INTERVIEW[a]

Complaint	Djimtilo Males No.	%	Djimtilo Females No.	%	Ouli Bangala Males No.	%	Ouli Bangala Females No.	%	Ouarai Males No.	%	Ouarai Females No.	%	Boum Khebir Males No.	%	Boum Khebir Females No.	%	Faya-Largeau Males No.	%	Faya-Largeau Females No.	%
Aches and pains	8	*32.0*	16	*44.4*	5	*33.3*	4	*23.5*	5	*50.0*	8	*36.4*	4	*21.1*	6	*30.0*	3	*33.3*	7	*38.9*
Nausea, vertigo	2	8.0	9	*25.0*	0		0		0		1	4.5	0		0		1	11.1	0	
Cough	5	*20.0*	1	2.8	3	*20.0*	5	*29.4*	0		2	9.1	1	5.3	3	15.0	2	*22.2*	3	*16.7*
Fever	2	8.0	2	5.6	0		0		2	20.0	2	9.1	4	21.1	3	15.0	1	11.1	3	*16.7*
Arthritis	4	16.0	0		0		0		0		0		0		1	5.0	1	11.1	0	
Injury	2	8.0	0		0		0		0		0		0		0		0		0	
Gonorrhea	0		2	5.6	0		0		0		1	4.5	0		0		0		0	
Kidney ailment	1	4.0	1	2.8	1	6.7	0		0		1	4.5	0		0		0		0	
Edema	1	4.0	1	2.8	1	6.7	0		0		0		1	5.3	0		0		0	
Otitis	0		1	2.8	0		0		0		0		0		0		0		0	
Tumor	0		1	2.8	0		0		0		0		0		0		0		0	
Hernia	0		1	2.8	0		0		0		0		0		0		0		0	
Epilepsy	0		1	2.8	0		0		0		0		0		0		0		0	
Gastro-intestinal	0		0		1	6.7	4	*23.5*	3	*30.0*	1	4.5	7	*36.8*	7	*35.0*	0		1	5.6
Ulcers, abscess	0		0		1	6.7	2	11.8	0		0		0		0		0		0	
Eye disease	0		0		1	6.7	1	5.9	0		3	*13.6*	2	10.5	0		0		0	
Hemorrhage	0		0		1	6.7	0		0		0		0		0		0		0	
Anemia	0		0		0		1	5.9	0		0		0		0		0		0	
Heart ailment	0		0		1	6.7	0		0		1	4.5	0		0		0		0	
Mastitis	0		0		0		0		0		1	4.5	0		0		0		0	
Goiter	0		0		0		0		0		1	4.5	0		0		0		0	
Jaundice	0		0		0		0		0		1	4.5	0		0		1	11.1	1	5.6
Pox	0		0		0		0		0		0		0		0		0		3	*16.7*
Total	25	100.0	36	100.2	15	100.2	17	100.0	10	100.0	22	99.7	19	100.1	20	100.0	9	99.9	18	100.2

[a] The two most frequent conditions in each subgroup are italicized.

portance of eye diseases among their friends and relatives, they apologized that they had forgotten to state that, indeed, these were serious health problems of their children. When reminded that they themselves appeared to have advanced eye diseases that would lead to blindness, they simply replied that they were old, not sick.

History of Diarrhea

A comparison among the villages of the prevalence of diarrhea on examination day, estimated from statements made in interviews, is shown in Table 4–63.

With the exception of Boum Khebir, the age trend of diarrhea is characteristic of areas with poor sanitation; the highest prevalence is found in children, followed by a more or less abrupt decrease after the age of ten. Attempts to identify at least some of the major determinants of diarrhea in children were unsuccessful. Whereas some degree of association was found between the recovery of certain enteric bacilli and the presence of diarrhea, as described in the section on Enteric Bacteria, no other specific host or environmental factor was recognized that would explain the cause of diarrhea in the majority of persons afflicted.

Life Histories of Severe Diseases

Shown in Table 4–64 are life histories of some specific diseases about which information was obtained in routine health interviews. For most of the conditions listed there were pronounced regional differences in prevalence, which often corresponded with the results of other more objective tests applied in the study. Of the treponematoses, yaws was reported most frequently from Boum Khebir, where by specific laboratory tests and by clinical evidence the infection was also found to be hyperendemic. On the other hand, syphilis (including endemic syphilis?) was more frequent in Djimtilo and Faya-Largeau (the two Arab communities) than in the southern villages of the Sara, Goula, and Laka tribes. A life history of sleeping disease was reported with surprising frequency in interview statements by the residents of Boum Khebir; but, without further supporting evidence from either reliable laboratory tests for residual antibodies of *Trypanosoma gambiense* or clinical studies, it cannot be decided whether the "sleeping disease" mentioned by the residents is identical with African trypanosomiasis or

TABLE 4–63. PREVALENCE OF DIARRHEA ON THE DAY BEFORE INTERVIEW

Age (years)	Djimtilo			Ouli Bangala			Ouarai			Boum Khebir			Faya-Largeau			All Villages		
	No. in Group	Diarrhea No.	%	No. in Group	Diarrhea No.	%	No. in Group	Diarrhea No.	%	No. in Group	Diarrhea No.	%	No. in Group	Diarrhea No.	%	No. in Group	Diarrhea No.	%
Birth–9	108	13	12.0	129	52	40.3	139	41	29.4	139	13	9.3	70	31	44.3	585	150	25.6
10–19	64	1	1.6	110	31	28.2	71	6	8.5	63	5	7.9	34	12	35.3	342	55	16.1
20–29	48	1	2.1	67	17	25.4	61	4	6.6	51	3	5.9	32	10	31.3	259	35	13.5
30–39	76	2	2.6	51	20	39.2	36	1	2.7	35	5	14.3	21	6	28.6	219	34	15.5
40–49	29	2	6.9	24	4	16.7	21	3	14.3	30	0		22	5	22.8	126	14	11.1
50+	48	0		18	3	16.7	33	4	12.1	64	7	10.9	24	6	25.0	187	20	10.7
Total	373	19	5.1	399	127	31.8	361	59	16.3	382	33	8.6	203	70	34.5	1,718	308	17.9

TABLE 4–64. LIFE HISTORIES OF SEVERE DISEASE AS ELICITED BY SPECIFIC
QUESTIONS IN THE HEALTH INTERVIEWS

History of:	Djimtilo (N = 373) %	Ouli Bangala (N = 392) %	Ouarai (N = 362) %	Boum Khebir (N = 382) %	Faya-Largeau (N = 203) %
Yaws	0.3	3.3	0	43.5	0.5
Syphilis	19.3	0.8	1.7	1.0	14.9
Sleeping disease	0.8	0.5	0.6	12.3	1.5
Leprosy	0	12.8	6.4	5.0	0
Accidents: Males	7.0	12.2	16.4	13.2	37.5
Females	0.9	7.4	10.8	7.2	31.5
Both	3.5	9.4	13.5	9.9	34.0

could have been caused by arbovirus infections producing encephalitis or by other agents that cause a typhus-like disease.

The high percentage of persons in Ouli Bangala who mentioned episodes of Hansen's disease in their medical histories can be interpreted by the coexistence of true leprosy with certain similar manifestations of severe onchocerciasis. The latter disease includes deforming skin manifestations, such as *facies leonina*, that may be confused with lepromatous leprosy.

The accidents listed in the table reveal interesting regional and sex differences. Most of the accidents among the males were falls or cuts, whereas the major injury among the females was burns. In Faya-Largeau, which had the highest accident rate, almost 40 percent of the injuries to both sexes were listed as the result of blows. Other important accidents included wounds caused by perforating splinters.

Also included in this section is a table (4–65) which summarizes the prevalence of miscellaneous diseases that were not routinely registered in the study protocol but were detected in the physical examinations and listed in a category reserved for "other diagnoses." Of specific interest are two conditions, hernia and meningitis. The cases of meningitis have already been discussed in the section on Meningococcal Meningitis. The interesting variations in the frequency of hernias, mostly inguinal hernias in males, suggest a preponderance of the condition in the three southern communities, especially in Ouarai. This speculation gains considerable support from the reports of Dr. David Seymour, surgeon of the Mid-Baptist Hospital in Koumra, the administrative seat of the subprefecture to which Ouarai belongs. According to his records, which comprise the experience of many years, incarcerated hernias among males were the most important single reason for admission to his hospital. No specific constitutional factor was recognized in the population samples which could explain the preponderance of hernias among the Saras of the Koumra area of Chad.

TABLE 4–65. PREVALENCE OF MISCELLANEOUS DISEASES NOT INCLUDED IN STUDY PROTOCOL

Condition	Djimtilo (N = 379) Cases	Ouli Bangala (N = 399) Cases	Ouarai (N = 364) Cases	Boum Khebir (N = 374) Cases	Faya-Largeau (N = 204) Cases
Hernia	2	9	14	8	2
Congestive heart disease	3	0	0	1	1
Bronchitis	4	8	4	2	0
Pneumonia	1	5	0	1	0
Otitis media	2	0	1	0	0
Tonsillitis	1	0	0	0	0
Meningitis	0	2	1	0	0
Icterus	0	2	1	1	0
Spastic hemiparesis	0	1	0	1	0
Facialis paresis	1	1	0	1	0
Kwashiorkor	0	2	0	0	0

Eye Diseases and Conditions

Trachoma and onchocerciasis are the two most important eye diseases in Chad. Both are the clinical manifestations of endemic infections discussed previously. Table 4–66 summarizes the prevalence of selected eye diseases and conditions for regional comparisons by presenting age-adjusted percentages. The geographical distribution of blindness is closely related to that of trachoma in Djimtilo and Faya-Largeau and of onchocerciasis in Ouli Bangala. Superior pannus, a typical manifestation of trachoma, and, to a lesser degree, entropion were found concentrated in the areas where trachoma was endemic. Among the cases of conjunctivitis listed, follicular hypertrophy was detected only among the residents of Djimtilo and Faya-Largeau. The high prevalence of corneal opacities in Ouli Bangala was the result of ocular onchocerciasis in the area (von Noorden and Buck, 1968). While most of the cataracts in Djimtilo, Ouarai, Boum Khebir, and Faya-Largeau occurred with equal frequency in both sexes and were present only in persons who were older than fifty years, those in Ouli Bangala were found scattered throughout the entire adult population and occurred most often among males. The majority of the cases represented secondary cataracts caused by ocular onchocerciasis (von Noorden and Buck, 1968).

TABLE 4–66. PREVALENCE[a] OF SELECTED EYE CONDITIONS BY VILLAGE

						Cataract	
Village	Blind-ness[b]	Entro-pion	Con-junc-tivitis	Su-perior Pannus	Corneal Opaci-ties	Uni-lateral	Bi-lateral
Djimtilo (N = 379)	4.2	8.3	23.4	13.8	6.2	1.4	1.4
Ouli Bangala (N = 395)	9.3	0	3.7	0.4	22.4	3.9	7.1
Ouarai (N = 364)	2.6	1.7	10.0	0.6	8.6	1.2	1.7
Boum Khebir (N = 374)	3.6	0.2	6.4	0	12.9	1.0	0.9
Faya-Largeau (N = 207)	7.8	1.3	16.3	17.8	8.6	3.9	1.3

[a] Percentages listed are age adjusted.
[b] Includes blindness of one or both eyes.

Skin Diseases and Conditions

This section summarizes the findings of the great variety of skin diseases and conditions that were recognized in the study (Table 4–67). Some of the more specific skin manifestations of the treponematoses, dermatomycoses, leprosy and onchocerciasis have been discussed in the context of the individual diseases to which they belong, while others, such as depigmentations and ulcers, were analyzed for associations with the results of tuberculin and syphilis tests for clues to their possible etiology (see Treponematoses, Onchocerciasis, Tuberculosis and Other Mycobacterial Infections, and Fungal Infections).

The high prevalence, great variety, and mimicry of skin diseases in the tropics make them one of the most important disease categories for both the epidemiologist and clinician. Table 4–67 gives a detailed list of the major conditions detected in the study. True scabies was relatively infrequent. The high percentage of persons with onchocercal dermatitis resembling scabies (*gâle filarienne*) ac-

TABLE 4–67. PREVALENCE[a] OF SKIN DISEASES AND CONDITIONS

Conditions	Djimtilo (N = 379)	Ouli Bangala (N = 399)	Ouarai (N = 364)	Boum Khebir (N = 374)	Faya-Largeau (N = 204)
Scabies	9.5	41.7[b]	1.2	1.7	0
Pediculosis	1.3	0.2	0.6	0	0
Dermatomycoses					
Tinea capitis	6.9	19.1	7.7	5.4	11.5
Tinea corporis	2.0	3.9	0.6	0.6	0
Tinea versicolor	20.2	13.8	41.0	27.2	5.4
Scars and keloids					
Ornamental keloids	47.6	28.3	67.0	9.6	0
Post-traumatic keloids	35.2	24.4	21.0	16.3	11.6
Paper-thin round scars	3.4	2.3	48.9	33.9	4.7
Pyoderma	9.5	21.5	1.9	1.5	5.0
Ulcers	3.6	13.1	1.9	2.1	2.2
Depigmentations[c]	24.9	50.2	43.8	18.5	43.5
Venereal diseases					
Gonorrhea	0.7	0.7	0	0	0
Chancroid	0.3	0	0	0	0
Syphilis	0.9	0.8	0	0	0
Yaws	0	0.2	0	1.7	0
Leprosy	0	1.7	0.3	1.5	0
Miscellaneous					
Hyperkeratosis	0.6	0	0	0	5.8
Macular rashes	0.5	0	0	0	0.6
Lichenoid dermatoses	0	0.7	0.3	0.3	0
Verrugae	0	0.7	0.3	0	0
Herpes zoster	0.3	0	0	0	0

[a] Percentages listed are age adjusted.
[b] Includes *gâle filarienne* of onchocerciasis.
[c] See also Table 4–43.

counts for the majority of the cases included in this category in Ouli Bangala. The diagnosis of pediculosis was made only when lice or their nits were found on a person in the sample. The dermatomycoses have been presented previously (see Fungal Infections). There were interesting geographical variations in the prevalence of keloids which were mainly related to differences in the practice of initiation rites among the various tribes represented in the population samples (see Social Ranking, pp. 34–39).

The high percentage of the residents of Ouarai and Boum Khebir who had round or oval paper-thin scars with sharp demarcation lines on their extremities was surprising. The scars resembled those left by cutaneous leishmaniasis, but there was no further evidence available from the study that could be used to narrow the range of differential diagnostic possibilities. Some of the villagers in Ouarai mentioned that the scars had resulted from ulcers that were most prevalent during the rainy season. The seasonal variation in the size of the phlebotomus population, vectors of leishmaniasis, usually is minimal in the wet season.

The large excess of pyoderma among the children and young adults of Ouli Bangala is related to onchocercal dermatitis. The often intense and chronic itching caused by this skin condition furthers excoriation from scratching and promotes superinfections causing pyoderma.

Ulcers were registered if they measured at least two by two centimeters. Although some were caused by trauma, the etiology of most remained obscure. It has already been mentioned in the section on Tuberculosis and Other Mycobacterial Infections that there was a significant correlation between the presence of ulcers and reactivity in skin tests with *Mycobacterium gause*.

A subclassification of skin depigmentations by size and into those that were or were not accompanied by scarring is shown in Table 4–43. In the section on Treponematoses, various types of leucoderma were examined for associations with the results of syphilis tests in order to obtain clues to their etiology.

Of the venereal diseases listed it can be assumed that the prevalence estimates of gonorrhea are probably much too low, because the physical examinations included only an inspection of the genitals. The cases recognized were all detected in the afternoon clinics, which were open to all sick persons included in the population samples. The few cases included in the category "miscellaneous" are listed for the sake of completeness, but the numbers are inconspicuous.

5

MATERIALS AND METHODS

Anthropology

Two field methods were used to obtain information in this study. The precoded survey schedule, initially used in Peru (Buck, Sasaki, and Anderson, 1968), was shortened and modified to make it applicable to Chad. The questions were translated into French, with both French and English appearing in the final form. These questionnaire schedules were used during the interviews of household heads.

The second method was the interviewing of key informants (Tremblay, 1957). These were individuals who had detailed knowledge about specific aspects of the culture and social system of the country. They included village chiefs, medical practitioners, religious leaders, and others with specialized skills or high social standing.

Relevant information was also obtained by the Chadian nurses of our medical team and included demographic data, household size and composition, marital status, religious affiliation, occupation, and travel histories.

An innovation not used in Peru was tried in Chad, walkie-talkies, which the anthropologist, sanitary engineer, and entomologist carried into the field. These instruments made it possible for fieldworkers to keep in constant communication with each other and with the base camp. The method was satisfactory when used within a range of less than half a mile.

Field Procedures and Village Reception

Prior to our entry into the villages the subprefects were notified by letters and phone calls from the office of the Ministry of Health. The advance team, composed of the anthropologist, sanitary engineer, and Hopkins and Chadian nurses, made initial courtesy calls on the subprefects and proceeded to the villages for site selection and meetings with the chiefs and village elders.

The structure of government administration, which combined the modern French system at the higher levels with the traditional at the village levels, was advantageous to the work of the research project. The Ministry of Health issued and distributed a newsletter concerning the Hopkins team to administrative officers in the provinces, as well as to medical officers in the larger cities. The Ministry emphasized the cooperative aspects of the project, and subprefects furnished uniformed guards to serve as symbols of national representation. The village chiefs also selected individuals who were stationed at the camp sites throughout the night to help guard the camp from looting by native travelers. Since all sites visited presented different situations, each will be detailed separately.

Djimtilo

Djimtilo was visited several days prior to the establishment of the camp since it was only about a two-and-a-half-hour ride from Fort Lamy. The people identified themselves as the Arab Salamat, who are Muslims and speak Arabic. These people are the descendants of the Arabs who invaded Chad in the fifteenth century and intermarried with the indigenous Sudanese population (Murdock, 1959, p. 410).

When the team arrived in the village, a site measuring 200 square meters had already been cleared. Throughout our period of residence full cooperation was received. Visits to the camp by the sultan, who was also the canton chief, and his honor guard, and later by the minister of health and French health advisers, were viewed by the villagers as significant events and added to their desire to participate in the field study.

Because no local person was available to work with the anthropologist, an English-speaking Nigerian from Fort Lamy served as his interpreter.

Ouli Bangala

The residents of Ouli Bangala are primarily members of the Laka tribe. Because the village is located on the main road which links the large town of Moundou with Baiboukoum, capital of the sub-prefecture, it has long had contact with western influences. The more affluent men wear western clothing, the evangelical church had had an effect on the local aboriginal culture, and a sizable number of men understand the French language. Women have been less affected by such contact; although some wear clothing made of brightly colored imported prints, most still garb themselves with daily changes of fresh leaves.

Our camp was situated by the Lim River, where water was easily obtained and was shaded from the sun by tall trees. The site was avoided by local residents during the evening and night because of their belief in the presence of witches and ghosts. The illusions, probably created by mists, are seen mainly during the wet season and are believed to be the cause of illnesses.

The sample was defined by a map plotted by the sanitary engineer, and the enumeration of families began with those living closest to the Lim River and proceeded toward the center of the village. All of the households belonging to Ouli Bangala I were included, as were a few families of newcomers who lived in the eastern, or Ouli Bangala II, section of the village. During the course of our field work, families who lived on the western side of the river began to move into unfinished houses located within the sample area, hoping to be included in the study. These families were migrants from the bush and were still considered outsiders by the villagers. They were not included in the sample, but emergency cases were given medical treatment.

Four school teachers conducted most of the interviews; they were bilingual, speaking French and the native dialect. Interviews with key informants were conducted by the anthropologist with the help of a Chadian French- and English-speaking interpreter who lived in a neighboring village. This interpreter also served in Ouarai.

Ouarai

Ouarai is one of the many Sara villages located near Koumra. The Sara tribesmen have long been recognized as good soldiers, having served in the French armed forces in Africa and in Southeast Asia (Thompson and Adloff, 1960, p. 90).

While it was revealed during the pilot study that the village was composed of two parts, negotiations had been undertaken only with the chief of Ouarai I. It was not known at the time that there was a rift between the independent chiefs of Ouarai I and Ouarai II.

The chief of Ouarai I was a retired veteran of the French army. He, like most people in the region, had had some contact with the American Mid-Baptist Mission Hospital located at Koumra. The medical doctor from this hospital accompanied the advance team to the village and assisted in the selection of the campsite. A local official, a relative of the chief, immediately assumed the role of foreman and hired as camp aides mainly those affiliated with Ouarai I.

A definite sample area was selected which included almost all Ouarai I residents, as well as a few Ouarai II families.

The village did not have a school, a fact which handicapped the interviewing program. The English-speaking interpreter who worked with the anthropologist in Ouli Bangala secured as interviewers members of the village who were literate in the French language. These persons obtained the necessary quota of interviews.

Boum Khebir

Boum Khebir is inhabited by the Goula tribe, which was relatively unknown to the western world until recent years (Pairault, 1966). Western and Islamic religious influences have been negligible in the village because of its inaccessibility, and only since the independence of the country in 1960 has the village been affected by national policies. Few men and fewer women wear western clothing, and older women still wear wooden or metal buttons in their perforated upper lips.

The village chief had received a message from the subprefect's office several days prior to the arrival of our team. The originally selected campsite was being used as the central gathering place for cotton, and another location had to be found. This site was about a quarter of a mile from the village and provided much privacy.

The villagers received the team cordially and accepted without protest the examination schedule and the limitation of the sample size. Intrusions by foreigners engaged in research was not unknown to these people; during the preceding year a World Health Organization team had been operating in Boum Khebir, and between 1959 and 1961 a French anthropologist had been in residence. A

Chadian nurse assigned to the health station of the village had been a classmate of one of the nurses assigned to the team, and he helped to establish rapport in the village.

A local teacher and the secretary of the subprefect conducted the interviews with the help of a community resident who spoke Arabic, as well as French and the Goula dialect.

Faya-Largeau

The two villages selected in the vicinity of Faya-Largeau were located several kilometers from the town and represented the *Quartier* Camero of the Kamadja tribe and the *Quartier* Garba of the Anakaza people. Medical examinations were conducted at the General Hospital of the prefecture. Although attempts were made to secure interviews with household heads, the absence of a special interpreter made this almost impossible. One teacher appeared for several days after his school duties were completed, but because he lacked the incentive to work he was dismissed. Data for the two villages have been taken primarily from the health interviews.

Interviewers and Interpreters

Languages in Chad are numerous. The elite and the more educated speak French, while the average person speaks the local dialect. It was thus essential to obtain interpreters who spoke English as well as French and the local language. In the village of Djimtilo a Nigerian who was recruited in Fort Lamy served as the anthropologist's interpreter. He had been employed for years by the Nigerian Embassy and had also worked with the Peace Corps. In the absence of school teachers, he and the anthropologist administered the survey schedules. His services were terminated after the work was completed in Djimtilo because he could not speak the languages of the southern tribes, Laka, Nar, and Goula.

In Ouli Bangala, through fortunate circumstances, an English-speaking school boy of the Laka tribe applied for the job of interpreter. He had completed his secondary training and was awaiting assignment to a higher school. The survey schedule was administered by four French-speaking school teachers. Two days were spent in training; thereafter the teachers did the interviewing. Here, as in Ouarai and Boum Khebir, the interviewers were paid on a contract basis.

The English-speaking school boy from Ouli Bangala was retained as an interpreter in Ouarai. There was no school located in Ouarai, so teachers were not available. The school boy and a French-speaking member of the community conducted the survey interviews.

In Boum Khebir one teacher was available to do the field interviewing. Since he had little knowledge of the Goula language, he had a French-speaking student interpret for him. In the intensive interviewing of key informants one of the team nurses and the secretary to the subprefect served as interpreters.

ENVIRONMENTAL HEALTH

The evaluation of factors in the environment which may have affected the health of the survey population was based on observations and measurements, supplemented by data elicited from interviews. The information was obtained from a random sample of the population included in the survey because time did not permit interviews with all the families. Precoded survey schedules were drawn up for use in the field.

Water Supply

Since the quality of water is so important to health, its evaluation was given prominence in the environmental health survey. Samples were taken from all sources of domestic water supplies and were analyzed physically, chemically, and bacteriologically. The physical and chemical analyses included determinations of temperature, color, turbidity, and pH, as well as amounts of ammonia nitrogen, nitrite nitrogen, nitrate nitrogen, chloride, sulfate, fluoride, iron, manganese, calcium hardness, total hardness, and dissolved oxygen. The testing was done with the Direct Reading Engineer's Laboratory (DR-EL) supplied by the Hach Chemical Company. An assessment of odor also was included and was, of necessity, scored on a subjective basis.

The bacteriological analysis of the water was performed with field monitoring kits supplied by the Millipore Corporation. Water samples were passed through membrane filters in the monitors; M-Endo medium was then added and the samples were incubated in a field incubator. The temperature control of the incubator was not within the exact limits set forth in *Standard Methods* (American Public Health Association, 1965), but it was close enough to give an estimate of the numbers of coliform organisms present in the samples. Since all the water sources were subjected to a large amount of natural pollution, the efficacy of our techniques was considered adequate for field conditions.

Some of the water samples were too heavily polluted to make an accurate coliform count without dilution. Sterile water, at least to the exclusion of coliform colonies, was produced as a diluent in the following manner. Raw water was treated by coagulation with ferric sulfate and sedimentation; then the pH was adjusted to slightly above 7.0 by adding sodium carbonate. This water was chlorinated with calcium hypochlorite to a free chlorine residual of two milligrams per liter after a three-hour contact period. A non-ionic polyelectrolyte was also used as a coagulant aid (Kawata, 1967). A requisite quantity of water was drawn and filtered through filter paper to remove suspended floc particles. The filtered water was then dechlorinated with sodium thiosulfate and passed through clean demineralizing resin. A check was made of the treated water by the use of control monitors; they showed no organisms on M-Endo medium. The treated water was not harmful to coliform bacilli, as shown by the growth of typical colonies when it was added to raw water samples.

Waste Disposal

The waste disposal survey included disposal of both human excreta and household refuse. The evaluation was based on observations, but was supplemented by interviews when information was not readily available from observation. Defecation habits were noted with the following points in mind: the use of latrines, if any; principal defecation sites and their proximity to closely populated areas; and types and amount of shade over these sites, as well as the moistness, pH, and texture of their soil. Household refuse was studied for composition and for evidence of fly breeding.

Aquatic Environment

Because onchocerciasis and schistosomiasis are endemic in Chad, the evaluation of environmental conditions affecting the biology of their respective vectors was important. Observations were made of the type of each body of water, the nature of its bottom, the extent of pollution, the amount of aquatic vegetation, the presence of

aquatic birds, the degree of exposure to the sun, and the extent to
which the people came into contact with the water. Furthermore,
each water source was tested for certain physical and chemical
characteristics, as shown in Table 2–2. Special efforts were made to
collect snails from rivers, creeks, and ponds from which water for
household use was fetched; the presence or absence of egg masses
was also noted. The snails were identified by Dr. G. Mandahl-
Barth at the Snail Identification Center of the World Health
Organization in Charlottenlund, Denmark.

Household Sample Survey

An attempt was made by observation and interview to evaluate
the factors within the houses and in their immediate environs which
might affect the health of the inhabitants. The storage of water for
domestic needs, an estimate of the quantity of water used per person
per day, and the nature of the terrain and the distance to the water
source during the dry and rainy seasons were studied. Latrines,
when present, were graded for their cleanliness; evidence of defecation and urination in areas adjacent to the houses was recorded.
Information concerning bathing practices and the use of footwear
was elicited by interview and the results were scored.

The dwellings in each village were classified according to construction material. Total floor space and floor areas used for sleeping were measured; from these figures the per capita floor space
was derived to give an indication of the degree of crowding. Evidence of animals kept in the sleeping areas, provisions for ventilation, and the spacing and density of vegetation between structures
were noted. The cleanliness of the houses and their surroundings
and the extent of fly and rodent infestation were scored. The use of
bed nets and other means of protection against biting insects was
also ascertained. Rodents were caught alive in Havahart traps that
were set in selected houses, using rolled oats as bait. The trapped
rodents were killed with carbon tetrachloride by enclosing the trap
completely in a plastic bag so that ectoparasites could be recovered.
The identification of ectoparasites was made by the team entomologist. Rodent specimens were preserved and sent to the U.S. National Museum for identification by experts.

Also included in the sanitation survey were systematic observations for the evaluation of food sanitation, including the storage of

cooked food, methods of cleaning utensils and plates, and means of garbage disposal. The types of domestic animals kept in each household and their numbers were registered.

Mapping

Maps of the study villages were prepared as definitions of the sample areas and to facilitate the locating of houses, prominent structures such as schools and clinics, roads, water sources, principal defecation sites, and other landmarks. These maps were also used for the analysis of geographical variations in the prevalence or severity of selected diseases among subsamples of the village populations. A small plane table, an aiming compass, and a steel tape were employed for mapping. Distances were determined by taping, by using a range finder, and, on occasion, by pacing. In Ouli Bangala and Boum Khebir much of the mapping was done from the back of a Land Rover because the houses were very close to the roadways.

Entomology

Entomological specimens were collected in Djimtilo, Ouli Bangala, Ouarai, and Boum Khebir. The following methods were used in the collection of medically important arthropods.

Light Traps. Battery-powered miniature light traps of the Communicable Disease Center design were placed and operated in each of the survey areas. The larger specimens (including mosquitoes) were first removed for pin mounting. The remaining specimens were then aspirated into alcohol vials so that the tiny ceratopogonids (biting midges) and psychodids could be recovered.

Human Bait. Insects attracted to man were collected from the skin or clothing by direct aspiration or by net as they approached, followed, or hovered around the individual. Special collections were also made using human bait.

Malaise Trap. This trap was used only in Djimtilo.

Net and/or Aspirator. Many habitats were sampled by sweeping a net through or around vegetation, over ground or water, and along trails. The sweepings were directed toward either a particular group of insects or a single individual, or they were done at random. The aspirator was used primarily to collect individual insects. This method was applied regularly for the collection of insects from the tents in camp.

Aquatic Habitat Sampling.   Aquatic habitats where insect breeding was suspected were sampled by the dipping method. The collected larvae were identified if possible. In addition, attempts were made to rear adults from this immature stage.

Ectoparasites.   When available, wild and domestic animals were searched for ectoparasites. Rodents, captured alive in Havahart traps in the houses, were combed for ectoparasites after they were killed with carbon tetrachloride. Complete enclosure of the traps in clean plastic bags permitted the collection of ectoparasites that had fallen off the rodents.

All collections were numbered and recorded. Specimens were labeled as soon as possible. The labels included separate recordings for date, location, collection number, and the name of the collector.

Insect pins of sizes 3, 5, and minuten were used exclusively. Insects too small for size 5 were pinned by size 3; smaller specimens were either double-mounted on a minuten or tipped on a paper point. After labeling, the pinned specimens were stored in Schmitt boxes, each of which contained between 200 and 500 insects, depending on specimen sizes.

Specimens which are better preserved in alcohol were placed in vials at the time of capture. They were stored in one-liter jars which were subsequently filled with alcohol.

Although some preliminary and definitive species determinations were made in the field, the bulk of this work was done at the British Museum (Natural History), London; at the Laboratories of Medical Entomology, The Johns Hopkins University School of Hygiene and Public Health; and at the U.S. National Museum in Washington, D.C. Some specimens were identified elsewhere by specialists concerned with particular groups.

MEDICAL

Population Samples

In each of the five accessible study communities, denominator information was obtained by two methods. First, the sanitary engineer of the team prepared a complete map of the village in which each house, regardless of occupancy, was listed. Next, the population sample was defined by selecting natural boundaries that enclosed either all parts of the main village or, if the village was very large, a representative segment. Excluded were small hamlets, individual houses, and satellite communities which, although part of the village politically, were found scattered over a wide area. After the sample area was defined, all houses were given consecutive numbers; these were then listed on the map and painted on the houses. Thereafter all families were visited by a census team of two specially trained Chadian nurses who were fluent in the local language and who were assisted by local residents, most of whom were members of the community power structure.

The census included the enumeration of individual households. All persons belonging to this smallest independent socioeconomic unit in the community were listed by name, age, sex, and degree of family relationship to the household head. A specially designed code system permitted easy separation of pedigrees in the predominantly polygynous families.

Medical information for the study was obtained by five principal methods: interviews, standardized physical examinations, laboratory tests, skin tests, and chest radiography. In addition, special ophthalmological examinations, including eye microscopy with a slit lamp, were carried out by experienced specialists in two of the communities (Ouli Bangala and Faya-Largeau). The actual field procedures which were administered to and requested from all individuals in the study comprised a health interview, a physical examination, two skin tests with different types of tuberculin, a venipuncture for drawing approximately ten milliliters of blood, acquisition of a fresh stool and urine specimen, and, for children under ten years of age, a rectal swab for bacteriological examination. In addition, chest roentgenograms were taken routinely for all persons six years of age and over. Furthermore, skin tests with histoplasmin were given to the individuals of two communities (Boum Khebir and Faya-Largeau); lepromin tests were included in the routine examination of only one study population (Boum Khebir), where skin snips from earlobes for examination of acidfast bacilli were also acquired by a Holth cornealscleral biopsy instrument.

The participation of individuals in various aspects of the study was selectively affected by a variety of factors, including the inconvenience of following a particular procedure, beliefs and taboos, and age- and sex-related technical difficulties in obtaining specimens. In order to obtain maximum participation the study program was explained to the people of each of the five communities in public meetings, during home visits, and through informal persuasion by influential members of the local power structure who supported the project. The residents were told that, while it was desirable that they avail themselves of all tests, they were free to refuse participation in any part of the study they might find objectionable. The venipunctures, skin tests, stool swabs, and the delivery of stool and urine specimens might be particularly objectionable.

With this initial approach and subsequent, almost continuous, efforts to reach and convince reluctant members of the study population, the over-all response was very high in all five communities. Table 5–1 lists the age-adjusted rates of participation in specified test procedures for each village. More detailed information on participation by age in individual tests is given for each community in Tables 5–2, 5–3, 5–4, 5–5, and 5–6.

Household and Medical Interviews

Two Chadian nurses interviewed the household heads and their wives in their homes. The information elicited included personal data, residence and nutritional histories, occupations during the dry and rainy seasons, migration and seasonal travel, and the number of children who were born and died during the year preceding the examination. The standardized protocols consisted of precoded questions printed in French. When completed, the individual questionnaires were kept as field records. During the course of the interviews the project was again explained to the respondents. Special invitation and registration cards listing each participant's name, age, sex, household number, individual code, and operation number were issued. Small containers for individual stool and urine specimens were distributed with the instruction that they be brought to the clinic for laboratory analysis. Each day a limited number of families, comprising from thirty-five to fifty individuals, were invited to the medical camp for examination and health interviews on the following day.

A second interview was held when the families arrived at the camp for the medical examination. The precoded questions of this health schedule were also printed in French and were concerned with residence histories, vaccinations against smallpox and yellow fever and with BCG, past and present illnesses, animal bites, and the habit of chewing cola, hashish, and betel.

TABLE 5-1. PARTICIPATION OF POPULATION SAMPLES IN SPECIFIED TEST PROCEDURES BY LOCALITY

Locality	Census Population	Participation of Population Samples, in Percentages							Skin Tests		Onchocerciasis Skin Snip
		Interviews	Physical Examination	Stool	Urine	Blood	Stool Culture[a]		Made	Read	
Djimtilo	379	98.9	99.5	96.3	96.8	97.9	98.2		95.0	92.6	not taken
Ouli Bangala	401	99.7	99.7	94.0	96.7	98.7	97.0		92.2	85.0	93.0
Ouarai	365	99.4	99.4	92.9	95.3	99.4	96.4		95.3	84.3	9.6[b]
Boum Khebir	379	98.4	98.7	91.8	94.4	95.8	92.7		94.4	92.5	11.9[b]
Faya-Largeau	217	94.9	94.9	88.5	75.1	91.2	77.9		77.9	72.4[c]	not taken

[a] Children from birth to nine years of age only.
[b] Selected cases only.
[c] Because of our flight schedule, the last two days of examinations in Faya-Largeau did not include skin tests.

TABLE 5-2. PARTICIPATION IN SPECIFIED TEST PROCEDURES OF AN EPIDEMIOLOGICAL STUDY BY AGE, DJIMTILO

Age	No. in Census	Interview		Physical		Stool Sample		Urine Sample		Blood		Stool Culture		Skin Tests Made		Skin Tests Read		Onchocerciasis Skin Snip	
		No.	%	No.	%	No.	%	No.	%	No.	%	No.	%	No.	%	No.	%	No.	%
Birth–6 mos.	12	11	91.7	11	91.7	8	66.7	7	58.3	10	83.3	11	91.7	0		0		0	—
7–12 mos.	5	5	100.0	5	100.0	4	80.0	4	80.0	2	40.0	5	100.0	0		0		0	—
1–9 yrs.	92	92	100.0	92	100.0	87	94.5	90	97.7	90	97.7	91	98.8	91	98.8	89	97.8	0	—
10–19 yrs.	66	65	98.5	66	100.0	66	100.0	65	98.5	66	100.0	0	—	66	100.0	66	100.0	0	—
20–29 yrs.	50	49	98.0	50	100.0	50	100.0	50	100.0	50	100.0	0	—	50	100.0	49	98.0	0	—
30–39 yrs.	76	76	100.0	76	100.0	75	98.7	76	100.0	76	100.0	0	—	76	100.0	73	96.1	0	—
40–49 yrs.	29	28	96.6	28	96.6	26	89.7	26	89.7	28	96.6	0	—	28	96.6	26	92.8	0	—
50–59 yrs.	27	27	100.0	27	100.0	27	100.0	27	100.0	27	100.0	0	—	27	100.0	27	100.0	0	—
60 + yrs.	22	22	100.0	22	100.0	22	100.0	22	100.0	22	100.0	0	—	22	100.0	21	95.5	0	—
Total	379	375	98.9	377	99.5	365	96.3	367	96.8	371	97.9	107	98.2	360	95.0	351	97.5	0	—

TABLE 5–3. PARTICIPATION IN SPECIFIED TEST PROCEDURES OF AN EPIDEMIOLOGICAL STUDY BY AGE, OULI BANGALA

| Age (years) | No. in Census | Interview | | Physical | | Stool Sample | | Urine Sample | | Blood | | Stool Culture | | Skin Tests | | | | Onchocerciasis Skin Snip | |
| | | | | | | | | | | | | | | Made | | Read | | | |
		No.	%	No.	%	No.	%	No.	%	No.	%	No.	%	No.	%	No.	%	No.	%
Birth–9	132	132	100.0	132	100.0	119	90.1	121	91.7	129	97.7	128	97.0	110	83.3	102	92.7	107	81.1
10–19	110	110	100.0	110	100.0	108	98.2	109	99.1	109	99.1	0	—	107	97.3	103	96.3	109	99.1
20–29	67	67	100.0	67	100.0	65	97.0	66	98.5	67	100.0	0	—	65	97.0	55	84.6	67	100.0
30–39	51	51	100.0	50	98.0	47	92.1	51	100.0	50	98.0	0	—	49	96.0	44	90.0	49	96.0
40–49	24	23	95.8	24	100.0	22	91.7	24	100.0	24	100.0	0	—	22	91.7	21	95.5	24	100.0
50–59	12	12	100.0	12	100.0	11	91.7	12	100.0	12	100.0	0	—	12	100.0	11	91.7	12	100.0
60+	5	5	100.0	5	100.0	5	100.0	5	100.0	5	100.0	0	—	5	100.0	5	100.0	5	100.0
Total	401	400	99.7	400	99.7	377	94.0	388	96.7	396	98.7	128	97.0	370	92.2	341	92.2	373	93.0

TABLE 5–4. PARTICIPATION IN SPECIFIED TEST PROCEDURES OF AN EPIDEMIOLOGICAL STUDY BY AGE, OUARAI

Age (years)	No. in Census	Interview		Physical		Stool Sample		Urine Sample		Blood		Stool Culture		Skin Tests				Onchocerciasis Skin Snip	
														Made		Read			
		No.	%	No.	%	No.	%	No.	%	No.	%	No.	%	No.	%	No.	%	No.	%
Birth–9	139	139	100.0	139	100.0	123	88.5	126	90.6	139	100.0	134	96.4	124	89.2	112	90.3	1	0.7
10–19	74	73	98.6	73	98.6	70	94.6	73	98.6	73	98.6	0	—	73	98.6	65	89.0	11	14.9
20–29	62	61	98.3	61	98.3	60	96.7	61	98.3	61	98.3	0	—	61	98.3	55	90.2	6	9.7
30–39	36	36	100.0	36	100.0	33	91.6	35	97.2	36	100.0	0	—	36	100.0	30	83.3	4	11.1
40–49	21	21	100.0	21	100.0	21	100.0	21	100.0	21	100.0	0	—	21	100.0	18	85.7	9	42.9
50–59	19	19	100.0	19	100.0	19	100.0	19	100.0	19	100.0	0	—	19	100.0	16	84.2	1	5.3
60+	14	14	100.0	14	100.0	13	92.8	13	92.8	14	100.0	0	—	14	100.0	12	85.7	3	21.4
Total	365	363	99.4	363	99.4	339	92.9	348	95.3	363	99.4	134	96.4	348	95.3	308	88.5	35	9.6

242

TABLE 5-5. PARTICIPATION IN SPECIFIED TEST PROCEDURES OF AN EPIDEMIOLOGICAL STUDY BY AGE, BOUM KHEBIR

Age (years)	No. in Cen-sus	Interview		Physical		Stool Sample		Urine Sample		Blood		Stool Culture		Skin Tests				Onchocerciasis Skin Snip	
														Made		Read			
		No.	%	No.	%	No.	%	No.	%	No.	%	No.	%	No.	%	No.	%	No.	%
Birth–9	137	134	97.8	135	98.5	122	89.0	125	91.2	130	94.9	127	92.7	119	86.9	118	99.2	7	5.1
10–19	62	62	100.0	62	100.0	59	95.1	60	96.7	60	96.7	0	—	62	100.0	62	100.0	5	8.1
20–29	52	52	100.0	52	100.0	48	92.3	50	96.2	52	100.0	0	—	52	100.0	50	96.2	12	23.1
30–39	34	34	100.0	34	100.0	33	97.1	34	100.0	34	100.0	0	—	34	100.0	32	94.1	9	26.5
40–49	30	30	100.0	30	100.0	28	93.3	29	96.7	29	96.7	0	—	30	100.0	29	96.7	4	13.3
50–59	25	25	100.0	25	100.0	21	84.0	22	88.0	22	88.0	0	—	25	100.0	25	100.0	1	4.0
60+	39	36	92.3	36	92.3	37	94.9	38	97.4	36	92.3	0	—	36	92.3	35	97.2	7	17.9
Total	379	373	98.4	374	98.7	348	91.8	358	94.4	363	95.8	127	92.7	358	94.4	351	98.0	45	11.9

243

TABLE 5-6. PARTICIPATION IN SPECIFIED TEST PROCEDURES OF AN EPIDEMIOLOGICAL STUDY BY AGE, FAYA-LARGEAU

Age (years)	No. in Census	Interview		Physical		Stool Sample		Urine Sample		Blood		Stool Culture		Skin Tests				Onchocerciasis Skin Snip	
														Made		Read			
	sus	No.	%	No.	%	No.	%	No.	%	No.	%	No.	%	No.	%	No.	%	No.	%
Birth–9	75	72	96.0	72	96.0	63	84.0	58	77.3	64	85.3	56	74.6	53	70.6	46	86.8	0	—
10–19	38	35	92.1	35	92.1	35	92.1	22	57.9	35	92.1	0	—	32	84.2	31	96.9	0	—
20–29	34	31	91.2	31	91.2	30	88.2	26	76.5	31	91.2	0	—	25	73.5	23	92.0	0	—
30–39	22	22	100.0	22	100.0	22	100.0	18	81.8	22	100.0	0	—	20	90.9	20	100.0	0	—
40–49	22	22	100.0	22	100.0	21	95.4	18	81.8	22	100.0	0	—	20	90.9	20	100.0	0	—
50–59	16	14	87.5	14	87.5	13	81.3	12	75.0	14	87.5	0	—	11	68.8	9	81.8	0	—
60 +	10	10	100.0	10	100.0	8	80.0	9	90.0	10	100.0	0	—	8	80.0	8	100.0	0	—
Total	217	206	94.9	206	94.9	192	88.5	163	75.1	198	91.2	56	74.6	169	77.9	157	92.9	0	—

Physical Examinations

The physical examinations were standardized and restricted to systematic observations and measurements of selected physiological and pathological signs and symptoms. Results were recorded on precoded forms. Routine measurements included body weight and height, as well as skinfold thickness at the mid-posterior mid-point of the arms held in 90° flexion. Also recorded were gross deformities and incapacitations; conditions of the hair, lips, and skin indicating nutritional deficiencies and infections; specified categories of eye infections and diseases; types of edema; presence and degree of hepato- and splenomegaly; and scars resulting from smallpox disease and vaccinations. To permit the registration of findings not included in the schedule, five categories for "other diagnoses and conditions" were established.

Skin Tests

Two tuberculins, PPD-S and PPD-G (Gause strain), were used in the skin tests. One-tenth of a milliliter, or the equivalent of five TU of each antigen, was injected intracutaneously into the skin of each forearm. A reading schedule for the random selection of injection sites for the two antigens was kept by a team member who was not involved in the reading of the tests. All reactions were read by one person forty-eight hours after the injection of the antigen, and the sizes of induration of these reactions were recorded. In addition, histoplasmin skin tests were applied in two communities. The three antigens were obtained from the U.S. Public Health Service, Operational Research Section, Tuberculosis Program. Lepromin was furnished by the Leprosy Research Team of the Department of International Health (Dr. Carl E. Taylor).

Chest Radiography

A mobile Viso Model 10 Chest Radiography System, supplied with a Du Pont high-speed intensifying screen and a radioactive Ytterbium 169 power source, was employed. Kodak Royal Blue X-ray film in fifty-foot rolls was used in the system. The unit was pretested in the Department of Radiology of The Johns Hopkins Hospital. A rotating time schedule for exchanging the power head permitted monthly replacements of the energy source at the half-life point of the isotope. The field operations were smooth and un-eventful. After completion of the routine examinations in a given village, all residents except children under the age of six, who were excluded because of technical limitations, appeared on an appointed day for their chest X-rays. They were lined up by height from tall-est to shortest in order to reduce the time that normally would be spent raising and lowering the X-ray cassette to suit the height of each individual. Exposed X-ray films from each village were shipped directly to the Department of Radiology of The Johns Hopkins Hospital, where they were developed and read. The field team was notified by telegram whether the chest roentgenograms taken in a village were of relatively high or low quality. This permitted flexi-bility in finding the optimal exposure time in connection with a standard timetable of energy emission furnished by the manufac-turers of the radioisotope Ytterbium.

LABORATORY

Field Laboratory

Whereas the methods and equipment used in the field laboratory were essentially those that had been used in Peru (Buck, Sasaki, and Anderson, 1968), certain improvements and additions were made. These modifications were based on field experiences in Peru or be-came necessary for the study of specific disease problems in Chad. Emphasis continued to be placed on compact, sturdy, light-weight, and durable equipment and supplies.

The heavy kerosene-operated incubator, which gave excellent service in Peru, was not used in Chad, because the hot climate and relatively slight changes in altitude in the latter country permitted the use of a more practical item. A polyfoam insulated box with a durable fiber jacket was selected. Internal dimensions of the box were approximately fourteen by twenty-three by twenty-three inches. During the day and until about 9:00 P.M. the ambient tem-perature was sufficient for incubation purposes. During the evening two gallons of hot water in metal containers with two small holes in each lid were added to the box. These served to maintain the tem-perature at a satisfactory level for enteric organisms until the follow-ing day. In addition, moisture escaping from the holes in the lids helped to maintain a humidity level which enhanced the growth of the organisms.

The Linde Division of Union Carbide supplied two liquid nitrogen transport tanks (LD-30), two large nitrogen refrigerators (LR-40), and one small nitrogen refrigerator (LD-30). All units gave excellent service, but retention time of the liquid nitrogen in the small refrigerator was outstanding. This was attributed to the unit's narrow neck when compared to the large refrigerators. The wide neck and large cover required for insertion of the specimen containers into the large units resulted in a much greater liquid nitrogen loss, particularly during transit over rough terrain and during air transport. Schedules for the delivery of liquid nitrogen were prearranged with L'Air Liquide Corporation, Paris. The excellent services of this company, the airlines, and the personnel in the U.S. Embassy in Fort Lamy were instrumental in maintaining the schedule.

The medical team collected ten milliliters of blood by venipuncture from each individual examined. Before clotting, small portions were taken for transfer to a special tube containing acid-citrate-dextrose (ACD) solution, for making thick and thin smears, for filling two capillary tubes for hematocrit readings, and for determining the hemoglobin level. The remainder was allowed to clot and the serum was withdrawn. Stool cups and urine containers were distributed by the health interviewers on the afternoon prior to the examinations. The specimens were delivered to the medical examination tent by each individual on the following morning.

Hemoglobin

Hemoglobin determinations were made routinely, using a battery-operated hemoglobinometer obtained from the American Optical Company, Buffalo, New York.

Hematocrit

The Strumia capillary tube method (Strumia, Sample, and Hart, 1954) was employed, using a capillary tube head in the table model centrifuge. Some difficulty was encountered with breakage of the tubes in the centrifuge head. It was not possible to correct the problem in the field, but it was subsequently solved with the use of a softer cushioning inner rim in the head.

Blood Smears

For each person a thick smear and a thin blood film were prepared on clean glass slides. The blood was allowed to air dry in screened slide boxes. Once dry, the thin film was fixed in methyl alcohol and the thick smear was laked in distilled water. The slides were then stained with Giemsa, washed, air dried, and stored in dust-proof slide boxes.

Red Blood Cells Preserved in ACD

Samples of approximately two milliliters of whole blood were transferred under sterile conditions to tubes containing 0.2 milliliter of ACD solution. These tubes were purchased from the Becton-Dickinson Company, Columbus, Nebraska. The appropriately labeled tubes were placed in racks and stored in the refrigerator (4° C).

Serum Specimens

Venipunctures were performed using ten-milliliter Becton-Dickinson vacutainers. After blood was dispensed for the above procedures, the remainder was allowed to clot and the vacutainer tubes were centrifuged. The serum was removed with sterile disposable one-milliliter pipettes fitted with suction bulbs and was placed in sterile polypropylene test tubes (Falcon Plastics, Los Angeles, California). As soon as groups of the sera had been processed they were put into a liquid nitrogen refrigerator.

Rectal Swabs: Bacteriology

Rectal swabs were obtained from all children under ten years of age. The swabs were plated onto MacConkey and SS agar plates and incubated for twenty-four hours at 37° C. After the incubation period, representative colonies that had not fermented lactose were selected and transferred to screw-capped tubes containing nutrient agar. The plates were then reincubated for twenty-four hours and again were screened for any additional non-lactose-fermenting colonies. The inoculated tubes were incubated for twenty-four hours, checked for growth, and stored at ambient temperature for shipment.

Stool Specimens: Parasitology

Stool specimens were collected in disposable cardboard cups. Approximately one gram of feces was emulsified in a polypropylene vial containing about three milliliters of merthiolate-formalin solution that did not contain the iodine used in the published MIF technique (Sapero and Lawless, 1952). The specimens were stored at ambient temperature until shipped.

Urine Specimens: Parasitology

Each participant was instructed to void a complete early morning urine specimen into a polypropylene container. These containers were fitted with snap-on lids and were virtually spill proof; in addition, they were calibrated on one side in milliliters. Upon receipt of the specimen in the laboratory, the volume was recorded and tincture of merthiolate was added (approximately one milliliter per one hundred milliliters of specimen). The specimen was transferred to a 150-milliliter funnel fitted with a length of plastic tubing and a clamp. Specimens of less than ten milliliters were kept in the original container. All specimens were allowed to sediment overnight. The following morning ten milliliters of the sedimented urine were transferred to a centrifuge tube via the plastic tubing. The specimens of less than ten milliliters, which had remained in the original containers, were shaken and poured directly into the centrifuge tubes. Following centrifugation, approximately seven milliliters of the supernatant urine was discarded by decanting and the sediment was shaken in the tube until well dispersed. The dispersed sediment was then poured into a polypropylene vial. Specimens were stored at ambient temperature until shipped.

Skin Snips for Microfilariae

In selected villages skin snips were routinely collected and examined for microfilariae. The methods employed have been presented in detail elsewhere (Buck *et al.*, 1969). A corneal biopsy instrument (Holth Cornealscleral Punch, two millimeters) was used for the superficial skin biopsy of a site located above the iliac crest. The instrument performed well, gave snips which were relatively uniform in size and thickness, and did not cause excessive bleeding, which might have led to the passive transfer of blood-borne microfilariae. The snips were readily transferable to welled microscope slides. A small drop of 0.85 percent normal saline solution was placed in each well and then covered with transparent plastic tape. When the specimens arrived in the laboratory tent they were immediately examined under the low power of a compound microscope. If microfilariae were present, they were identified and counted. The findings were graded as follows: specimens containing from one to five microfilariae were recorded as 1+, those containing from six to ten as 2+, from eleven to twenty as 3+, and more than twenty as 4+. If no microfilariae were found upon initial observation, the slides were placed in a moist chamber for thirty minutes and then re-examined. Then, if no microfilariae were observed, the specimens were macerated by pressing on the tape. If microfilariae still were not observed, the findings were recorded as negative. Representative specimens were removed from the slides and stored in 10 percent formalin for later use as pathological specimens.

Miscellaneous Procedures

On one occasion physicians removed an onchocerciasis nodule from a patient. The nodule was quick-frozen and stored in a liquid nitrogen refrigerator. It was transported with the frozen serum specimens back to the base laboratory as a source of antigen for serological tests.

The field laboratory had limited capacities for performing miscellaneous tests other than those routinely run as part of the survey. These tests were requested by the physicians when indicated as an aid in the diagnosis of unusual or acute conditions. They included red and white blood cell counts, differential white blood cell counts, urinalyses, and bacteriological and mycological smears, stains, and cultures. Examinations for stool, urine, and blood parasites, which were routinely made only on the specimens sent to Baltimore, occasionally were also required for immediate diagnosis. All of the procedures were performed by standard laboratory methods.

Shipment of Specimens

At the end of the study in each village the preserved stool and urine specimens, the stained blood films, the frozen sera, the ACD-preserved blood cells, and the enteric cultures were transported to Fort Lamy. The last two were immediately shipped to Baltimore via previously arranged air routes. The frozen sera were placed in a mechanical freezer ($-20°$ C) and the preserved stool and urine specimens were stored in a cool place in the U.S. Embassy. At the end of the entire study, the frozen sera were placed with dry ice in the polyfoam box which had served as the field incubator. The box, along with the preserved stool and urine specimens, was transported as excess air baggage by a member of the team returning to Baltimore.

Base Laboratory

The base laboratory was located in the Department of Epidemiology, The School of Hygiene and Public Health of The Johns Hopkins University. It included three laboratory rooms, a glassware and media kitchen, and quarters for a limited number of animals. The methods and equipment were selected specifically for the current type of study. Wherever feasible, microtechniques and miniaturized equipment were used. All procedures were standardized to be comparable to those in appropriate control laboratories, including the National Communicable Disease Center (NCDC) and the Walter Reed Army Institute of Research (WRAIR). Continuing efforts have been made to familiarize the laboratory personnel with all techniques and equipment employed in the study. Whenever necessary, personnel were given training. Essentially the tests were performed at the base laboratory, the single exception being the hemoglobin electrophoresis and genetic studies, which were performed by Dr. Samuel H. Boyer of The Johns Hopkins Hospital. In addition, several other laboratories assisted by supplying antigens that were not available commercially.

Blood Smears

The Giemsa-stained blood smears were examined for blood parasites under the appropriate powers of a compound microscope. Representative specimens of microfilariae which were found and identified by base laboratory personnel were verified by Dr. Leo A. Jachowski, Jr., of the University of Maryland. In addition, red blood cell morphology and white blood cell differential counts were reported when indicated.

Red Blood Cells Preserved in ACD

The aseptically collected samples were refrigerated (except during the two or three days they were in transport) until they were examined in Baltimore, usually from five to fifteen days later. The determinations of hemoglobin phenotypes were made in the laboratory of the Division of Medical Genetics (Dr. Samuel H. Boyer) of The Johns Hopkins Hospital. Laboratory procedures involved the washing of erythrocytes, the preparation of hemolysates, and electrophoretic assays on starch gel (Boyer *et al.*, 1967). Presence of fetal hemoglobin (F) on starch gel was verified by agar-gel electrophoresis (Marder and Conley, 1959).

Additional blood samples were obtained from the two individuals with hemoglobin$_{Chad}$, as well as from other members of their family, through the assistance of Dr. Pierre Ziegler, director of the Service des Grandes Endémies, Fort Lamy. Separation and estimates of the proportions of various hemoglobins in hemolysates from this family were made by column chromatography on diethylaminoethyl Sephadex (A–50, Pharmacia) (Huisman and Dozy, 1965). Globin was prepared from individual hemoglobins and globin chains subsequently were separated (Clegg, Naughton, and Weatherall, 1966). Individual S-beta-aminoethylcysteinyl derivatives of chains were digested with trypsin. The resulting peptides were separated and their composition analyzed by methods referred to or elaborated upon elsewhere (Boyer *et al.*, 1967).

Serum Specimens

When the frozen serum specimens were received in the base laboratory, they were removed from the shipping box containing dry ice and were immediately stored in a mechanical deep freezer ($-80°$ C). Prior to testing, each serum was thawed and dispensed into appropriate aliquants for the various types of tests. In this manner it was possible to perform each type of test in protocols convenient for the given test without repeatedly freezing and thawing the parent specimen. The parent specimen was again stored at $-80°$ C.

Chemistry

Total protein and cholesterol determinations were performed by spectrophotometric methods (Henry, Sobel, and Berkman, 1957;

Mann, 1961). The Microzone-Analytrol method (Grunbaum, Zec, and Durrum, 1963) was used for serum electrophoresis.

Flocculation and Card Tests

The Venereal Disease Research Laboratory (VDRL) cardiolipin flocculation test (Harris, Rosenberg, and Riedel, 1946) and the cercarial antigen schistosome flocculation test (Anderson, 1963) were performed. Antigen for the schistosome test was prepared in the base laboratory from cercariae obtained through the courtesy of the World Health Organization and the U.S. Army Tropical Research Medical Laboratory (USA TRML). Two card tests, one for trichinosis and the other for brucellosis, were performed with antigens and equipment supplied by Hynson, Westcott, and Dunning, Inc., Baltimore, Maryland.

Fluorescent Antibody Tests

The Fluorescent Treponemal Antibody-Absorption (FTA-ABS) test was performed as part of the battery of serological tests for treponematoses. The method (Hunter, Deacon, and Meyer, 1964) was essentially that of the test originator and the reagents used were from commercial sources. Test performance had been standardized to correspond with those of NCDC. The methods used in reporting the results are presented in Table 5–7.

TABLE 5–7. METHODS FOR RECORDING RESULTS IN THE FTA-ABS TEST

Intensity of Fluorescence	Reading	Report
None or vaguely visible	− or ±	Non-reactive (−)
Weak but definite	1+	Weakly reactive (Wr)
Moderate to strong	2+, 3+, or 4+	Reactive (R)

Treponema pallidum Immobilization (TPI) Test

The TPI test (Nelson and Diesendruck, 1951) was performed only on selected sera. Non-specific immobilization (failure of treponemes to survive in the control tube due to toxic substances in the patient's serum) proved to be a serious problem. Attempts to overcome non-specific immobilization (NSI) by precipitating the euglobulins with diluted hydrochloric acid (Neurath *et al.*, 1946) and testing the reconstituted precipitate resulted in a reduced sensitivity of the TPI procedure and was therefore abandoned. Reagents for the TPI test were from commercial sources, and WRAIR served as the reference laboratory. Table 5–8 presents the method used for recording the TPI test results.

TABLE 5–8. METHODS FOR RECORDING RESULTS IN THE TPI TEST

Result	Report
<70% motile in control with patient's serum	Non-Specific Immobilization (NSI)
% specifically immobilized[a]	
0–20	Non-reactive (−)
21–70	Weakly reactive (Wr)
71–100	Reactive (R)
<25% hemolysis in residual C' check	Anticomplementary

[a] $\dfrac{\% \text{ motile in control} - \% \text{ motile in test}}{\% \text{ motile in control}} \times 100.$

Hemagglutination Test for Onchocerciasis

Antigens were prepared (Chaffee, Bauman, and Shapilo, 1954) from the microfilariae and also from the adult *Onchocerca volvulus* obtained from the patient in Chad. *Dirofilaria immitis* adult worm antigen (Melcher, 1943) was made available by WRAIR. The NCDC hemagglutination test for parasitic diseases (Kagan, Norman, and Allain, 1960) was modified (Buck *et al.*, 1969) in the base laboratory for use with microtiter equipment (Cooke Engineering Co., Alexandria, Virginia). The modified test retained the same proportion of cells-to-serum dilution as the original procedure. Sera from selected villages were tested in six dilutions (1:50, 1:100, 1:200, 1:400, 1:800, and 1:1,600). The titer was recorded as the highest serum dilution showing at least 50 percent agglutination of antigen cells and no agglutination in the tannic acid–cells control. Freezing proved to be detrimental to both *Onchocerca* antigens; therefore, only the *D. immitis* antigen test results could be reported.

Leptospiral Agglutination Test

A macroscopic slide agglutination test which uses four commercially obtainable leptospiral antigen pools (Galton *et al.*, 1958) served as a screening procedure. Pool 1 contains *Leptospira ballum*, *L. canicola*, and *L. icterohemorrhagiae* antigens. Pool 2 consists of *L. bataviae*, *L. grippotyphosa*, and *L. pyrogenes* antigens. Pool 3 is made up of *L. autumnalis*, *L. pomona*, and *L. sejroe*. Pool 4 contains *L. australis*, *L. hyos*, *L. mini georgia*, and *L. icterokremastos*. Individual antigens may be used in testing those sera which react with the pooled antigens, but no attempt was made in this study to identify antibodies beyond the pool number.

Complement Fixation (CF) Tests

The complement fixation test (Kent and Fife, 1963) used in the base laboratory was a spectrophotometric system, employing the 50 percent end point of hemolysis for reagent standardization. For qualitative tests with microtiter equipment, the volumes allotted for sera and reagents were reduced to 0.025 milliliter. The sheep cells used in the tests were obtained from WRAIR, and the other components required were from commercial sources, with the exception of certain antigens. The sources of the eleven antigens used in the current study are given in the following paragraphs.

Reiter Treponeme Antigen. This antigen was included as part of the battery of tests for treponemal infections. The antigen was obtained from a commercial source.

Schistosoma mansoni Adult Antigen. The adult worms used in the preparation of this antigen were obtained through the courtesy of the World Health Organization and USA TRML. The method of preparation was the same as that used in the preparation of antigen from cercariae (Chaffee, Bauman, and Shapilo, 1954) for the slide flocculation test.

Mycotic Disease Antigens. These antigens—histoplasmin, coccidioidin, and the yeast phase of *Blastomyces dermatitidis*—were prepared, standardized, and supplied by WRAIR.

Rickettsial Disease Antigens. All four of the antigens, corresponding control antigens, and control sera came from commercial sources. Rocky Mountain spotted fever (RMSF) and Q fever antigens were purchased. However, the Lederle Laboratories Division of the American Cyanamid Company, Pearl River, New York, generously donated the murine typhus and epidemic typhus antigens, which were not available commercially.

Plague Antigen. Plague antigen was obtained from WRAIR, where it has been prepared by their standard methods.

Measles Antigen. Measles antigen and the corresponding control antigen were obtained commercially.

Amoebiasis Antigen. This antigen was donated by WRAIR and had been prepared experimentally by a commercial source.

Anticomplementary Activity. Preliminary CF tests showed that approximately 85 percent of the sera from all the villages except Faya-Largeau were anticomplementary. Limited investigation revealed that the sera had high levels of macroglobulins (Mayer, 1968), and the routine determination of the albumin/globulin ratio indicated that essentially all of the sera contained inverted ratios. The addition of egg albumin to these sera reduced the anticomplementary activity in the CF test in the majority of instances, but approximately 16 percent of the sera remained unsatisfactory for testing. Table 5–9 shows by locality the percentage of sera remaining anticomplementary. Djimtilo and Boum Khebir had the highest residual of anticomplementary sera, 26.5 and 27.3 percent respectively. Faya-Largeau, on the other hand, showed only 1.0 percent anticomplementary activity, and these sera had not required treatment with egg albumin. Table 5–10 shows anticomplementary activity by age and by sex. The percentage of females (18.4) with anticomplementary components was slightly higher than that of males (13.5), and in both sexes the percentage increased with age.

TABLE 5–9. PERCENTAGE OF SERA WITH ANTICOMPLEMENTARY
ACTIVITY IN COMPLEMENT FIXATION TESTS BY LOCALITY

Locality	No. of Sera Examined	Anticomplementary Activity	
		No.	%
Djimtilo	347	92	26.5
Ouli Bangala	381	41	10.8
Ouarai	337	31	9.2
Boum Khebir	344	94	27.3
Faya-Largeau	193	2	1.0

Hemagglutination Inhibition (HI) Tests for Viral Diseases

Arboviruses representing various groups were selected by Dr. Winston H. Price, The Johns Hopkins University, as being of possible importance in Chad. The arboviruses included in the study are presented in Table 5–11. Standard Methods (Clarke and Casals, 1958; Clarke, 1964) were used in antigen preparation and in performing the HI tests.

TABLE 5–10. PERCENTAGE OF SERA WITH ANTICOMPLEMENTARY
ACTIVITY IN COMPLEMENT FIXATION TESTS BY AGE AND SEX

Age (years)	Males			Females		
	No. Examined	Anti-Complementary		No. Examined	Anti-Complementary	
		No.	%		No.	%
Birth–4	97	6	6.2	100	10	10.0
5–9	154	8	5.2	129	9	7.0
10–19	152	16	10.5	188	29	15.4
20–29	85	15	17.6	177	29	16.4
30–39	87	20	23.0	125	37	29.6
40+	142	32	22.5	165	49	29.7
Total	717	97	13.5	884	163	18.4

TABLE 5–11. VIRUSES USED IN THE STUDY

Group A	Group B	Group Bunyamwera
Chikungunya	Yellow Fever	Bunyamwera
Semliki Forest	Uganda S	Germiston
Sindbis	West Nile	
O'nyongnyong	Zika	

Mouse Neutralization Test for Viral Diseases

The constant virus-varying serum procedure was employed on sera selected from the results obtained in the virus neutralization tests. Antigens were diluted in 60 percent Human Accessory Factor to contain 100 LD_{50} per dose. The 100-LD_{50} dose for each antigen had been determined by antigen titration of the virus in mice. The Human Accessory Factor was serum obtained from a healthy donor who had not previously had an infection of the virus and who had not been immunized with the virus. Both the Human Accessory Factor serum and the patient's serum were diluted with 0.75 percent bovine serum albumin (BSA), Serum Fraction V (pH 9.0). All test sera were incubated for thirty minutes in a water bath at 56° C. Following incubation, fourfold dilutions of the sera were made in the 0.75 percent BSA, and an equal volume of the antigen containing 100 LD_{50} was added to each serum dilution. The mixture was incubated for one hour in a water bath at 37° C. For all tests except Sindbis virus, 0.03 milliliter of each antigen-serum mixture was inoculated intracerebrally into each of four weanling mice weighing between eight and ten grams apiece. For Sindbis virus, 0.01 milliliter of the mixture was employed in three-to-four-day-old suckling mice. All mice were observed for up to twenty-one days. The titer of the serum was calculated as the serum dilution at which 50 percent of the mice were protected.

Rectal Swabs: Bacteriology

Non-lactose-fermenting cultures were received from the field at the end of the study in each village. The cultures were transferred from the nutrient agar transport medium onto MacConkey's agar to confirm that they were either non-lactose- or slow-lactose-fermenting organisms. Typical colonies were inoculated into urease medium. All urease negative organisms were subjected to motility tests and to biochemical reactions with the following: methyl red, phenylalanine, indol, citrate, lysine, KCN, gelatin, glucose, lactose, sucrose, mannite, and triple sugar. Whenever indicated, serological identification was made, using *Shigella* and *Salmonella* grouping sera. Standard laboratory methods (Bailey and Scott, 1966) were followed, and the classification system of Kauffmann (1966) was employed for a new sero-type of *Salmonella* that was found. Enteric pathogens and closely related organisms were forwarded to NCDC for verification and/or identification.

Stool Specimens: Parasitology

The merthiolate-formalin-preserved stool specimens were prepared by the ether concentration method (Blagg *et al.*, 1955). The sediment from each concentrated specimen was examined with a compound microscope. All protozoa, helminth eggs, and/or larvae were recorded. When hookworm eggs were found, a rough estimate of their numbers was made. These categories were defined as: few, from one to ten eggs per twenty-two-by-twenty-two-millimeter cover glass; moderate, more than ten eggs per cover glass but less than one egg per low power field; and numerous, more than one egg per low field. As previously indicated, iodine was not used in the preservation or concentration procedures.

Urine Specimens: Parasitology

The merthiolate-preserved urine specimens were washed from the transport vial into fifteen-milliliter graduated tubes and centrifuged. All but 0.5 milliliter of the supernatant fluid was withdrawn. The sediment was mixed by shaking the tube, and 0.03 milliliter was placed on a clean slide. A twenty-two-by-twenty-two-millimeter cover glass was placed on the specimen, and the area under the entire cover glass was searched microscopically for ova and parasites. The ova of *S. hematobium* were counted. When microfilariae were found they, too, were counted. A combination of the techniques used in the field and base laboratories permitted a fairly accurate estimate of the total number of organisms either in the entire specimen or on a per-milliliter basis.

BIBLIOGRAPHY

Ajello, L. 1968. Comparative morphology and immunology of members of the genus *Histoplasma;* a review. *Mykosen* 11:507–14.

Albrink, M. J., and Meigs, J. W. 1964. Interrelationships between skinfold thickness, serum lipids and blood sugar in normal men. *Amer. J. Clin. Nutr.* 15:255–61.

American Public Health Association. 1965. *Standard Methods for the Examination of Water and Wastewater.* 12th ed. New York.

Anderson, R. I. 1963. Serologic diagnosis of *Schistosoma mansoni* infections. I: Development of a cercarial antigen slide flocculation test. *Amer. J. Trop. Med.* 9:600–603.

Anderson, R. I.; Sadun, E. H.; and Schoenbechler, M. J. 1963. Cholesterol-lecithin slide (TsSF) and charcoal card (TsCC) flocculation tests using an acid soluble fraction of *Trichinella spiralis* larvae. *J. Parasit.* 49:642–47.

Bailey, W. R., and Scott, E. G. 1966. *Diagnostic Microbiology*, pp. 125–46. St. Louis, Missouri: The C. V. Mosby Co.

Basu, B. C., and Rao, S. S. 1939. Studies on filariasis transmission. *Indian J. Med. Res.* 27:233–49.

Blagg, W.; Schloegel, E. L.; Mansour, N. S.; and Khalaf, G. I. 1955. A new concentration technic for the demonstration of protozoa and helminth eggs in feces. *Amer. J. Trop. Med.* 4:23–28.

Boyd, M. F. 1949. *Malariology.* Philadelphia and London: W. B. Saunders Co.

Boyer, S. H.; Crosby, E. F.; Fuller, G. F.; Ulenurm, L.; and Buck, A. A. 1968. A survey of hemoglobins in the Republic of Chad and characterization of Hemoglobin Chad: $\alpha_2^{23 \text{ Glu}} \rightarrow {}^{\text{Lys}}\beta_2$. *Amer. J. Hum. Genet.* 20:570–78.

Boyer, S. H.; Hathaway, P.; Pascasio, F.; Bordley, J.; Orton, C.; and Naughton, M. A. 1967. Differences in the amino acid sequences of tryptic peptides in three sheep hemoglobin β chains. *J. Biol. Chem.* 242:2211–32.

Boyer, S. H.; Rucknagel, D. L.; Weatherall, D. J.; and Watson-Williams, E. J. 1963. Further evidence for linkage between the β and δ loci governing hemoglobin and population dynamics of linked genes. *Amer. J. Hum. Genet.* 15:438–48.

Buck, A. A. 1961. Epidemiologic investigations of sarcoidosis, I: Introduction; material and methods. *Amer. J. Hyg.* 74:137–51.

Buck, A. A.; Anderson, R. I.; and Hewitt, J. J. 1966. *Report on pilot study in the Republic of Chad.* Geographic Epidemiology Unit, The Johns Hopkins University, School of Hygiene and Public Health, Baltimore, Maryland. Unpublished data.

Buck, A. A.; Anderson, R. I.; Kawata, K.; and Hitchcock, J. C., Jr. 1969. Onchocerciasis: Some new epidemiologic and clinical findings. *Amer. J. Trop. Med.* 18:217–30.

Buck, A. A.; Sasaki, T. T.; and Anderson, R. I. 1968. *Health and disease in four Peruvian villages: Contrasts in epidemiology.* The Johns Hopkins Monographs in International Health. Baltimore: The Johns Hopkins Press.

Buck, A. A.; Sasaki, T. T.; Hewitt, J. J.; and MacRae, A. A. 1968. Coca chewing and health. *Amer. J. Epid.* 88:159–77.

Chaffee, E. F.; Bauman, P. M.; and Shapilo, J. J. 1954. Diagnosis of schistosomiasis by complement fixation. *Amer. J. Trop. Med.* 3:905–13.

Chapelle, J. 1957. *Nomades Noirs du Sahara.* Paris: Librairie Plon.

Clarke, D. H. 1964. Further studies on antigenic relationships among viruses of the Group B tick-borne complex. *Bull. WHO* 31:45–56.

Clarke, D. H., and Casals, J. 1958. Techniques for hemagglutination and hemagglutination-inhibition with arthropod-borne viruses. *Amer. J. Trop. Med.* 7:561–73.

Clegg, J. B.; Naughton, M. A.; and Weatherall, D. J. 1966. Abnormal human haemoglobins. Separation and characterization of the α and β chains by chromatography, and the determination of two new variants, Hb Chesapeake and Hb J (Bangkok). *J. Molec. Biol.* 19:91–108.

Cochran, W. G. 1954. Some methods for strengthening the common Chi-square tests. *Biometrics* 10:417–51.

Comstock, G. W.; Kendrick, M. A.; and Livesay, V. T. 1966. Subcutaneous fatness and mortality. *Amer. J. Epid.* 83:548–63.

Connor, D. H., and Fletcher Lunn, H. 1965. *Mycobacterium ulcerans* infection. *Int. J. Leprosy* 33:698–709.

———. 1966. Buruli ulceration. *Arch. Path.* (Chicago) 81:183–89.

Davis, B. D.; Dulbecco, R.; Eisen, H. N.; Ginsberg, H. S.; and Wood, W. B., Jr. 1968. Pathogenesis of viral infections. *Microbiology*, p. 1210. New York: Harper & Row, Hoeber Medical Division.

Direction de la Météorologie Nationale. 1955. *Cartes Pluviometriques Moyennes des ex-territoires Français de L'Afrique-Noire.* Paris: Ministère des Travaux Publics et des Transports.

Edwards, D. A. W. 1950. Observations on the distribution of subcutaneous fat. *Clin. Sci.* 9:259–70.

Edwards, L. B., and Palmer, C. E. 1958. Epidemiologic studies of tuberculin sensitivity. I: Preliminary results with purified protein derivations prepared from atypical acid-fast organisms. *Amer. J. Hyg.* 68:213–31.

Edwards, P. Q.; Geser, A. G.; Kjolbye, E. H.; Meijer, J. H.; and Christensen, O. W. 1956. Histoplasmin testing in Africa and southern Asia. *Amer. J. Trop. Med.* 5:224–34.

Farooq, M.; Nielsen, S.; Samaan, S. A.; Mallah, M. B.; and Allam, A. A. 1966. The epidemiology of *Schistosoma haematobium and S. mansoni* infections in the Egypt–49 Project Area. *Bull. WHO* 35:293–318.

Furculow, M. L.; Emge, M. E.; and Bunnell, I. L. 1948. Depression of tuberculin and histoplasmin sensitivity associated with critical illness. *Public Health Rep.* 63, pt. 2:1290–98.

Galton, M. M.; Powers, D. K.; Hall, A. D.; and Cornell, R. G. 1958. A rapid macroscopic-screening test for the serodiagnosis of leptospirosis. *Amer. J. Vet. Res.* 19:505–12.

Great Britain Naval Staff. 1942. *French Equatorial Africa and Cameroons.* Geographical Handbook Series, Naval Intelligence Division.

Grunbaum, B. W.; Zec, J.; and Durrum, E. L. 1963. Application of an improved microelectrophoresis technique and immunoelectrophoresis of the serum proteins on cellulose acetate. *Microchem. J.* 7:41–53.

Gruvel, J. 1965. *Les glossines, vectrices des trypanosomiases au Tchad.* Institut d'Elevage et de Médecine Vétérinaire des Pays Tropicaux, Laboratoire de Farcha, Fort Lamy.

Hackett, L. W. 1944. Spleen measurement in malaria. *J. Natn. Malar. Soc.* 3:121–33.

Harris, A.; Rosenberg, A. A.; and Riedel, L. M. 1946. A microflocculation test for syphilis using cardiolipin antigen. Preliminary report. *J. Vener. Dis. Inf.* 27:169–74.

Henry, R. J.; Sobel, C.; and Berkman, S. 1957. Interferences with biuret methods for serum proteins. Use of Benedict's qualitative glucose reagent as a biuret reagent. *Anal. Chem.* 29:1491–95.

Hoeppli, R., and Gunders, A. E. 1962. A comparison of skin changes caused by onchocerciasis and aging. *Amer. J. Trop. Med.* 11:234–37.

Hoogstraal, H. 1956. *African Ixodoidea.* I: *Ticks of the Sudan.* Washington, D.C.: Department of the Navy, Bureau of Medicine and Surgery.

Hoogstraal, H., and Dietlein, D. R. 1964. Leishmaniasis in the Sudan Republic: Recent results. *Bull. WHO* 31:137.

Huisman, T. H. J., and Dozy, A. M. 1965. Studies on the heterogenicity of hemoglobin I_x. The use of tris (hydroxymethyl) aminomethane HCl buffers in the anion-exchange chromatography of hemoglobins. *J. Chromatogr.* 19:160–69.

Hunter, E. F.; Deacon, W. E.; and Meyer, P. E. 1964. An improved FTA test for syphilis, the absorption procedure (FTA-ABS). *Public Health Rep.* 79:410–12.

Kagan, I. G.; Norman, L.; and Allain, D. S. 1960. Studies on echinococcosis: Serology of crude and fractionated antigens prepared from *Echinococcus multilocularis. Amer. J. Trop. Med.* 3:248–61.

———. 1963. An evaluation of the bentonite flocculation and indirect hemagglutination tests for the diagnosis of filariasis. *Amer. J. Trop. Med.* 12:548–55.

Kar, S.; Elliston, E. P.; and Taylor, C. E. 1964. Field method for concentrating for *Mycobacterium leprae* in skin biopsy specimens. *Int. J. Leprosy* 32:18–23.

Kauffmann, F. 1966. *The Bacteriology of Enterobacteriaceae,* pp. 156–62. Baltimore: The Williams & Wilkins Co.

Kaufman, L., and Blumer, S. 1968. Development and use of a polyvalent conjugate to differentiate *Histoplasma capsulatum* and *Histoplasma duboisii* from other pathogens. *J. Bact.* 95:1243–46.

Kawata, K. 1967. Providing a safe water supply in the African bush. *Public Health Rep.* 82:1057–62.

Kent, J. F., and Fife, E. H., Jr. 1963. Precise standardization of reagents for complement fixation. *Amer. J. Trop. Med.* 12:103–16.

Lechat, M. 1961. *Étude des mutilations lepreuses.* Brussels: Editions Arcia S. A.

Leveque, C. 1967. Mollusques aquatiques de la zone est du Lac Tchad. *Bulletin de l'I.F.A.N.,* vol. 29, ser. A, no. 4, pp. 1494–1533.

McCuiston, C. F., and Hudgins, P. C. 1960. Serum electrophoresis in sarcoidosis, tuberculosis and disease due to unclassified mycobacteria. *Am. Rev. Tuberc. Pulm. Dis.* 82:96–100.

McDonough, J. R.; Hames, C. J.; Garrison, G. E.; Stulb, S. C.; Lichtman,

M. A.; and Hefelfinger, D. C. 1965. The relationship of hematocrit to cardiovascular states of health in the Negro and white population of Evans County, Georgia. *J. Chron. Dis.* 18:243–57.

Mann, G. V. 1961. A method for measurement of cholesterol in blood serum. *Clin. Chim. Acta.* 7:275–84.

Marder, V. J., and Conley, C. L. 1959. Electrophoresis of hemoglobin on agar gels. Frequency of hemoglobin D in a Negro population. *Bull. Johns Hopkins Hosp.* 105:77–88.

Mascher, W. 1951. Tuberculin-negative tuberculosis. *Am. Rev. Tuberc. Pulm. Dis.* 63:501–25.

Mayer, M. M. 1968. Professor of Microbiology, The Johns Hopkins School of Medicine, Baltimore, Maryland. Personal communication.

Melcher, L. R. 1943. An antigenic analysis of *Trichinella spiralis. J. Infect. Dis.* 73:31–39.

Merveille, P.; Andebond, G.; and Cecaldi, J. 1954. L'histoplasmose existe-t'elle en Afrique Equatoriale Française? *Bull. Soc. Path. Exot.* 47:566–72.

Ministry of Public Health. 1966. *Les Quatorze Prefectures Sanitaires.* Étude Bureau Technique, Départment Santé Publique, Fort Lamy.

Murdock, G. P. 1959. *Africa.* New York: McGraw-Hill.

Natelson, S. 1961. *Carotene in microtechnics of clinical chemistry.* 2d ed. Springfield, Ill.: Charles C Thomas.

National Research Council. 1966. *Public health problems in 14 French-speaking countries in Africa and Madagascar: A survey of resources and needs,* vol. 1. Washington, D.C.: National Academy of Sciences, Division of Medical Services.

———. 1966. *Public health problems in 14 French-speaking countries in Africa and Madagascar: A survey of resources and needs,* vol. 2. Washington, D.C.: National Academy of Sciences, Division of Medical Services.

Nebout, M. 1969. Situation épidémiologique de la trypanosomiase au Tchad. *Med. Trop.* (Marseille) 29:229–41.

Nelson, G. S.; Guggisberg, C. W. A.; and Mukundi, J. 1963. Animal hosts of *Trichinella spiralis* in East Africa. *Ann. Trop. Med. Parasit.* 57:332–46.

Nelson, R. A., Jr., and Diesendruck, J. H. 1951. Studies on treponemal immobilizing antibodies in syphilis. I: Techniques of measurement and factors influencing immobilization. *J. Immun.* 66:667–85.

Neurath, H.; Erickson, J. O.; Volkin, E.; Craig, H. W.; and Cooper, G. R. 1946. Biologic false positive reactions in serologic tests for syphilis. II: Preparation and properties of serologically active serum euglobulin fractions obtained by isoelectric precipitation. *Am. J. Syph. Gonorrhea Vener. Dis.* 31:374–96.

Nishimura, S.; Mori, T.; Kohsaka, K.; Kishi, Y.; and Innami, S. 1965. Studies on acid-fast bacilli detected in non-leprosy human skin tissues. *La Lepro* (Tokyo) 34:358–59.

Otto, G. F.; Berthrong, M.; Appleby, R. E.; Rawlins, J. C.; and Wilbur, O. 1954. Eosinophilia and hepatomegaly due to *Capillaria hepatica* infection. *Bull. Johns Hopkins Hosp.* 94:319–36.

Pairault, C. 1966. *Boum-le-Grand: Village d'Iro.* Paris: Institute D'Ethnologie.

Parrot, L., and Bellon, J. 1952. Notes sur les phlébotomes. LXIV: Phlébotomes du Ouaddai. *Archs. Inst. Pasteur Algér.* 30:137.

Pepys, J. 1955. The relationship of nonspecific and specific factors in the tuberculin reaction: A review. *Am. Rev. Tuberc. Pulm. Dis.* 71:49–73.

Pollitzer, R. 1954. *Plague.* World Health Organization Monograph Series, no. 22. Geneva.

Ranque, J. A., and Rioux, J. A. 1961. La schistosome vesicale dans la palmerai de Faya-Largeau. In *Mission épidémiologique au Nord Tchad*, ed. J. A. Rioux, Comité de Coordination Scientifique du Sahara. Paris: Arts et Metiers Graphiques.

Rodger, F. C. 1962. A review of recent advances in scientific knowledge of the symptomatology, pathology, and pathogenesis of onchocercal infections. *Bull WHO* 27:429–48.

Russell, P. F.; West, L. S.; Manwell, R. D.; and MacDonald, G. 1963. *Practical Malariology.* London: Oxford University Press.

Sapero, J. J., and Lawless, D. K. 1952. The "MIF" stain preservation technique for the identification of intestinal protozoa. *Amer. J. Trop. Med.* 2:613–19.

Schier, W. W.; Roth, A.; Ostroff, G.; and Schrift, M. H. 1956. Hodgkin's disease and immunity. *Amer. J. Med.* 20:94–99.

Schultz, M. G.; Kagan, I. G.; and Warner, G. S. 1967. Card flocculation test in the field of diagnosis of trichinosis. *Amer. J. Clin. Path.* 47: 26–29.

Scrimshaw, N. S. 1960. *Iodine deficiency (goiter) in control of malnutrition in man.* New York: American Public Health Association.

Scrimshaw, N. S.; Taylor, C. E.; and Gordon, J. E. 1959. Interactions of nutrition and infection. *Amer. J. Med. Sci.* 237:367–403.

Sigales, N. S. 1967. General Hospital reports. Doba, Republic of Chad. Personal communication.

Spruyt, D. J.; Elder, F. B.; Messing, S. D.; Wade, M. K.; Ryder, B.; Prince, J. S.; and Tseghe, Y. 1967. Ethiopia's health center program —its impact on community health. *Ethiopian Med. J.*, vol. 5 (supplement).

Stolt, H. M. 1954. Histoplasmin sensitivity and pulmonary calcification in Kenya. *Brit. Med. J.* 4852:22–25.

Strumia, M. M.; Sample, A. B.; and Hart, E. D. 1954. An improved microhematocrit method. *Amer. J. Clin. Path.* 24:1016–24.

Thompson, V., and Adloff, R. 1960. *The emerging states of French Equatorial Africa.* Stanford, Calif.: Stanford University Press.

Tremblay, M. 1957. The key informant technique: A non-ethnographic application. *Am. Anthrop.* 59:688–701.

United Nations. 1967. *Demographic Yearbook 1966.* New York.

Vachon, M. 1961. A propos du scorpion des Palmerais Borkouanes. In: *Mission épidémiologique au Nord Tchad,* ed. J. A. Rioux, Comité de Coordination Scientifique du Sahara. Paris: Arts et Metiers Graphiques.

von Noorden, G. K., and Buck, A. A. 1968. Ocular onchocerciasis: An ophthalmological and epidemiological study in an African village. *Arch. Ophthal.* 80:26–34.

Wijsmuller, G. 1963. *Naturally acquired tuberculin sensitivity in New Guinea.* Amsterdam: N. V. 'T Koggeschip, Drukkers En Vitgerersbedrijf.

World Health Organization. 1955. Sensitivity of human populations to human and avian tuberculins. Tuberculosis Office. *Bull. WHO* 12: 85–99.

———. 1962. *First report.* Expert Committee on Trypanosomiasis. Technical Report Series, no. 247. Geneva.

———. 1963. *International standards for drinking water.* 2d ed. Geneva.

———. 1964. *Soil-transmitted helminths.* Expert Committee on Helminths. Technical Report Series, no. 277. Geneva.

———. 1965. *Third report.* Expert Committee on Bilharziasis. Technical Report Series, no. 299. Geneva.

———. 1966. *Geographical distribution of schistosomes,* pp. 68–70 (Working Paper). Expert Committee on Bilharziasis. Geneva.

———. 1967. *Measurement of the public health importance of bilharziasis,* p. 25. Technical Report Series, no. 349. Geneva.

Ziegler, P. 1967. *Rapport sur l'activité du Service des Grandes Endémies pendant l'année 1966.* Ministry of Public Health, Fort Lamy.

———. 1968. *Rapport sur l'activité du Service des Grandes Endémies pendant l'année 1967.* Ministry of Public Health, Fort Lamy.

LIST OF TABLES

269

LIST OF FIGURES

INDEX

Agriculture. *See* Economic activities

Albumin/globulin ratio, 109–10; abnormal, 109–10; mean values by study village, 110

Amebiasis: complement fixation test for, 166–67; prevalence by village, 164, 166–67; reported for 1966, 101. *See also* Intestinal parasites

Animal bites, 124–27; frequency of, 126–27; types of, 125–27

Anopheles, 90–91; *A. funestus*, 90–132; *A. gambiae*, 90, 132; *A. pharoensis*, 90; *A. nili*, 90. *See also* Malaria

Anthropology, methods, 227–32; field procedures, 228; interpreters, 231, 232; interviewers, 227, 231–32; key informants, 227; modifications for each study site, 228–31; precoded survey schedule, 227

Arbovirus infections, 208–12; antigens used in tests, 208; correlation of HI and neutralization test findings, 211–12; hemagglutination inhibition tests, 208–12; neutralization tests in mice, 209–12; prevalence of reaction in HI tests, 208–10; yellow fever vaccinations, 123, 212

Arthropods of medical importance, 83–97; *Anopheles*, 90–93, 132–34; attracted to human feces, 88–89; *Ceratopogonidae*, 91; *Chloropidae*, 95; collection of, 86, 235–36; *Culex*, 90–93; *Culicidae*, 90–91; diptera, 86; dipterous families, 87; *Glossina*, 86, 136; *Hippoboscidae*, 96; *Phlebotomus*, 86, 89–90; *Psychodidae*, 89–

90; *Rhagionidae*, 94; *Sciomyzidae*, 95; *Simulidae*, 91; *Simulium*, 86, 91; *Tabanidae*, 91–94; ticks, 96–97, 199. *See also* Entomology

Ascaris lumbricoides. *See* Intestinal parasites

Bacterial diseases and infections, 167–98; brucellosis, 193–95; enteric bacteria, 195–97; leprosy, 185–86; leptospirosis, 195; meningococcal infections, 197–98; plague, 193; treponematoses, 186–92; tuberculosis, 167–85. *See also individual bacterial diseases*

Birth rate, 127–30; polygyny and, 129; regional differences in, 127–29; total estimated, 127–29. *See also* Fertility

Bites. *See* Animal bites

Blood pressure, 113–16

Boum Khebir: climate and terrain, 12, 14, 86; customs, 38; economics, 56–61; education, 51–54; excreta disposal, 70–71; housing, 49, 51, 75–79; language, 231; location, 4, 12; map, 13; medical and health services, 54; nutrition, 102–13; political organization, 47–48; population, 12, 18, 19; religions, 38, 43–44; tribes, 14; water supply, 63, 66–67

Boutonneuse fever: vectors of, 96–97. *See also* Rickettsioses

Brucellosis, 193–95; prevalence of, 193–94; reported for 1966, 101; serological test for, Djimtilo, 193

Capillaria species, 165; rat eating and, 104–5, 165

279